Foreign policy in the European Union

Theory, history and practice

BEN SOETENDORP

LONGMAN
London and New York

Pearson Education Limited
Edinburgh Gate
Harlow, Essex CM20 2JE, United Kingdom
and Associated Companies throughout the world.

*Published in the United States of America
by Pearson Education Inc., New York*

*Visit us on the World Wide Web at:
http://www.awl-he.com*

D
1060
S64

First published 1999

ISBN 0–582–32893–4

British Library Cataloguing-in-Publication Data

A catalogue record for this book is available from the British Library

Library of Congress Cataloging-in-Publication Data

Soetendorp, Ben, 1944–
    Foreign policy in the European Union: theory, history, and
practice / Ben Soetendorp.
        p.   cm.
    Includes bibliographical references and index.
    ISBN 0–582–32893–4 (ppr)
    1. European Union countries—Foreign relations. I. Title.
D1060.S6   1999
327.47—dc21   98–52187
                                                         CIP

Typeset by 35 in 10/12pt Times
Printed in Malaysia, CLP

Contents

Abbreviations

CAP	Common Agricultural Policy
CCP	Common Commerce Policy
CFSP	Common Foreign and Security Policy
CGAC	(Portuguese) Government Commission for Community Affairs
CICE	(Portuguese) Interministerial Commission for the European Community
CJTF	Combined Joint Task Force
CMCA	(Portuguese) Council of Ministers for Community Affairs
CMEA	Council for Mutual Economic Assistance
Co-Co	Coordination Committee for European Integration
COREPER	Committee of Permanent Representatives
COREU	European Correspondents network
CSCE	Conference on Security and Cooperation in Europe
EBRD	European Bank for Reconstruction and Development
EC	European Community
EC/EU	European Communities/European Union
ECMM	European Community Monitoring Mission
ECSC	European Coal and Steel Community
EDC	European Defence Community
EEC	European Economic Community
EFTA	European Free Trade Association
EMS	European Monetary System
EMU	Economic and Monetary Union
EP	European Parliament
EPC	European Political Cooperation
ESDI	European Security and Defence Identity
EU	European Union
Euratom	European Atomic Energy Community
FCO	Foreign and Commonwealth Office
FDP	(German) Free Democratic Party
FRG	Federal Republic of Germany
GATT	General Agreement on Tariffs and Trade

GDR	German Democratic Republic
IFOR	Implementation Force
MBFR	Mutual Balanced Force Reductions
NATO	North Atlantic Treaty Organization
OAPEC	Organization of Arab Petroleum Exporting Countries
OECD	Organization for Economic Cooperation and Development
OEEC	Organization for European Economic Cooperation
OSCE	Organization for Security and Cooperation in Europe
PASOK	(Greek socialist party)
PHARE	Poland and Hungary: Assistance for Restructuring Economies
PLO	Palestinian Liberation Organization
SEA	Single European Act
SECE	(Spain) Secretariat of State for the European Community
SGCI	Secrétariat Général du Comité Interministériel
SPD	(German) Social Democratic Party
SU	Soviet Union
TEU	Treaty on European Union
UNPROFOR	United Nations Protection Force
US	United States
WEU	West European Union
WTO	World Trade Organization

Introduction

In the process of European integration, the effort to create a single European foreign policy has a distinctive character. While the West European states were willing to make great leaps forward towards the building of an economic and monetary union with a single market and a single currency, less progress has been made so far in the foreign policy field. It looks as if foreign policy and especially security policy remain the last great bastion of state sovereignty and that the member-states still consider foreign policy making the reserved domain of the European nation-states. But the creation of an institutionalized framework for the making of a common foreign policy at the level of the European Union (EU) has made European foreign policy more than just the aggregation of fifteen national foreign policies. It has actually blurred the distinction between national foreign policies and a common European foreign policy. More and more foreign policy issues are treated as common foreign policies, binding national governments to the common decision taken, and making it harder for the member-states to pursue national foreign policies that are at odds with the other EU countries.

The aim of this book is to find out to what extent the individual member-states – each with a different history, different interests and different styles of foreign policy making – still dominate the common foreign policy making in the EU, and how the common foreign policy making in the EU framework constrains the foreign policy behaviour of the individual member-states.

After a short introductory chapter the first part of the book reviews the diverse foreign policy patterns of the individual member-states towards European integration (Chapters 2 and 3); describes their various styles of foreign policy making (Chapter 4), and then examines the institutional arrangements for joint foreign policy making created by the member-states at the EU level (Chapter 5). The second part of the book looks closely at the practice of common foreign policy making in a number of issue areas, focusing on the three dimensions of the EU's foreign policy. Chapter 6 deals with the diplomatic dimension; Chapter 7 treats the economic dimension and Chapter 8 looks into the military dimension. This will help us to understand the reality of European foreign policy making, to comprehend the relationship between the foreign policies of the member-states of the EU and the foreign policy of the EU as a whole, to grasp its unique nature and to explore the prospects for developing a single European foreign policy.

Before proceeding it is important to make some observations about the term 'foreign policy'. To start with, foreign policy is defined in this book as the individual and the collective plans and actions of national governments oriented towards the external world (Rosenau, 1987: 3). It refers to the collection of goals, strategies and instruments, as well as the everyday actions selected by governmental policy makers (Rosati, 1993: 2). However, two remarks have to be made in this respect. First, as Northedge reminds us, it is useful to think of a government's policy more in terms of a government's position. 'Foreign policy represents an infinite sequence of positions on the daily flow of international issues reaching the Foreign Minister's desk' (Northedge, 1969: 28). Second, because many of the foreign policy decisions are taken in cooperation with other West European states, these positions, as William Wallace has claimed, are rather negotiating positions: 'decisions about desired decisions to guide its negotiators in the process of multilateral bargaining' (Wallace, 1975: 295).

Foreign policy is also conceived to be a boundary activity linking the internal and external environment of a state (Evans and Newnham, 1990: 123). Foreign policy analysis is therefore a 'bridging discipline', as Rosenau calls it, which must concern itself with politics at both the national and the international level. It has to deal with the increasing relevance of economics to the conduct of foreign policy, and has to handle the continuing erosion of the distinction between domestic and foreign issues (Rosenau, 1987: 1–3). As the distinction between 'high politics' (security issues) and 'low politics' (economic issues) has become blurred and increasingly irrelevant, the more traditional components of foreign policy, that is diplomacy and security, and foreign economic policy will be treated in this book as a whole.

Chapter 1

The puzzle of European foreign policy making

European integration in the area of foreign policy has always been part of the extensive process of European integration. But as we will illustrate in more detail in Chapter 5, the integration effort in the field of foreign policy has followed, from its start in the early 1970s, a separate road. With the exception of exclusively economic aspects of external relations, cooperation in the foreign affairs field took place within the intergovernmental system of European Political Cooperation (EPC), outside the competence and the institutional framework of the European Economic Community (EEC). The member-states were able to agree on decision-making procedures that will allow the governments to cooperate in the foreign policy field, but were careful to retain their sovereignty.

The Common Foreign and Security Policy (CFSP), the formal title for EPC in the Treaty on European Union (TEU) agreed in Maastricht in 1991, maintains its distinguished intergovernmental character. In the new established European Union (EU) the involvement of EU institutions, other than the European Council of Heads of State and Government and the Council of Ministers, is kept to a minimum. During the intensive process of intergovernmental negotiations over the TEU as well as its revision by the Treaty of Amsterdam in 1997, the strengthening of the EU's common foreign and security policy has been a declared fundamental aim of the EU member states. But in the intergovernmental negotiations over the two treaties, it proved impossible to transfer national sovereignty in the making of a common foreign and security policy to the European Community level. The member-states persist in maintaining national sovereignty in the field of foreign and security policy, and are prepared to accept only some intensification of institutional arrangements and decision-making rules for joint foreign policy making to contribute to a more effective and coherent external policy of the Union as a whole. Contrary to the establishment of a supranational European central bank and the proposed replacement of a traditional symbol of sovereignty like a national currency by a single European currency, which demonstrates the willingness of the member-states to share national sovereignty in the very sensitive area of monetary policies, there is no evidence yet for the readiness of national governments to transfer their authority in the foreign policy field to a supranational European foreign ministry equipped with the machinery and capabilities to fulfil the international ambitions of the Union.

In this chapter we will seek no clear-cut theoretical explanation for this behaviour. We will rather discuss some of the answers that international relations literature in general and the regional integration school of thought in particular provide, for an understanding of the rather puzzling behaviour of the European states. We will do so by focusing on two questions. First we will consider the central question of the willingness of the EU member-states to engage in a common foreign policy making, which deals with the dimension of voluntarism in the European integration process. Second, we will address the question of the specific nature of the foreign policy-making process in the EU, of which the two-layer structure and the intergovernmental bargaining are the essential features.

The willingness to create a common foreign policy

Our starting point for understanding the key question of why sovereign states are willing voluntarily to constitute a common foreign policy is realism, the most dominant approach in international relations theory and traditionally very sceptical about European integration. For realists, interstate anarchy constitutes the substantive rationality of states. International institutions such as the EU are, in their view, of little importance to states, as competition and conflict among states constrains interstate cooperation even when they share common interests (cf. Kegley, 1995: 151). Consequently realism considers the securing of national sovereignty a fundamental value that shapes the basic foreign policy goals of each nation-state. But realist thinkers do not exclude the participation of some states in a process of integration which might lead to the loss of their national sovereignty. The influential realist scholar Morgenthau, for example, who emphasized that national sovereignty will continue to be the central driving force in the international system, did not rule out the willingness of states to transfer their national sovereignty to supranational organizations. However, he made such a readiness conditional upon the mutual recognition of the national interests of the nations concerned, and an expectation of benefits that outweigh the loss of the nation's freedom of action (Morgenthau, 1952: 972–3). Writing in the early 1950s, Morgenthau regarded the establishment of the EEC as an attempt by the member-states to compensate, through united effort, for the loss of power of the individual European nations, as well as an attempt by France and the other European states to control the natural superiority of Germany in Europe (Morgenthau, 1973: 509).

Some decades later, the readiness of France to lose its independence in monetary policy making in exchange for the creation of a European Economic and Monetary Union (EMU), is explained by a contemporary realist thinker such as Grieco almost along the same lines. Grieco regards the large leap forward of European economic and monetary unification through the institutions of the EU, simply as an attempt by France (and other European states) to reduce German domination of European monetary affairs and to regain a degree of control over monetary policies. Addressing the more general current tendency of states to undertake international cooperation through institutionalized arrangements, Grieco offers his so-called binding thesis. It says that if states share a common interest and undertake negotiations on rules constituting a collaborative arrangement, then the weaker but still influential partners will seek to ensure that the rules so constructed will give them effective influence and prevent their domination by stronger partners (Baldwin, 1993: 331). Indeed, as Grieco argues, the EMU structure will ensure greater symmetry in power among the EU members in the monetary domain. The binding thesis may also explain why the smaller EU countries are the keenest on strong institutional arrangements in the movement towards a common foreign policy. Such a firm structure protects them against a potential directorate of the larger states.

Pure self-interest

That pure self-interest is the driving force behind the transfer of power and sovereignty from national governments to a new centre of authority is in fact the central assumption in regional integration theory. Haas, the most distinguished thinker on regional integration, had already argued in one of the first theoretical assessments of the West European integration endeavour that a shift of loyalty will take place only if more satisfaction is expected from the new institutions of the Community than from the existing institutions of the nation-states. All progress towards integration has to be based, in Haas's view, on agreements between the political elites of the member-states, reached by the accommodation of individual interests (Haas, 1958: 13). The benefits of the economies of scale, which have made the EU a powerful trading bloc that commands the largest share of world trade, were obviously the most important reason for the member-states to create a common external trade policy. Thus, the loss of sovereignty with respect to foreign trade policy was amply compensated by the bargaining power that the member-states acquired as a unified actor in international trade negotiations *vis-à-vis* the United States and Japan. Moreover, as we will illustrate in detail in the next two chapters, the addition of a foreign policy dimension to economic cooperation has served some very specific foreign policy interests of the larger as well as the smaller member-states.

However, regional integration scholars have stressed the gradual nature of the integration process. They believe that cooperation in one area will lead to cooperation in other areas. Such a spillover of integration from one policy sector to another is very likely in the foreign policy area. According to Schmitter, a prominent regional integration theorist, once agreement is reached and made operative on a policy or set of policies, the member-states will be forced to hammer out a collective external position. In the process of externalization, the member-states will rely increasingly on the new central institution of the Community (Schmitter, 1969: 165). There is little doubt that the rise in the economic power of the EC/EU and the necessity to recover control over the economic effects of foreign policy decisions of individual member-states, generated major impulses towards the development of a joint foreign policy and reinforced the successive attempts to improve the international performance of the EC/EU as a single actor.

The view that egoistic self-interest of states is the basic rationale for the willingness of states to establish cooperative networks and to build communities beyond the state is also one of the main features of the interdependence approach in international relations theory, and a key element in its offshoot international regime theory. Interdependence theory does not deny the importance of anarchy in international relations, nor does it disregard that states are the principal actors in world politics and that they behave on the basis of their conception of their own self-interests. But as scholars like Milner and Keohane have argued, the centrality of anarchy to world politics has been overemphasized at the expense of other essential features of international relations such as the interdependence of the actors and the significant role of international institutions in changing conceptions of self-interest (Baldwin, 1993: 162, 270).

A demand for international institutions

Interdependence theory highlights patterns of interaction among states that lead them to international cooperation, stresses the implications of the emergence of transnational and other non-state actors on the global stage, and emphasizes the increased importance in interstate relations of trade problems, monetary politics and other economic issues (Keohane and Nye, 1989). According to Keohane, a central theorist of international institutionalism which incorporates interdependence and regime theory, conditions of interdependence generate a demand for international institutions to enable governments to achieve their interests through limited collective action. International institutions serve state objectives by facilitating the making and keeping of agreed sets of rules, norms and decision-making procedures, referred to as international regimes. These sets of governing arrangements are designed to regulate international behaviour within issue areas, and to control the effects of interdependence through the provision of information which reduces uncertainty and reductions in transaction costs. Keohane argues that even if the costs of interstate cooperation remain substantial, governments will create and use such institutions as long as the institutions enable states to achieve valued objectives unattainable through unilateral or bilateral means (Baldwin, 1993: 274). This is why Britain, in spite of its dislike of supranationalism, agreed to deepen the institutional setting of the EC through a European Union. It helped Britain to control the power of Germany, which it feared after German unification.

Most students of international regimes are quite optimistic about the willingness of governments to enter into interstate cooperation that constitute international regimes, and argue that the existence of regimes is fully consistent with the realist view of international politics. Stein, for example, suggests that it is the self-interest of autonomous governments in a state of anarchy that leads them to move from independent decision making to joint decision making in international regimes. When national governments are confronted with dilemmas of common interests or common aversions, jointly reached outcomes are in both cases preferable to decisions made independently (Stein, 1990: 39; Baldwin, 1993: 53).

However, it is important to bear in mind the observation made by Lipson that international cooperation is more likely in areas of economic issue than in those concerning military security (Baldwin, 1993: 71). As we will see in Chapter 5, the institutional arrangements and decision-making rules concerning the common external economic relations of the EU are indeed much more comprehensive than the institutional arrangements and decision rules regarding the common foreign and security policy.

Thus, summarizing the scholarly debate over the willingness of the member-states to create a common foreign policy, we may argue that the will to cooperate is rooted in what international relations theorists of various schools of thought see as self-interest of the member-states. But as we have emphasized, self-interest also conditions their willingness to pool and mix their national sovereignty with Community powers. This circumscribed voluntarism explains why foreign policy in the EU is only loosely integrated, compared to other policy areas.

The specific nature of European foreign policy making

As indicated at the beginning of this chapter, we will turn now to see how international relations literature, and regional integration scholarship in particular, can be helpful in understanding European integration in the foreign policy field by discussing the specific nature of the foreign policy process in the EU. In this respect two essential features catch the eye: the two-layer structure and the intergovernmental bargaining. To put it in other words, foreign policy (with the exception of external economic relations issues) continues to be a policy area where national decision making remains important, which has made foreign policy making in the Union a complex interplay between the national and the European levels of foreign policy making. In addition, joint decision making at the EU level is basically a bargaining process between the governments of the member-states wherein the involvement of supranational bodies such as the European Commission and the European Parliament is very limited. This has created different institutional arrangements and distinct decision rules to govern the process of European foreign policy making in the traditional foreign policy activities of diplomacy, defence, trade and development cooperation (which we will describe in detail in Chapter 5).

A two-layer system

In the search for useful theories and concepts to capture the nature of policy making in the EU, we will start with the notion of the two-layer system. Discussing the end state of the European integration process, regional integration scholars have concluded already, in relatively early stages of the European integration process, that it will not lead to a regional supranational state that is analogous to the national state. Integration, they argue, should be seen as a merger of national and community decision-making systems. Instead of thinking in terms of the Community's capacity to impose decisions forcibly on the member governments, integration has to be considered as some sort of symbiosis between the Community and the national systems (Lindberg and Scheingold, 1970: 32; Haas, 1970: 634).

Thus, integration theorists studying the European Community realized the close relationship between the national and European levels in the process of European integration. Haas, for example, emphasized, in addition to the process of supra-national community building at the EC level and the crucial role of supranational institutions in this respect, the important role played by national elites in the transfer of authority from the national to the supranational level. However, in the initial study of the policy-making process in the EC, much of the analysis of policy making in the EC focused on the institutional context at the EC level, without reference to the domestic sources of European policy making. Bulmer was one of the first students of European integration who explicitly concentrated on the impact of factors at the national level on the functioning of the Community. He argued, for instance, that the negotiating behaviour of individual member-states in the EC is influenced by the domestic policy-making structures (termed the national policy style) and the attitudes held within the member-states regarding the EC (Bulmer, 1983). In a joint study with Paterson, he has demonstrated that the internal policy-making style and the priority given by political parties, public opinion and socioeconomic interest groups to domestic issues over European integration, are significant barriers for a German leading role in the EC (Bulmer and Paterson, 1987). In another study, a British study group has illustrated that the position of Britain as a semi-detached member is a result of the gap between steady governmental adjustment to working within the EC and slow political adaptation to EC membership (George, 1992). Moravcsik, a firm proponent of the domestic politics approach in the study of Euro-pean politics, has even claimed that 'EC politics is the continuation of domestic policies by other means' (Moravcsik, 1991: 25). Using a domestic politics approach to explain EC policy outcomes, Moravcsik has proposed a theoretical construct which stresses that member-states' national interests and intergovernmental bargains domin-ate EC politics.

Intergovernmental bargaining

The emphasis on the significance of domestic politics in the analysis of EC politics and the importance of intergovernmental bargaining in the analysis of policy out-comes in the EC, has generated a demand for a better understanding of the effects of the interaction among the national and the European levels on policy making in the EU. One promising avenue for such an understanding is the logic of a two-level game, introduced by Putnam in an effort to explain how domestic and international politics interact during diplomatic negotiations. Putnam suggests that the politics of many international negotiations can be conceived as a two-level game, where each central negotiator must play simultaneously at two game boards and satisfy both his foreign and domestic counterparts with the bargaining outcome (Putnam, 1988). In a collective study the metaphor of a two-level game proved to be a useful starting assumption to explain how domestic constraints, that is the need to gain the neces-sary domestic majority to ensure ratification for the agreement, influence the pro-cess as well as the outcomes of international negotiations (Evans, Jacobson and Putnam, 1993).

The image of the negotiator as 'Janus-faced' is seen by many observers of EU politics as a practical conception of the policy-making process in the EU. Bulmer has referred to Putnam's work when he has argued in favour of approaching EPC or the EC as a two-tier bargaining model which has to take into account the dynamics of national foreign policy making as well as those at the level of the EPC itself (Bulmer, 1991). A similar view is taken by Sandholtz who maintains that each member-state tries to assure negotiation outcomes that are as close as possible to its national interests but also emphasizes that EC membership has an impact on the way that member-states define their interests, or, as Sandholtz puts it: 'States define their interests in a different way as members of the EC than they would without it' (Sandholtz, 1993: 3). In a later study Moravcsik also modified his earlier intergovernmental framework, taking into account the impact of the institutional context of the EC on the way that the member-states define their national interests. He has formulated what he calls a liberal intergovernmentalist view of decision making in the EC, which integrates assumptions from liberal theories about national preference formation and theories about intergovernmental negotiations and institutional creation. Major EC decisions are shaped, according to Moravcsik, in a process of domestic preference formation primarily determined by constraints and opportunities imposed by economic interdependence, and a process of interstate strategic bargaining of which the outcomes are determined by the relative bargaining power of governments and the functional incentives for institutionalization created by high transaction costs and the desire to control domestic agendas (Moravcsik, 1993: 481, 517).

In the current study of policy making in the EU it has become common to regard the policy-making process in the EU as an interaction between national and European levels of policy making and bargaining between policy makers as the predominant form of political interaction (cf. Wallace and Wallace, 1996: 32). As more and more scholars find it necessary to include in their analysis, in addition to the national level and the European level, the subnational level and in some issue areas even the international level, policy making in the EU is treated increasingly in terms of multilevel governance, where bargaining takes place within policy networks involving a broad range of actors at the subnational, national, European and international levels (cf. Wallace and Wallace, 1996; Richardson, 1996). Whereas a multilevel explanatory framework may be relevant for the analysis of the vast majority of the day-to-day, often technical decisions which fall within the scope of the EC institutional structure, such a framework is certainly less appropriate for the analysis of foreign policy decisions. Under the existing institutional structure of the EU, foreign policy decision making (with the exception of external economic issues) takes place in the separate CFSP institutional framework of the EU, in which intergovernmental arrangements prevail (this will be illustrated in Chapter 5).

In this connection it should be pointed out that, because of the different degree of institutionalization in the foreign policy sectors of diplomacy, defence, external trade and development cooperation, we have to differentiate between the different policy sectors when we approach the question of foreign policy making in the EU. As a matter of fact, there is not one but two separate regimes for common foreign policy making in the Union. This is not an unexpected development. As indicated by Schmitter in a recent analysis of the probable end states of the European integration process, the most likely outcome is an arrangement where each member-state will be allowed to select the common policies that it is willing to accept, so that instead of a single Europe with a single centre of authority, there would be many Europes, composed of a different set of members, as well as multiple regional institutions acting autonomously and producing different common policies. This may lead to the creation of a 'trading Europe', a 'diplomatic Europe', a 'military Europe' and an 'environmental Europe', each with a different level and intensity of integration (Traxler and Schmitter, 1995: 197). Many other students of European integration have made similar observations about the future development of the EU, using a broad range of terminology, such as a 'multispeed Europe', a 'flexible Europe', a 'core Europe', a 'variable geometry' or a 'Europe à la carte', to describe the diversity of policy regimes for the management of European cooperation across different policy areas (cf. Wallace and Wallace, 1995).

The degree of institutionalization is in fact very much related to the question of the willingness of the member-states to cooperate in a common foreign policy. We may argue that the degree of institutionalization in each regime reflects in essence the extent to which the member-states are willing to cooperate in a certain policy sector. After all, the main function of a regime is actually to clarify the rules in a certain issue area according to which governments (or any other actor involved in the policy-making process) should behave. As we shall see in detail in Chapter 5, the weak policy regime created by the member-states for the making of the CFSP clearly has the intention to impose some safeguards against the erosion of national sovereignty in a policy sector where, in the view of some member-states, vital national interests are (or could be) at stake.

This brings us to the concept of regime or, to be more precise, the notion of decision regime, which occupies a central place in this book. This is not the place to address the unresolved question of whether the EU should be considered a new international entity transforming its member-states into a new supranational state, or whether the EU should be regarded as simply a novel version of a well-developed international organization. In other words, judging by the present cooperation and coordination of policies among state actors and other relevant non-state actors in the various issue areas, is the EU a would-be state, an international organization or an international regime? I will illustrate the difficulty of defining the exact nature of the EU by referring to two opposite characterizations of the EU given by Nugent on the one hand and Moravcsik on the other. According to Nugent, 'the EU is more than merely another international organization in which countries cooperate with one another on a voluntary basis for reasons of mutual benefit. Rather it is an organization in which states have voluntarily surrendered their right, across a broad range of important sectors, to be independent in the determination and application of public policy' (Nugent, 1994: 207). Moravcsik holds a different view. He conceives the EC/EU as an international regime for policy coordination which goes, however, further than nearly all other international (functional) regimes by 'pooling decision-making through arrangements for qualified majority voting and delegating authority over representation, formal agenda-setting and enforcement to semi autonomous institutions' (Moravcsik, 1993: 514).

Given the degree of institutionalization in the CFSP sector, the EU is certainly not a would-be state. We realize that in many issue areas, including the external trade and development cooperation policy sectors, the EU should be seen more as an international organization than an international regime. But in the foreign policy issue area as such, the EU could indeed be considered a regime. We describe a regime as sets of implicit or explicit agreed-upon principles, norms, rules, procedures and programmes that govern the interactions of actors in specific issue areas (cf. Krasner 1983: 2; Levy, Young and Zürn, 1995: 274). As mentioned above, in this book we will refer to the institutional arrangements and decision rules that govern the process of foreign policy making in the distinctive foreign policy sectors in the EU as a 'decision regime'. The same concept would be applied to describe and analyse the foreign policy patterns and decision-making style that influence foreign policy outcomes in the individual fifteen member-states.

A decision regime

The notion of a decision regime is borrowed from Kegley who has employed the concept of regime in the comparative study of foreign policy. Arguing that regime formation is probable in any situation where there is a need for a set of rules of the game among actors, to regulate collective problem solving, Kegley utilizes the term 'regime' to analyse the rules and procedures that structure the process of foreign policy making within states. His point of departure is the proposition that the game of foreign policy making tends to be played according to identifiable shared decision rules, which he calls a decision regime (Kegley, 1987: 261). He makes a useful distinction between two types of decision regimes. The first one conditions the procedures for foreign policy making and is termed a 'procedural decision regime'. It refers to a leadership consensus regarding the process by which foreign policy is made. The second type of decision regime sets out the goals of foreign policy and is called a 'substantive decision regime', by which Kegley means 'a set of consensually based rules for action which limit a state's range of permissible options in its conduct abroad. Such a regime refers to those important sets of issues on which policy makers hold in common values or rules that legitimate principles for the making of foreign policy decisions' (Kegley, 1987: 255–6). While procedural regimes involve those rules that specify how to decide and who will do so, substantive regimes concern those rules that define what to decide. As he indicates, the formation of such substantive decision regimes may vary by the policy sector, so that the rules and the principles for the management of foreign policy may vary across issue areas.

In essence, decision regimes are composed of cognitive beliefs of decision makers emerging, according to Kegley, from an ongoing political process. This makes the identification of a decision regime difficult but, as he reminds us, 'in theorizing about the sources of foreign policy behaviour, we should begin with individuals, because only persons think, prefer and act' (Kegley, 1987: 249). All the domestic and international factors that might influence foreign policy outcomes must be filtered through clusters of beliefs of the decision makers who actually do the deciding. Empirical information regarding the procedural rules of decision regimes can be traced, as Kegley indicates, by various observational methods. For example, the reconstruction and close examination of the decision-making process, the analysis of official documents and newspapers and also interviews of participants make such data available. To identify substantive decision regimes, Kegley suggests uncovering the general pattern of the states' diplomatic practice. A substantive regime exists when the positions taken by the state on global issues are governed by repetition and regularity. Such a pattern of continuity in foreign policy conduct, he argues, indicates that its foreign policy decision makers operate from a consistent set of shared beliefs. But in addition to identifying the general pattern of the states' over-all diplomatic activity, empirical evidence about the substantive rules of decision regimes is also revealed, according to Kegley, by observing a number of specific indicators such as the policy declarations and doctrine announcements of its leaders, the voting behaviour in international organizations, the formation of tacit and overt political coalitions with other states and the formal agreements and treaties to which the state commits itself (Kegley, 1987: 258–60).

The concept of decision regimes has, in my view, the potential capacity to uncover the continuing patterns of interactions between the two levels of foreign policy making. It will help us to explore the complex relationship between the foreign policy-making processes and foreign policy outcomes within the national states and the EU, thus providing a useful instrument to expose the rules of the game that limit and shape the game of foreign policy making in the new Europe.

Part I

The institutional foreign policy setting

Chapter 2

National foreign policy patterns: the first-rank states

Paraphrasing Stanley Hoffmann's argument that in order to understand an international system one must know what the distinctive features of well-differentiated national states are (Hoffmann, 1987: 54), we may say that in order to understand European foreign policy we have to identify the main distinguishing characteristics of the overall diplomatic patterns of the different EU member-states towards European integration. In this chapter (and the next) we will make some historical generalizations that seize the broad nature and the main direction of the member-states' foreign policy in this respect. The conception of a country's foreign policy as a patterned behaviour is based on the supposition that a government's foreign policy is a goal-seeking behaviour and that some continuity and consistency in the policy goals and their underlying assumptions may be deduced from the observed external behaviour of a country over the long run, irrespective of the changes in government (cf. Kegley and Wittkopf, 1987: 5–7).

It is obvious that the challenge of European integration had dominated the foreign policy agendas of decision makers in the West European states in the postwar period. But as we will illustrate in this chapter (as well as the next chapter), the West European governments differ in the way that they have chosen to cope with this question and diverge in the guiding premises and fundamental beliefs upon which these choices are based. Consequently, the member-states vary in the substantial set of foreign policy goals and means through which successive governments in each country have treated West European integration. In this chapter we will deal with the three large member-states: France, Germany and Britain. The other twelve member-states will be dealt with in the next chapter. This examination has no pretension to be exhaustive, but simply to trace the general direction of the member-states' foreign policies towards European integration in general and the cooperation in the foreign policy field in particular.

The French quest for European leadership

France has become throughout the postwar period the great champion of European integration. French policy makers initiated the process of sectoral integration in western Europe and determined subsequently, in close cooperation with the West German leaders, the course of that process. The French design for some kind of a united states of Europe of which France was to be the focal point, was already drawn during the Second World War. The plans elaborated on earlier French ideas in favour of European integration and concrete designs for a custom union which were launched in the interwar period by two former French premiers, Aristide Briand and Édouard Herriot. Briand proposed in 1929 and 1930 a confederal bond between the states of Europe as a solution to the problem of European security and a way of controlling Germany by embracing her in a web of European cooperation. The responses of the other major European powers to the French plans at that time were sceptical, as the French scheme was considered more as a design to ensure French continental hegemony (Urwin, 1991: 5–7; Young, 1993: 8). In the French planning of postwar European cooperation the German problem again overshadowed French thinking. But this time the French plans laid more emphasis on French cooperation with the smaller European states. General Charles de Gaulle, the leader of the first provisional postwar French government (before he came back to power in 1958), saw France as the ideal power to defend the interests of the small European states against the Great Powers (Young, 1993: 9, 34).

During the war the French policy makers produced two main alternative schemes for future European cooperation. The first option sought the creation of a European customs union with Belgium, the Netherlands and Luxembourg (Benelux), or the establishment of an economic federation which may include, in addition to the Benelux, the western part of Germany, Italy and Spain. The main concern was to improve the postwar trading conditions among these countries. A second, more ambitious plan aimed at founding a European entity that would make the states of Europe a single economic unit. The loss of national sovereignty was the price for economic welfare. In this early French thinking about the postwar structure of western Europe, France was provided a leading role. The exclusion of Germany from a dominant position in the future was sought by the division of Germany in several states and tying its parts into the postwar economic arrangements. A remarkable fact, which is already noticeable in this early stage in French reflection on the favourable schemes of future cooperation in western Europe, is the absence of Britain in most of the French designs.

During the first postwar years France failed to implement any of these plans. De Gaulle saw at that time a danger in including Germany in any scheme that was aimed at the creation of a broad economic custom union in western Europe. He feared that such a federation would strengthen the German economy and consequently its influence in western Europe. De Gaulle preferred to start with some kind of federation or confederation with Belgium and the Netherlands, and to settle for controls that would secure the benefits from the German coal, iron and steel industry in the Saar, Rhineland and Ruhr for the economic reconstruction of the three countries (Young, 1993: 9–14). The most serious attempt, a French initiative for close cooperation with its northern neighbours by means of a custom union with the Benelux countries, was faced with a rather reserved attitude from both the Netherlands and Belgium. The two countries feared French domination and were therefore reluctant about any scheme for collaboration that did not include the British. The

Benelux countries were actually more interested in the recovery of their commercial links with Germany as a result of their economic dependency on the German market and wanted, contrary to the French, to include Germany as well in the formation of such a free trade union. Plans for cooperation with its southern neighbours, Italy and Spain, were not feasible because of the strong domestic opposition to such a proposal from several political parties and various interest groups. There was also little likelihood of a revival of the prewar close links of France with the other smaller states in central Europe such as Poland and Czechoslovakia (Young, 1993: 77–82; Milward, 1984: 222–55).

In these first postwar years the French strategy towards European integration was already dictated by a combination of national economic and foreign policy interests. The French foreign policy goal of seeking a partition and permanent weakening of Germany, turning it into a confederation of states without a central government, was in fact very closely linked to the domestic economic objective of postwar reconstruction. A central part of this national economic recovery plan, which the head of the Planning Commissariat Jean Monnet preferred to call the Modernization Plan, was the French ambition to replace Germany as the largest producer and exporter of steel in western Europe. To realize such an aspiration, France, which already controlled in its own occupation zone the coal mines of the Saar area, had to seize some kind of direct or indirect control over the German coal mines and steel industry in the Ruhr area as well. Monnet considered two conditions indispensable for the success of his plan. First, the French had to guarantee access to the German coal and coke resources. Second, the French had to secure a low level of German steel production (Milward, 1984: 127–67).

In June 1948, the French presented their plan to internationalize the Ruhr area. Their aim was to separate the Ruhr region from the rest of Germany and to place the German iron and steel firms as well as the German coal mines under an international regime. But the British and the Americans followed a different course. The two Western powers wanted to create a federal German state with a strong central government. They had already merged their two occupation zones in May 1947, and wished the French to join them in their treatment of Germany as one economic entity. As the price for French agreement to a merger of its occupation zone with the two other Western zones, the British (who actually controlled the Ruhr as part of their occupation zone) and the Americans were willing to establish an International Ruhr Authority. However, the two powers ensured that the Authority's powers were so weak that the French were in fact deprived of direct or indirect management of the Ruhr coal and steel resources.

The French failure to realize sufficient control of the Ruhr resources by means of an International Ruhr Authority made the French policy makers change their tactics and opt for another solution: an association of Germany in a larger European framework which would make German steel part of a European steel cartel. In that way, France would also be able to guarantee indirect control over the German coal mines and steel industry (Milward, 1984: 162–3). As Milward has rightly argued, the French plan for a European Coal and Steel Community (ECSC), named after the French Foreign Minister Robert Schuman who launched the proposal in 1950, originated in the French shortcoming in mid-1948. It was in fact thought out in the

Planning Commissariat, led by Monnet, as an alternative to the International Ruhr Authority to safeguard the modernization plan. The Schuman plan pooled the basic French and German coal and steel production and established a new High Authority that would control the entire French–German production of coal and steel. Its decisions would be binding on France, Germany and the other countries who may join the ECSC (Milward, 1984: 395–7).

The establishment of the ECSC in 1951 gave France an opportunity to exercise leadership in this very first stage of European integration. Britain's unwillingness to commit itself to the proposed European framework and the willingness of West Germany to collaborate in such an economic association, as well as the readiness of the Benelux countries and Italy to participate in the ECSC, presented the French government with a unique possibility to couple the satisfaction of its domestic economic needs with the chance to fulfil a decisive role in the process of western European integration. Also very important in this respect was the support given to the establishment of the ECSC by the United States, which had already pressed the western European governments for some time to realize some kind of economic integration. The launching of the Schuman Plan strengthened the American Minister of Foreign Affairs Dean Acheson in his conviction that the key to progress towards economic integration in western Europe was at that time not actually in British but in French hands (Milward, 1984: 391).

Because of the political weakness of the successive French governments during the Fourth Republic, especially after the French débâcle with the European Defence Community (to be discussed in Chapter 8), French policy makers kept the process of European integration simmering over a low flame. New initiatives for further integration had to originate in the other five ECSC member-states. But from the experience with the European Defence Community (EDC), the other five countries had to draw the lesson that any progress towards European integration depended on their willingness to accommodate to the French conception for further integration. Thus, France not only managed to establish itself as the power that was indispensable to any advance on the road to European integration, but it also became the country that fulfilled a decisive and leading role in mapping out the route and the direction of this process.

France was still committed to the idea of sectoral integration when, in 1955, the Benelux countries took the initiative for negotiations on further economic integration aimed at the founding of a broader European Economic Community (EEC), creating a common market which would embrace the whole economy. During the intergovernmental negotiations on the EEC, the French policy makers accepted the plan for a common market only after the other five countries agreed to a gradual stage-by-stage transformation into a common market. In that way the French hoped to realize indirectly their sector-by-sector approach to European integration and ensured that the proposed common market would apply not only to industrial goods, which at that stage was more advantageous to the Germans than to the French, but would include agricultural products as well so that the large agricultural sector in France would be one of the main beneficiaries of the common market. In exchange for the French participation in the EEC, the other five countries had to accept the French demand for further sectoral integration and to embrace the French proposal for a European Atomic Energy Community (Euratom) to supplement the ECSC. It provided France with a unique opportunity to dominate this crucial future energy sector, since France was the only EEC member that already possessed a nuclear programme (cf. Urwin, 1991: 76).

The French move from supranationalism towards intergovernmentalism

With de Gaulle's return to power in 1958 France recovered its leadership role in western Europe. De Gaulle believed that France was not only destined to play a leading role in Europe but that France, as the largest and at that time the most powerful member-state, was also the only country entitled to fulfil such a role. He had, however, no intention of transferring French sovereignty to a supranational European authority and tried to impose his conception of a united Europe on the other five EEC members. In the Gaullist view, as Northedge has noted, 'only national states have the authority to carry out policies and to inspire the loyalty of armies'. Supranational institutions were regarded by de Gaulle as 'myths, fictions and empty show', or as 'the chimera' of 'an intolerable and impracticable fusion' (Northedge, 1969: 192). Thus, cooperation with the other five EEC members was considered by de Gaulle simply as a vehicle to promote France's foreign policy goals. Illustrative of de Gaulle's conception of a united Europe is his abortive attempt to establish a European political community in 1960.

De Gaulle's proposal for a 'union of states' had two fundamental aims: first, to strengthen the political cooperation and coordination of foreign and defence policies among the EEC member-states under French leadership, outside the existing institutional frameworks of NATO and the EEC; second, to create an institutional framework for French–German cooperation. The French initiative led to the Fouchet Plan, as the original draft treaty for a 'Union of States' was called. The proposed Fouchet Plan had, completely in line with the Gaullist conception of a 'Europe des Patries' (a Europe of fatherlands), basically an intergovernmental structure. It suggested the creation of a council of heads of governments or foreign ministers that would establish the practice of regular summit meetings, the founding of a permanent secretariat composed of officials from the member-states and the institution of an assembly whose members would be appointed by the national parliaments. To emphasize the intergovernmental character of the new enterprise, decisions would be taken unanimously (Urwin, 1991: 105).

The Fouchet plan aroused, however, strong opposition from the Benelux countries which feared French domination as long as the British were absent from such a scheme. Faced with Dutch rejection, de Gaulle abandoned his original plan for a broad confederation and moved towards a bilateral, closer political cooperation with the other major West European partner: West Germany. The Franco-German Treaty of Friendship and Reconciliation (also known as the Elysée treaty) was signed in 1963. It includes provisions for institutional cooperation that actually were suggested in the Fouchet Plan. But de Gaulle's views on a 'Union of States' provided not only an institutional framework for French–German cooperation; they also inspired later French initiatives for institutional developments within the EC. The creation of a European Council of Heads of State and Governments and the establishment of the European Political Cooperation, as well as the inclusion of a separate pillar for a Common Foreign and Security Policy in the Treaty on European Union along intergovernmental rather than federal lines, resemble in fact some of the recommendations that were put forward in the abortive Fouchet Plan.

Whereas the French leader considered the EEC mainly as a useful instrument to extend France's leadership in Europe, a combination of economic and foreign policy interests was nevertheless at the core of the Gaullist policy towards the EEC. Despite his opposition to any significant transfer of powers to EEC institutions which may imply a surrender of French sovereignty, de Gaulle was not hostile to the EEC as such. He saw in economic integration an important instrument to advance the industrial development of his country and a major tool to modernize the large French agricultural sector (Dinan, 1994: 42–3). He supported, for instance, the formulation of a common agricultural policy which benefited the French farmers, but he did not hesitate to clash with the European Commission or the other member-states when the formulation of such a policy threatened French sovereignty. His decision to boycott the meetings of the EEC Council of Ministers from June 1965 to January 1966 is a good example of this double-edged policy. De Gaulle's 'empty chair policy' was in fact the culmination of a collision between the French leader and the European Commission which, under the chairmanship of its first president Walter Hallstein, tried to act as some kind of a European government.

Hallstein dismissed national sovereignty as a doctrine of 'yesteryear' and regarded himself as a kind of European prime minister (Urwin, 1991: 102). In an attempt to increase the supranational character of the EEC, Hallstein tried in 1965 to link an agreement on a common agricultural policy among the six member-states (hereafter referred to as the Six) to an approval of two other issues: first, the acceptance of increased control of the European Parliament over the EEC budget, and second, an endorsement of the Commission's demand for an independent source of income. The clash with the Commission and the other European partners deepened at the end of 1965 when the Commission wanted to make a start with decision making by qualified majority in the Council of Ministers on certain matters. Although the Commission's intention did not go beyond an implementation of the provisions of the Treaty of Rome to which France was a party, this was regarded by de Gaulle as another step that implied a transfer of decision-making powers from the member-states to the EEC institutions. De Gaulle had to compromise, however, since his 'empty chair policy' paralysed not only the decision-making capacity of the EEC. It also blocked the acceptance of the common agricultural policy which was very beneficial to the French farmers who composed an important part of his electorate. He lifted his boycott of the EEC, but not before an agreement was reached that granted France (as well as any other member-state) a *de facto* power to veto any proposed decision that was contrary to a member-state's vital national interest (Northedge, 1969: 206; Urwin, 1991: 113). The outcome of that compromise had, however, far-reaching consequences for the nature of European integration and the way it has developed. The Luxembourg compromise, as it is known, was in fact an agreement to disagree and made decision making along intergovernmental lines, instead of a supranational mode of decision making, actually the most fundamental unwritten rule for EC decision making for many years to come.

The French aspiration of European leadership did not change after de Gaulle's departure from the political stage in 1969. The creation of a European Council of Head of States and Governments in 1974, on a French initiative and whereby only the French participate with both their president and prime minister, provided his successors with a forum to exercise a leading role for France in the EC. However, the French leaders had to acknowledge Germany's increasing economic power in Europe. They tried therefore to counterbalance Germany's economic weight through an intensification of the French–German relations, seeking joint French–German political leadership of an integrated Europe.

The French–German leadership has become a *de facto* French–German directorate within the EC, which was at the centre of many of the significant initiatives that have deepened the process of European integration. Almost all the important decisions in the history of the EC have been prenegotiated by the two countries and have been presented as a joint initiative, thought up by the powerful French–German coalition. The French President Georges Pompidou and West Germany's Chancellor Willy Brandt were the motor behind the movement towards a closer coordination of the foreign and monetary policies of the member-states in the 1970s. The start of the European Political Cooperation (EPC) in 1970 was a result of an initial agreement between the two leaders, while their successors, Valéry Giscard d'Estaing and Helmut Schmidt, were responsible for the emergence of the European Monetary System (EMS) in 1979. The two countries were also at the core of the revival of the Community in the 1980s and early 1990s. Close coordination on common positions between the French President François Mitterrand and the German Chancellor Helmut Kohl made it possible for the member-states to conclude two major reforms of the original Treaty of Rome: the Single European Act (SEA) of 1986 and the Treaty on European Union (TEU) signed in Maastricht in 1992. The two revisions completed and broadened the scope of the single European market and improved the decision-making capacity of the Community. The SEA and the TEU extended the competence of the EC/EU to related economic, monetary and social policy areas and included a timetable for the establishment of an Economic and Monetary Union (EMU). The two revisions incorporated institutional innovations which were developed on a French initiative outside the institutional framework of the original Treaty of Rome, namely the EPC and the European Council. But the French had to give in to the German wish to open the way for a more frequent application of qualified majority voting, and to strengthen the powers of the European Parliament through the introduction of the 'cooperation procedure' and the 'co-decision procedure' in some policy areas.

Despite the French–German connection, based on a carefully crafted balance between French and German interests, France still differs from Germany on the extent of power that it is ready to transfer to supranational institutions. It continues to hold on to the basic Gaullist approach which prefers to keep the distribution of powers in favour of the member-states, especially in the foreign policy area. But as in the early days of European integration, France is still willing to initiate a further pooling of sovereignty with Germany and other European states, if it serves the ultimate French goal of controlling Germany's power. Faced with increasing financial dominance of Germany's central bank over European financial markets, France was ready to accept the loss of sovereignty in the determination of its national economic and fiscal policies as a consequence of the EMU, since this replaced the German Bundesbank by a European Bank controlled by all EMU member governments. Hence, the French–German alliance has been not only the foremost instrument for French leaders to exercise European leadership, but it has also become the main vehicle for France to seek French solutions to basically European problems.

Germany's search for legitimacy and equality

The Federal Republic of Germany (FRG) which included, until the reunification in 1990, only the western part of the country was, as a consequence of the German defeat in the Second World War, much more humble in its foreign policy behaviour. Contrary to France, West Germany has not sought European leadership. The far-reaching aspiration of restoring the territorial unity of the country and the long-term ambition to recover the central role that Germany occupied on the European stage since its first unification in 1871, were subordinated to the more modest short-term objectives of reclaiming sovereignty and recapturing international respect, regaining economic power and achieving an equal position with the other European powers. Successive governments of the Federal Republic exploited almost every opportunity offered in the course of postwar history to promote those objectives. The rise of the cold war between East and West and the process of European integration offered West Germany an opportunity to bring about a reconciliation with its western neighbours and to integrate into the western European military political and economic systems. The later *détente* in the East–West relationship gave West Germany a chance to accommodate to the postwar reality in eastern Europe and to reach, by means of a self-assertive *ostpolitik*, a *modus vivendi* with their eastern neighbours. Finally, the collapse of communism and the end of the cold war made it possible for the West German leadership to accomplish the ultimate goal of German reunification.

In contrast to France, Germany had to build its foreign policy from scratch. Germany emerged from the Second World War as a weak country, occupied by the victorious allies, deprived of statehood and sovereignty. Besides the loss of its military and economic power, the country also lost its territorial and administrative unity. The Allies subjected the German occupied zones to various controls which imposed severe restraints on the country's freedom of action. But the German leaders' main concern in the first postwar years was to restore local self-government and to recover their control of the country's internal affairs. West Germany began to exercise some control over its foreign affairs only after the creation of the Federal Republic in 1949 by the merger of the three Western occupied zones. It took, however, another two years before the obstacles for the founding of a West German Foreign Ministry were removed, while sovereignty was not reestablished until 1955. As a result, the Federal Republic's foreign policy was in fact framed in the first postwar years by Konrad Adenauer, West Germany's first Chancellor who acted as his own foreign minister until 1955.

Adenauer laid the foundation for West Germany's postwar foreign policy of reconciliation and cooperation with France and was the architect of Germany's orientation towards the West. He realized that the most important goal of German reunification was not possible in the short term and was convinced that a unification in the longer run was conditional upon the support of the Western powers. The first postwar West German leader believed that the willingness of West Germany to incorporate its regained military and economic power into a larger European setting would remove the fears of a revival of a German threat to its neighbours, especially France. Adenauer considered integration into the western European political, military and economic systems of regional cooperation as the best strategy to overcome the profound distrust of Germany by France and Britain against whom Germany started two world wars. As Hanrieder has argued, integration and the restoration of sovereignty were closely connected, since the sovereignty for which Adenauer aimed was of a rather special kind. Once obtained, Adenauer was ready to tie Germany to the emerging European organizations and to transfer parts of Germany's restored legal sovereignty to the ECSC, the EEC and NATO (Hanrieder, 1989: 233). In the early 1950s, Adenauer's foreign policy priorities and his course of action were not endorsed by all West Germans. For instance, the German social democrat's leadership, the largest opposition party, gave its blessing to the policy of reconciliation, but attached at that time the highest priority to German unification. For this reason they preferred to keep more political distance from the emerging two power blocs and in consequence opposed both West Germany's participation in the ECSC and the Federal Republic's entry into NATO.

The French initiative for the creation of the ECSC was very warmly embraced by Adenauer. It offered him a first opportunity to implement his double-track policy of regaining national sovereignty and establishing West Germany's credentials as a reliable international partner. German willingness to place German and French coal and steel production under the common authority of the ECSC paved the way for the removal of the control and restrictions imposed on the German coal and steel industry by the occupation powers through the operation of the International Ruhr Authority. The replacement of the International Ruhr Authority by the ECSC's High Authority, the newly established supranational body, at the same time helped the Federal Republic to achieve equality with France. Likewise, the subordination of the West German military forces to a common Allied command within the framework of the Atlantic Alliance not only provided West Germany with the required security, but also opened the way for German rearmament and the acceptance of West German military parity within NATO. The further economic integration of West Germany into western Europe through the creation of the EEC, of which West Germany was a founding member was, from Adenauer's point of view, another major step in the process of reconciliation between Germany and its Western neighbours and the reinforcement of the Federal Republic's international credibility. But there was of course also another side to the willingness of Adenauer to integrate into the western European economic bloc. Membership of the EEC provided the

German industry with the benefits of an economy operating on a large scale and the advantages gained by an enlarged market. It not only gave the country the essential conditions for economic expansion and prosperity, but also made it possible for the new German state to rebuild its economic power base. In the longer run this would again make Germany the strongest member of the western European bloc in terms of economic power (cf. Milward, 1984: 389).

Germany's push for federalism

Like France, Germany has recognized the economic value of the EEC. But the German leaders wanted the EEC to be more than simply an economic common market. Although they had no intention of giving up German sovereignty altogether, unlike the French leaders, they were strong proponents of the pooling of national sovereignty and a political integration that goes beyond the simple coordination of the national foreign policies. Based on the German experience with a federal structure, the German politicians favoured the building of a political union that had as its ultimate aim a federal European state with the potential to become a united states of Europe. However, since de Gaulle argued more in favour of weakening rather than strengthening the institutions of the community, Adenauer, who made Franco-German cooperation the core of his European policy, had to be conscious of de Gaulle's resistance to a federal construct that limits the powers of the large member-states. As we have seen in our discussion of the French–German partnership, it was only after de Gaulle's resignation in 1969 that the West German leaders were able to push for a deepening of the integration process and to receive French consent for major steps forward.

Over the years, the German leaders have modified their enthusiasm for supranational institutions. Helmut Schmidt, for instance, argued that European integration could only advance through the will of statesmen and not through the many regulations produced by the Community's institutions (Paterson and Southern, 1991: 264). But despite such reservations about the role of the Community's institutions, successive West German governments, almost irrespective of their political composition, advocated the strengthening of the EC/EU institutions even if this implied cutbacks in national sovereignty.

Although Germany has developed in economic terms into a world power in its own right and has become the most powerful state in the EU, contributing financially to the EU more than any other member-state, the Federal Republic had no ambition to play a political leadership role in the EEC or the EU. In this respect the German leaders were always guided by what William Paterson has called the German leadership avoidance complex (Story, 1993: 166). As Paterson has noted, successive German governments have resisted the temptation to try to turn its economic and financial strength into an explicit political domination. Where political leadership has been employed, it was always exercised in cooperation with France. Moreover, German leaders have repeatedly stressed their determination to exercise international influence primarily through the multilateral framework of the EC/EU. Contrary to the French, who saw political cooperation in the foreign policy field mainly as an instrument to upgrade their international status, the Germans made European political cooperation the cornerstone of their foreign policy. More than their counterparts in France, German policy makers were convinced that no European country, including Germany, could satisfy its political and economic interests only as part of a powerful EU. Hence, as many observers of Germany's attitude towards European integration have remarked, Germany has advanced further than the two other large countries in leaving behind nineteenth-century principles of national sovereignty and national interests (Keohane, Nye and Hoffmann, 1993: 56).

The completion of German unification has not changed this basic pattern in Germany's postwar foreign policy. German politicians continued to argue that Germany had no single national foreign policy goal and that the foreign policy interests of a larger Germany are European (Ash, 1993: 386). Consequently, when the suggestion was made that, to reflect the new balance of power among the world powers, Germany and Japan should occupy a permanent seat in the United Nation's Security Council, the Germans responded that it is the EU rather than Germany that is entitled to hold such a seat. Although the German leaders have become more assertive in their foreign policy behaviour, they stressed their conviction that Germany should not go its own way but rather continue its integration into the European Community. The prevention of German hegemony was seen as a major goal of German foreign policy. Borrowing from Thomas Mann, the German leaders have repeatedly declared that they do not aspire to a German Europe but want to live in a European Germany (Ash, 1993: 386–9). Timothy Ash has, however, qualified this statement, arguing that this does not mean that the German leaders actually pursue a German Europe. Although the Federal Republic has constitutionally anchored its commitment to seek a European Union that is bound to federal principles, it also supports adherence to the principle of subsidiarity. The federalism that the German government advocates for Europe is German-style decentralized federalism rather than French-style centralized federalism (Ash, 1993: 388).

The same applies to the German endorsement of the European Economic and Monetary Union (EMU). The German leader approved the EMU initiative, which implies the founding of a central European bank and the introduction of a single European currency, which will replace the powerful national Bundesbank and the strong national currency (D-Mark), mainly for political reasons. Being aware of the French concern and British anxiety about German economic and financial dominance, Kohl wanted to demonstrate German willingness to tie itself further to the European Union and to subject itself to common European institutions. In this respect the German leader ignored the domestic opposition which regarded the EMU and the replacement of the D-Mark by a common European currency mainly as a means to weaken the strong D-Mark by coupling it to the much weaker French franc. Kohl realized that such a monetary union served, in the short term, more of a French than a German interest and that the establishment of a central European bank, where Germany is only one of the participants in decision making on common financial policies, would set limits to the freedom of the politically independent German Bundesbank. To ensure that such an EMU would serve the German interests as well and would not enlarge the paymaster role of Germany, the Federal government, in association with the Bundesbank, dictated several stringent conditions for participation in the EMU and the structure of the proposed European central bank modelled on the high German financial norms and the political independence of the central bank. The final agreed terms for entry into the monetary union follow these conditions closely and in fact extend the German fiscal policies to the EMU. More symbolic but of no less importance was the decision to locate the new European central bank in Germany, next to the German central bank. As Kohl has assured his opponents at home, the common European currency will be just as strong and stable as the German D-Mark (cf. Ash, 1993: 388).

The growth in Germany's assertiveness after unification is also reflected in the German desire to improve the effectiveness of the EU's global performance. Kohl, for example, made no secret of his conviction that, to make an enlarged EU more decisive, it was important to deepen the foreign policy-making process through the introduction of qualified majority voting in foreign policy matters. Although Kohl, like Adenauer in the 1960s, had to be sensitive to the French commitment to preserve the larger member-states' veto in such a vital policy area as foreign policy, he repeatedly stressed the need to change the voting procedures so that the EU would be able to make decisions and take actions that go beyond the lowest common denominator. German policy makers have also increasingly been involved with the EU's foreign policy agenda setting to secure German foreign interests. Germany has been, for instance, the driving force behind the EU's policy towards eastern Europe and the crucial EU decision to recognize Slovenia and Croatia as independent republics.

However, as the recent European Council meetings demonstrate, the heavy financial price of German unification has changed the almost unlimited German willingness to act as the primary paymaster of European unification. To satisfy domestic criticism, the German government has become much more hostile towards costly EU policies, and it repeatedly demands a decrease in the German financial contribution to the EU. Like the French and British leaders, the German Chancellor calls on EU institutions to stay out of decision making that is rightfully the property of national governments (*European Voice*, 18–24 June 1998). These are still modest changes in the basically positive attitude towards European unification, but it illustrates that there are nevertheless limits to the almost unconditional German championship of European integration and true belief in a European super-state.

The British aloofness from European integration

Britain, which had been a key actor in western Europe before 1945, chose to stay aloof from European integration until its reorientation towards the EC in the early 1960s. Being a major player on the world stage until the Second World War, the ambition to maintain a global status had preference over the possibility of fulfilling a leading role in the process of European integration. Britain was forced to play a secondary role in the postwar bipolar global order which has been dominated by the two new superpowers: the United States and the Soviet Union. Exhausted economically and squeezed militarily by two world wars, Britain could not compete with the economic and military power of the United States and the military strength of the Soviet Union. But the British leaders were not willing to accept such a decline in their country's international status and held on to their claim for a place at the table where international issues were settled. Britain's foremost foreign policy goal during the postwar period was to keep a leading role in world politics. Northedge has characterized this continuing British concern with its global status as the desire of all British governments to maintain a foothold in worldwide centres of international decision making (Northedge, 1969: 175–7).

As one of the 'Big Three', Britain, in contrast to France, fulfilled during the war a central role in the construction of the postwar international order. Its wartime leader, Winston Churchill, was a major architect of the many diplomatic, economic and military institutional structures that were established during the war to regulate the political and economic international relations after the war. Churchill believed that Britain could hold its prominent status, in spite of the shift in global power to the new superpowers, through its important position in three inter-linked circles. The first circle was described by Churchill as the British Commonwealth and Empire, the second circle was characterized by him as the English-speaking world which included the United States and the British Dominions, while the third circle was pictured as a united Europe (cited in Hanrieder and Auton, 1980: 177). In all three circles, which correspond to the three main arenas of Britain's postwar diplomatic activities, Britain had, according to Churchill, a great part to play and stood in fact at the very point of junction among them. Churchill's view, which mirrored the central global role that Britain had played in the past and hardly reflected the real position that Britain occupied in the postwar international environment, was widely shared by British policy makers.

The first postwar British governments tried to maintain Britain's greatness through the reconstruction of Britain's worldwide economic role and the building of an Atlantic community rather than a European community. Being still an imperial power with worldwide established economic interests, the British policy makers were determined to preserve Britain's special position in world trade and the financial markets. They were convinced that Commonwealth and empire would give Britain the extra weight needed to play a decisive role alongside the Americans in the structuring of the postwar economic order. As Milward argues, 'the fact remained that about a third of the value of world trade was invoiced in sterling, and that obviously did give the United Kingdom a far greater influence in determining the institutions and workings of the international economy than any other European country' (1992: 355).

The British goal was to maintain Britain's greatness by means of preserving the world role of the British currency and defending the sterling/dollar parity. The British policy makers aimed at the establishment of an economic partnership with the United States based on joint responsibility for the management of a stable international monetary and trade system and a shared interest in creating a stable global financial and economic order which would prevent a recurrence of the collapse of the international monetary system and the subsequent economic crisis in the 1930s. Even though the British pound could not maintain its significant position as the world primary currency in world trade and had to transfer its function to the stronger American dollar, sterling was seen as vital to world trade. In spite of the weakness of the British economy at the end of the war, the Americans considered Britain at that time still to be crucial to any international monetary regime. The Bretton Woods Agreements, which were signed in 1944 by 44 states and provided until 1971 the foundation for such an order, were basically an Anglo-American plan. In essence the plan aimed at the establishment of an international monetary mechanism which would guarantee fixed international exchange rates, thus providing a solid foundation for international trade. A key element in this respect has been the sterling/dollar parity and their function as the world's reserve currency (Spero, 1977: 32–6).

Both Labour and Conservative governments were therefore more concerned with Britain's ties with the Commonwealth and close economic cooperation with the United States than active participation in European economic integration. In the view of the first postwar Labour Foreign Secretary Ernest Bevin, Britain was not just another European country (Milward, 1992: 354). But in addition to the preference given to the Commonwealth and collaboration with the United States, British governments also followed a different strategy with respect to European cooperation. During the war Churchill already disapproved of the concept of a western European bloc which was launched in the war period by some Foreign Office policy makers. Such a Western bloc would include France, Belgium, the Netherlands, Luxembourg and the Scandinavian countries. Churchill was more in favour of a close cooperation of the western European states based on economic collaboration, avoiding economic integration into Europe (Young, 1993: 14). The Labour government that was in power during the first postwar years followed the same line.

Consequently, when France took the initiative for the establishment of a custom union in the late 1940s, the British government showed little interest. Contrary to the other western European states which, at the end of the war, considered a West European custom union essential for the growth of intra-West European trade as part of the economic reconstruction of western Europe, the British leaders decided in 1948 not to participate in a regional West European custom union (Milward, 1984: 236). British scepticism and lack of interest were grounded in the fact that the short-term economic disadvantages of joining such a custom union far outweighed the long-term commercial benefits. British trade with Europe composed at that time only a quarter of British trade compared to the sterling area's half. The influential economic ministries argued that Britain's economic reconstruction must be based on the preservation of its economic independence and the maintenance of its special ties to the Commonwealth. The existence of the common financial arrangements in the sterling area and the imperial trade preferences offered Britain the possibility of increasing trade and exports. British participation in such a custom union would ruin, in their view, the whole structure of the British Commonwealth trading arrangements unless the Commonwealth were also part of such a custom union. But British policy makers never discussed such an alternative with the other West European states (Young, 1993: 8, 22; Milward, 1984: 239, 249).

The British negative attitude towards British participation in a western European custom union repeated itself during the negotiations over the establishment of the ECSC and the creation of the EEC. Britain considered close cooperation with France in the leadership of western Europe after the war as inevitable. But the

British differed very much from the French in their views on the institutional framework that the cooperation among the countries of western Europe had to take. British politicians disliked from the very beginning the supranational tendencies in the process of European integration and kept aloof from that process. As Urwin has argued, throughout the postwar period the British attitude towards European integration was guided by a principle (already established in the early 1950s) according to which Britain wished to remain a decisive player in western Europe without committing itself in anyway to supranationalism (Urwin, 1991: 72). In the case of the ECSC, Britain, which had the largest coal and steel industries in Europe and exported much of its steel to the Commonwealth, had little to gain from joining the ECSC. Moreover, since the Labour government had just nationalized the coal and steel industries, it was politically unthinkable that the Labour government would turn over the control of the two key industries to some European authority (Young, 1993: 33; George, 1990: 20). British officials were willing to consider close cooperation with their European partners but rejected any proposal that implied the transfer of national sovereignty to a supranational European authority. British diplomats attended the first meetings of the six ECSC members when the Six started to discuss in 1955 the creation of a common market. They followed the deliberations in an attempt to steer the Six away from a federal structure which was unacceptable to the British government. But as the British policy makers realized that their efforts to tempt the Six away from their intention to create a European Economic Community had failed, they decided to disengage Britain from the negotiations over the establishment of the EEC. They conceived instead a plan for a European free trade area as opposed to a custom union, which is what the common market proposal basically was. This free trade area was based on an agreement to remove tariffs on trade among the participating countries, instead of a common external tariff against the outside world. It included no commitment to deeper economic integration and, contrary to the EEC plan, excluded any central institutions (Young, 1993: 45–50). Although British officials already recognized in 1955 the decreasing economic importance of the Commonwealth for Britain and the growing significance of the EEC, the British leaders were not yet ready to place as much emphasis on Europe as on the Commonwealth or, as another observer has argued, to narrow their horizons to Europe alone (cited in Young, 1993: 55).

Only after almost two decades did Britain's political leadership finally realize that it was in their country's interest to adjust their international ambitions to Britain's military capacity and economic resources. The need to withdraw from empire and to abandon its imperial possessions stripped Britain of its major raw material sources, food supplies and export markets. At the same time Britain's export of goods to Europe in the 1960s exceeded the export to the Commonwealth, which made Europe, in economic terms, more important to Britain than the Commonwealth. Thus, the shift in global economic interests made a reorientation of the British economy towards Europe indispensable and forced the British policy makers to abandon the reluctant stance that they had adopted towards European integration. Moreover, contrary to their expectations, the EEC had turned out to be an economic success, while their own alternative of a European Free Trade Association (EFTA) did not manage to develop into the focal trading group that British policy makers expected it to be. Thus, Britain had in the early 1960s no alternative but to come to terms with the EEC and to seek Community membership (Young, 1993: 173). To put it another way, the British leaders at last understood that their belief that Europe needed them more than they needed Europe or that the EEC could not be successful without British participation, was rather a misperception.

The British government decided in 1961 to apply for EEC membership, but Britain's admission to the EC was blocked by de Gaulle. Although the French president shared with British leaders an unwillingness to surrender sovereignty to any supranational body, de Gaulle repeatedly vetoed British entry. The French president was concerned about a potential increase in American influence in the Community through the British, given the importance that the British leaders ascribed to their country's special relationship with the United States. In de Gaulle's view, the British could not qualify for Community membership as long as they gave priority to their transatlantic loyalty over their faithfulness to the common cause of European integration. But the main obstacle to British membership was actually rooted in the French fear of a diminishing leading role for France in the event of British membership. As a result, negotiations regarding Britain's request for EEC membership could not start until 1970, when the French veto was removed by de Gaulle's successor, Georges Pompidou.

The British hanging on to national sovereignty

An important rationale for Britain's reorientation towards European integration was, in addition to the expected economic benefits of EC membership, the wish to influence the process of European integration in their preferred direction: economic integration without political integration. The British leaders underestimated, however, the fact that at this stage of European integration, Britain as a latecomer was unable to influence the basic direction of the integration process, which implied the pooling of sovereignty in some sectors and the loss of a limited amount of sovereignty to common institutions. To gain entry, the British had to accept the existing Common Agricultural Policy (CAP) as well as the prevailing budgetary system in the Community. Neither were favourable to Britain and both faced the British from the very beginning with the problem of becoming a large net contributor to the EEC budget. The size of the British contribution to the EEC budget and the spending of the EC/EU budget would remain one of the key issues that would lead to tensions between Britain and its partners. Britain gained, from the start of its participation in the work of the Community in 1973, the reputation of being an awkward partner (George, 1990: 60–2). British governments would make concessions on further integration only when it appeared to coincide with their own views on the way that the integration process should progress. Whenever such a development did not correspond, in their view, with British interests, they would try to block institutional advancement towards closer unity and hinder closer cooperation in specific issue areas. British officials were, for instance, very much in favour of cooperation in the area of foreign policy and the performance of the EC as a single actor in international trade matters. But British leaders refused to compromise on closer monetary integration which may jeopardize the international position of the British pound or the ability of the British government to pursue a monetary policy independently of its European partners. Another example is the British endorsement of qualified majority voting on issues related to the implementation of the single market or the conclusion of international trade agreements like the General Agreement on Tariffs and Trade (GATT). At the same time they refused to adopt qualified majority voting in other policy areas or the more general field of foreign and security policy. In the first case the British leaders considered the application of the voting rule of qualified majority as beneficial to their economy, while in the second case such a development was seen as a threat to national sovereignty.

From the start, the relationship between Britain and its European partners was therefore troubled by the double-edged attitude of the British leaders towards the EC/EU, a posture that has been adopted mainly because of domestic politics. Contrary to France and Germany where the basic attitude towards the process of European integration has never been dictated by domestic politics, although the policy towards the EC has been a significant topic on the domestic political agenda, in Britain the fundamental stance on European integration and the policy towards the Community has continuously been a predominant issue in the domestic political debate. All the different Conservative as well as the various Labour governments have had to deal with opposition and criticism over EC membership in Parliament as well as within their own parties. In the formulation of the British negotiation positions in the Community, British political leaders and officials have always to take into account simultaneously the demands of the domestic political electorate and the views of their European counterparts. Although this is to some extent also the case in France and Germany, in Britain the political sensitivity over European policies has been much greater. Almost every substantial step forward in the direction of deeper and broader European integration has been in dispute. This has made Britain a very difficult partner to cope with. In fact, since Britain's entry to the EEC, British leaders and officials have not been ready to accept significant agreements with their European partners or to compromise over important deals unless they felt that the negotiated result could carry the approval of a majority in Parliament and bear the consent of a majority in their own party. Edward Heath, the first British prime minister who managed to overcome French opposition to British membership, was himself a true believer in European integration and was convinced that being a member of the world's largest trading bloc would strengthen Britain's voice in the world. However, to overcome the opposition to EEC membership in his own country, Heath still had to win a vote in parliament. He pursued a strategy that actually postponed all the difficulties for later negotiations and survived in Parliament a six-day entry debate, the longest since the war. But, due to the antagonism in his own Conservative Party about membership and the negotiated terms of entry, Heath had to mobilize the support of some Labour members who were in favour of entry, to get the European Communities Bill accepted by Parliament. His successor, the Labour Prime Minister Harold Wilson, was faced with a divided Labour Party on the issue of EEC membership. Although Wilson himself saw no alternative to EEC membership, he was forced to treat the matter as a major domestic political issue and decided not only to renegotiate the terms of entry but also to win approval of the renegotiated outcome from Parliament and also from the British people by means of a referendum. Despite broad opposition in the Labour Party, Wilson obtained in Parliament a large majority in favour of the renegotiated terms thanks to the endorsement of the government's proposals by many members from the opposition Conservative and Liberal parties. The referendum also revealed a vast majority of people in support of continued membership. But this outcome caused little change in the basic attitude of successive British governments to the EC. Britain's leaders and officials persisted in their refusal to accept compromise agreements if they felt that the outcome was against British interests.

Most notorious in this respect has been the repeated rejection by the British Prime Minister Margaret Thatcher and her successor, John Major, of any attempt to deepen the integration within the EC. Under Thatcher's premiership the British attitude towards the EC has turned into a zero-sum game where any British concession in the direction of further integration was seen as another loss of national sovereignty. Moreover, she made the struggle against what she condemned as the interventionist, protectionist, bureaucratic and federalist tendencies in the EC, the spearheads of her EC policy. Her fight for large reductions in Britain's net contribution to the EC's budget was inspired not only by the determination to get a satisfactory deal on Britain's financial contribution but also by her desire to sort out the imbalance of the Community's finances, stopping what she regarded as a waste of money on the extravagant CAP. But Thatcher, like her predecessors, was not fundamentally against European integration. She considered the movement towards closer European cooperation as to be almost irresistible but opposed European federalism and wanted to ensure, in the same way that de Gaulle did in the 1960s, that any moves towards European integration would not damage British interests and would be based on active cooperation between independent sovereign states, each with its own customs, traditions and identity. As she believed that nation-states should retain as far as possible their power and sovereignty and should be free to decide their own destiny, she firmly opposed what she saw as the creeping expansion of the Commission's authority into new policy areas and an attempt to create a European super-state which would subordinate Britain's political system to the demands of a remote European bureaucracy in Brussels (Thatcher, 1993: 742–5).

This made Britain not only a troublesome partner but sometimes also inconsistent in its attitude. Thatcher was, for instance, in favour of the completion of the common market and improvements in the common foreign policy. In her memoirs she pays tribute to the contribution made by the British European Commissioner, Lord Cockfield, in the realization of a single market. But at the same time she blames him for going native, moving from deregulating the market to reregulating it under the rubric of harmonization. To achieve the economic benefits of the single market, Thatcher was ready to pay the price of applying more majority voting in the Community (which implies the loss of national sovereignty). While she was willing to agree to majority voting on matters related to the single market, she was not prepared to accept that decisions about issues which she still regarded to be of national interest, such as the harmonization of the national indirect taxation rates (the so-called VAT) or the elimination of frontier controls, would be decided by qualified majority voting (Thatcher, 1993: 547, 553). Like other European leaders, Thatcher also believed that European political cooperation would help to reinforce western Europe's global standing and would strengthen Britain's international position. But in her view, such cooperation should not lead to a loss of sovereignty or the erosion of national sovereignty. She wanted, as she put it, 'closer co-operation between member states, which would nonetheless reserve the right of states to go their own way' (Thatcher, 1993: 548). How this was possible, she could not explain.

Under her successor, John Major, Britain's diplomatic negotiating style in the Community changed but the content of policy remained the same. Major's unwillingness to commit Britain to participation in the EMU and his refusal to endorse the common social policies as agreed in the TEU was completely in line with traditional British adherence to national sovereignty and British opposition towards the Franco-German strategy of piecemeal integration, implying a gradual loss of sovereignty. The change in the negotiating style provided Britain with significant 'opt-outs' on EMU and social policy, but at the same time it manoeuvred the country into an isolated position in the Community. The 'opt-out' formula has in fact introduced the institutionalization of a 'two-speed Europe', putting Germany and France undeniably in the driver's seat and leaving Britain behind. The replacement of the Conservative government by a Labour government in 1997 has brought little change in this respect. The Labour leadership demonstrates a more constructive attitude towards European integration, but it still sticks to the basic former beliefs on EU policies. It seems that the tone has changed but the music is still the same. The new government, for instance, still refuses to commit itself to EMU membership, postponing the decision on whether to join the EMU to a later date. During Britain's presidency of the EU the new Prime Minister Tony Blair managed to reach a consensus among its partners on a statement saying that EU institutions should get involved in policy issues only if and insofar as the objective of the proposed action cannot be sufficiently achieved by national or local government. This would, however, bear little influence in policy areas where the powers of the EU are already established, since this would make treaty changes necessary as well as the unconditional support of France and Germany (*European Voice*, 18–24 June 1998).

So far the British have never been able to break into the French–German connection. Although the British share with the French a concern about maintaining national sovereignty and were also troubled by the economic dominance of Germany, French leaders have maintained their basic distrust of Britain which they have regarded from the start of British membership as an American 'Trojan horse' in the Community. Even after German unification, about which neither country was enthusiastic, the French preferred to prevent German domination of the Community by tying Germany down in the Community through a deepening of the integration process, rather than counterbalance the increasing power of a united Germany by closer cooperation with the British. Moreover, contrary to Britain, France was willing to pay the price of a further loss of French sovereignty by the transfer of additional national power to the EU institutions. British leaders were also unsuccessful in their attempts to build some kind of special relationship with the German leaders. Britain's troublesome attitude towards the Community aroused continuous irritation in the German leaders who considered the British attitude the main obstruction to progress in the process of European integration. As a result, Britain has been confronted time and again by the French and German leaders with Franco-German bargains which have confronted Britain's leaders with the dilemma of either approving a pre-arranged Franco-German plan or being left aside.

Chapter 3

National foreign policy patterns: the second-rank states

In this chapter we will deal with the other twelve member-states which will be clustered in three groups of countries: the Benelux states (Belgium, the Netherlands and Luxembourg); the Mediterranean countries (Italy, Spain, Portugal and Greece); and the fringe states (Denmark, Ireland, Sweden, Finland and Austria).

The Benelux countries: a passion for supranationalism

The three Benelux countries, Belgium, the Netherlands and Luxembourg, form together with the Franco-German alliance the core of countries that have always been in the forefront of European integration. Notwithstanding the reluctant attitude of the governments of the three Benelux countries towards supranational institutions in the first years after the Second World War, the overall postwar record of the three countries towards European integration shows a common passion for progress towards supranational arrangements. Although one can trace some idealism in this fervent support for supranationalism, it has had more to do with realism. To escape a domination of the larger states, the political elites in these three countries have developed a deep-rooted belief in the need to strengthen the supranational bodies of the Community, the European Commission, the European Parliament and the European Court, at the expense of the Council of Ministers. The smaller Benelux states felt that the Council, which had originally been created, on their insistence, to safeguard the interests of the smaller member-states, increasingly served the interests of the larger states rather than the interests of the smaller states. As deals among the larger states came to play a pivotal role in the practice of decision making in the Council, this body has turned into the symbol of the intergovernmental tendencies in the Community.

The Benelux countries in fact established the first postwar integrative organization in western Europe: a Benelux custom union. Whereas Belgium and Luxembourg already had an economic union in 1921, the movement towards economic cooperation among the Benelux as a whole started during the war. The governments of Belgium, the Netherlands and Luxembourg saw economic cooperation in postwar Europe as an essential condition for economic prosperity. To advance the postwar trade among Belgium, the Netherlands and Luxembourg, they signed an agreement in 1944 to form a custom union. However, the agreement to lift the custom barriers between the three countries was not effected until 1948 and even then it was not fully implemented. The main concern of the smaller European states after the war was economic recovery. The Dutch government in particular preferred a custom union on a broader scale and wanted to use for that purpose another organizational framework, namely the Organization for European Economic Cooperation (OEEC), which was established in 1948 to carry out the European Recovery Programme (the so-called Marshall aid programme). The Netherlands had already turned down a French proposal to create a custom union between France and the Benelux. The Belgian government was initially ready to collaborate but later shared the Dutch requirement that both Germany and Britain had to be included in any such scheme. In 1950 the Dutch Foreign Minister Stikker presented a plan for trade liberalization in western Europe with a much wider scope. It specified an industry-by-industry approach to western European integration and included proposals for tariff reductions among the members of the OEEC. However, the Stikker Plan received a cool reception from the other states and was soon overtaken by the Schuman Plan (Griffiths, 1980: 278; Milward, 1984: 446).

It is not surprising that Stikker initially expressed little enthusiasm for the French proposals regarding the ECSC. The Dutch foreign minister had reservations concerning the small scope of the ECSC both in terms of membership and policy areas. However, of more importance was the Dutch and Belgian objection to the great powers given to the supranational executive of the ECSC, the newly established High Authority which was supposed to operate independently of the member-states. On the insistence of the two countries, a Council of Ministers was created to counterbalance the powers of the High Authority and to safeguard the interests of the member-states. Although the Benelux desired, during the negotiations on the ECSC, that the directives to the High Authority be issued by the Council of Ministers, they had to settle for an arrangement that gave the Council only the powers to review the decisions of the High Authority, hence providing some control to the national governments over the functioning of the High Authority (Milward, 1984: 409, 417). There was at that early stage of European integration no sign of the belief in supranationalism that was later to become the hallmark of the Dutch approach towards European integration (Griffiths, 1980: 278–9). The Dutch and Belgian governments finally approved the ECSC agreement mainly for political reasons. Both countries realized that the ECSC could be considered vital to the security of western Europe as it could contribute to the ending of the rivalry between France and Germany. They were also sensitive to the American demand for further progress towards European integration which the American government saw as an essential part of the economic reconstruction of western Europe. Of no less importance for the Belgian endorsement of the ECSC were the indirect political and financial benefits offered by the ECSC. The new organization could help the Belgian government to carry out a much-needed reconstruction of the Belgian coal industry. The blame for this unpopular measure could be laid on an external authority, which in addition was also ready to provide the necessary funds for the reconstruction. Hence, as Milward has concluded, there is no trace of idealism in the Belgian decision to ratify the ECSC treaty (Milward, 1992: 83, 116).

To satisfy its commercial interests, in 1952 the Dutch government tried again to move towards a broader custom union than the Benelux, this time among the six members of the ECSC. The less ambitious Beyen Plan (named after Stikker's successor as foreign minister) reflected a change of attitude in the foreign policy of the Netherlands towards European integration. Beyen was less convinced than his predecessor about the necessity of including Britain in a West European custom union and wanted to exploit the success of the ECSC to extend the common market for coal and steel to other products as well. It was also a modest attempt to change the commercial protectionist policies of France and Italy, whose markets became potentially more important as a result of the changes in the Dutch postwar trade pattern. Whereas exports to Britain were declining, the exports to its ECSC partners, especially West Germany, were rising. Beyen's plan included proposals for a gradual, but automatic and irreversible, tariff reduction between the Six with a fixed date for the final completion of the custom union. It also suggested setting up a supranational authority (analogous to the High Authority) to supervise and enforce these tariff cuts (Milward, 1992: 187). But the Netherlands was unable to gain the support of the other ECSC members, not even Belgium.

Only after the French failure to establish a European defence community and a European community could the Dutch plan for a common market in western Europe have another chance. Combining his original plan with Monnet's new plans for further integration in the areas of transport, energy and nuclear technology, Beyen convinced the other two Benelux partners to present a joint Benelux initiative for a common market among the six ECSC members. The so-called Benelux memorandum played an important role in the renegotiations on the creation of the EEC. Under the chairmanship of the Belgian Foreign Minister Paul-Henri Spaak, the Six reached an agreement on economic integration in areas such as trade, transport, energy and agriculture, as well as an institutional framework to supervise the newly established EEC. However, this time the Benelux countries were less successful in realizing their aims than during the previous negotiations over the establishment of the ECSC. The Treaty of Rome, wherein the outcome of the negotiations was codified, did not immediately create a common market. It was more an agreement on the procedures to reach such an ultimate goal. Neither does the final institutional structure in the treaty reflect the supranational ideas implied in the Dutch proposals. The Dutch, for instance, wanted to entrust the supranational Commission with decisive powers over certain policy areas such as external trade or competition policy, and wished to allow the Council of Ministers to act only on initiatives from the Commission.

The Dutch demands were, however, not so much inspired by a belief in supra-nationalism as prompted by a clear self-interest. To assure the creation of a common market, the Dutch government wanted to make the implementation of such a market treaty based, and to entrust its enforcement to a supranational body like the Commission that was able to operate independently of the intergovernmental bargaining of the member-states in the Council of Ministers. Germany also favoured a great degree of supranationality in the institutional structure of the EEC, but was more inclined to meet the French unwillingness to give the Commission more powers compared to the Council. The final treaty appointed the Commission as the executive of the EEC, but the decision-making powers were delegated to the Council of Ministers. The Commission was only authorized to initiate proposals for further decision making in the Council. This outcome represented a compromise between the French and German positions and took almost no account of the Dutch demands. As Milward argues, once the French and German leaders 'had laid out the path for the negotiations the smaller countries simply had to take what was handed down to them by the French and Germans' (Milward, 1992: 217). It would repeat itself almost every time when the Community, standing on the crossroads of another stage in the integration process, had to decide whether to change the existing institutional balance in the Community in favour of more supranationalism or to maintain the status quo.

However, the Dutch refusal in the early 1960s to accept the French design for a political union, the so-called Fouchet Plan, proves that western Europe did not always have to be organized in the way the French demanded. The proposed Fouchet Plan was basically an attempt by the French President de Gaulle to found a West European political union which could be useful in reestablishing France's leadership role in the EEC and could serve as a counterbalance to the Atlantic alliance. The proposed political union could at the same time help de Gaulle to impose his concept of European integration on his EEC partners. It was supposed to be an intergovernmental union of states in which a council of heads of state or government, assisted by their foreign ministers, would play the key role; decisions would be taken unanimously to guarantee national sovereignty, and a European political commission comprised of officials from the national foreign ministries would prepare and implement the decision making. De Gaulle's plan for a political union was supported by Adenauer, but was strongly resisted by the Dutch Foreign Minister Joseph Luns. The Netherlands preferred to maintain the EEC essentially as an organizational framework for free trade. Although the realization of the Fouchet Plan would have weakened the EEC and its executive, the European Commission, Luns opposed the Fouchet proposals mainly because of the implications that such a political union may bear on the Atlantic alliance. Luns considered the proposed political union not only as a French alternative to the EEC but also as a French alternative to NATO. He saw in the plan essentially a French effort to undermine the Anglo-American leadership of the Atlantic alliance which he regarded as vital to West Europe's security. Instead of an outright rejection of the Fouchet Plan, Luns made his approval of the Fouchet Plan conditional upon Britain's entry into the EEC, mainly for tactical reasons. In this requirement Luns was joined by the Belgian Foreign Minister Spaak who, like Luns, believed that Britain could serve as a counterweight to the danger of a French–German hegemony (cf. Wertz, 1992: 21). In view of the French opposition to Britain's admission to the EEC, this condition was almost equal to a veto as an agreement over the Fouchet Plan needed the consent of all six EEC partners.

During the negotiations on the Fouchet proposals, the Netherlands and Belgium also played the supranational card. Arguing against the intergovernmental structure of the proposed political union, the Dutch and Belgian foreign minister made his country's participation in the union also conditional upon the strengthening of the existing supranational institutions of the EEC and the introduction of new supranational elements in the Fouchet Plan. Some historians have claimed, however, that this position did not have much to do with a forceful defence of supranationalism but was simply a cynical tactical manoeuvre on the side of Luns to block the development towards a political union (Griffiths, 1980: 281).

Although the Benelux presented themselves in the 1960s as the champion of supranationalism, during the 1970s the Benelux came to terms with the intergovernmental direction that the process of European integration had taken and learned to accept that they were unable to frame the EEC in a more supranational structure. During The Hague summit of 1969, the Benelux governments endorsed the French suggestion to start political consultations on foreign policy matters outside the EC's institutional framework. This was the first meeting of the EEC leaders after de Gaulle's departure from office in an attempt to set the process of European integration on track again. A year later, the Benelux supported the first arrangements for the coordination of the member-states' foreign policies which had a strong intergovernmental nature. Paradoxically, in spite of their declared antagonism towards the strengthening of intergovernmental cooperation in the Community, they accepted that the decision making of the ministerial meetings as well as the functioning of the national officials within the EPC were kept outside the institutional and organizational structure of the EC. Moreover, in 1974 the Benelux also approved a French proposal to institutionalize the regular summit meetings of the EC's heads of state or government through the establishment of the European Council. This meant not only the sanctioning of the introduction of more intergovernmental elements in the Community, but also a relative loss of power for the smaller EC members as it increased the bargaining advantages of the larger states. Such a proposition was earlier turned down by the Benelux when it was launched by de Gaulle in 1960.

The Netherlands made a last attempt to turn the direction of the development of the EC towards a more supranational structure when it presided over the negotiations of the TEU in 1991. Although the main task of the Dutch presidency was to conclude the drafting of a new treaty on a European union, which had already progressed under the former presidency, the Dutch government decided to disregard the negotiation results that had been achieved thus far and to present a new draft treaty. For the Dutch foreign policy makers, adherence to supranationalism was obviously not just rhetoric. The fundamental difference between the former draft and the Dutch draft was the proposed institutional structure. While the former draft suggested a hybrid structure of three pillars, one comprising the current EC, a second incorporating EPC under the new heading of CFSP and a third one embracing the new field of justice and home affairs, the Dutch proposed to create a single institutional structure for all the activities of the Union. Hence, in the former draft, cooperation in the area of foreign and security policy as well as cooperation in the fields of justice and home affairs were not subjected to the supranational institutions of the Union, whereas the Dutch draft integrated the two policy areas into the existing EC structure. In the former draft the provisions on the common commercial policy and the common foreign and security policy, for instance, were placed in different parts of the proposed treaty; in the Dutch draft they were placed in the same part that dealt with the external relations of the EC (cf. Laursen and Vanhoonacker, 1992: 14–17).

Belgium, like the Netherlands, also favoured a unified structure, but as the Belgian negotiators realized that such an approach had little chance in the face of French and British opposition, they preferred to ensure some linkages between the separate pillars and made a fruitless attempt to secure at least the merger of the three pillars in the near future (Laursen and Vanhoonacker, 1992: 40–6). With the exception of Belgium, all the other member-states rejected the proposed draft. Whereas the former draft was considered a compromise between the different positions of the member-states, the Dutch new proposals were seen as a self-willed attempt of the Netherlands to impose its own supranational views on the other countries. The Dutch government was forced to come up with a revised draft treaty that would be more in line with the earlier draft, and would serve as the basic draft for final negotiations on the Maastricht Treaty.

This unsuccessful campaign for a more supranational Union has made the Netherlands and Belgium more pragmatic in their efforts to turn the tide of intergovernmentalism in an enlarged EU. In the next intergovernmental conference where the Dutch had to preside again over the final intergovernmental negotiations of the revision of the TEU by the Treaty of Amsterdam, the Dutch government has taken a more pragmatic position towards the institutional structure of the Union. This time the government has not challenged the three-pillar structure of the Union as such. Instead, it has focused with Belgium on safeguarding the irreversibility of the achievements of European integration thus far, as well as the improvement of the functioning of the Union within its current structure. But the Netherlands still advocate a stronger role for the Commission in the preparation and implementation of the CFSP, and the extension of qualified majority voting to this policy area.

However, while the national consensus about the need to continue the process of European integration in all three Benelux countries still exists, one can nevertheless sense in the Netherlands a departure from the almost dogmatic belief in the advantages of European integration. As a result of this change of mentality among Dutch politicians and officials regarding the merits of European integration, it has become common among Dutch policy makers to express their doubts as to whether the Dutch government should approve initiatives of the Commission to start new European action programmes, given their misgivings about the lack of budgetary discipline of the European Commission and the European Parliament. It has become not unusual to employ in this connection the basic principle of subsidiarity as an argument against the transfer of certain responsibilities in a specific policy area from the national to the European level. In the Dutch memoranda prepared for the intergovernmental conference to review the TEU which started in 1996, the Dutch government has explicitly stated that European government and legislation are not an end in themselves. Emphasizing the basic principle of subsidiarity, saying that decisions should be taken as closely as possible to the citizens, the Dutch government argues that in its view the EU must take action only where the member-states are no longer able to offer satisfactory answers to social, economic and political questions. It has stressed that when the Commission submits a proposal, it is obliged to explain why regulations at European level are necessary. The more critical attitude of the Dutch government towards an extension of the activities of the Commission has much to do with the simple fact that the Netherlands has become the second large net contributor (in relative terms) to the EU, after Germany. The Dutch government realizes that the benefits of its EU membership for the economy as a whole outweigh the costs of being a large net contributor, but Dutch politicians also realize that since the financial contribution to the EU involves a diversion of funds from national priorities, there is a limit to the extent to which a position as a net contributor can be accepted by the public. This might be the beginning of some second thoughts about the merits of further integration and the start of some kind of political debate about the limits of European integration. In Belgium and Luxembourg the adoption of a more critical attitude towards the blessings of further integration seems very remote. This is not only because both countries still receive more payments from the EU than their financial contribution to that budget. It has also to do with the fact that both countries have less difficulty with the process of federalization. This applies especially to Belgium where the federal government is already involved in a substantial transfer of sovereignty in many policy areas from the federal government to the regional governments.

The Mediterranean member-states: turning their faces to Europe

Although Italy, Greece, Spain and Portugal entered the Community on different occasions, the four Mediterranean member-states have joined the EC not merely because of the economic benefits of EC membership. All four southern European countries joined the EC shortly after their departure from a period of fascism and a transformation from an authoritarian or dictatorial regime to a democratic system. Their leaders believed that EC membership would help them to regain international respect and to consolidate the newly established democratic institutions in their countries. The four Mediterranean countries differ, however, in the intensity of their enthusiasm towards European integration. While Italy is a fervent supporter of any new step in the direction of closer integration, Greece is less willing to surrender its sovereignty to the Community. Spain clearly does not fear tighter integration, while Portugal takes a more cautious attitude.

The Italian leaders' willingness to transfer national sovereignty to a supranational European authority is, besides the war experience, rooted in Italian political thought which saw Italian unity in the nineteenth century as a first stage in the uniting of Europe. Some of Italy's most influential leaders in the early postwar years, of which Alcide de Gasperi and Altiero Spinelli were the most prominent, were true believers in European federalism and were strongly committed to the idea of European unity. During the war the Italian resistance movement had already adopted some of Spinelli's documents arguing in favour of a federal structure in postwar Europe and leading to establishment of the European federalist movement. Spinelli was also the main drafter of a document published in 1944 in Geneva and circulated among resistance groups throughout Europe, proposing in postwar Europe a federal

Europe with a written constitution and a supranational government, parliament, court and army. Forty years later Spinelli would be, once again, the drafter of a detailed blueprint for a political union with a single supranational institutional framework that would be adopted by the European Parliament (Urwin, 1991: 8, 223). On many occasions in the history of European integration where stagnation or crises paralysed the integration process, Italian leaders and foreign ministers played a vital role in the launching of initiatives or the search for compromises. The joint German–Italian plan of 1981 for a European union, for instance, known as the Genscher–Colombo initiative, triggered the process that finally resulted in the SEA and the later TEU. Italian foreign policy makers were never hindered by constitutional provisions or by parliamentary opposition to the transfer of national sovereignty to the Community or the Union – to the contrary. With respect to the ratification of the TEU, for example, the Italian Parliament went as far as making its own ratification of the Treaty conditional upon the endorsement of the TEU by the European Parliament.

Despite this intellectual and political commitment to the cause of a united Europe and the strong advocacy of supranational institutions, Italy enjoys little authority among the other member-states. This lack of authority is essentially a result of the gap between Italy's federalist rhetoric and its poor performance in implementing decisions agreed at the EC level. Many observers of Italy's relations with the EC have noted the inability of the Italian government to translate EC directives into Italian law and the poor Italian compliance with judgments of the European Court (cf. Hine, 1993: 288; Story, 1993: 235). Italy has, however, tried to compensate for its lack of authority by associating itself with the larger states: France, Germany and Britain. This pragmatic attitude results in middle-of-the-road positions rather than the principled positions that one would expect from the Italian belief in supranational arrangements. During the negotiations of the TEU, for example, Italy initially favoured the Dutch design but finally joined the powerful Franco-German coalition in its rejection of the Dutch draft treaty. Italy also tries to act as a bridge builder between the Franco-German coalition and Britain or to join one of the larger states in a common enterprise such as the Genscher–Colombo initiative.

After the transformation of Spain into a constitutional democracy in 1975 and the revolution in Portugal in 1974, Spain and Portugal have turned their faces again to Europe. The absence from European politics was, however, not a deliberate choice of both countries but rather imposed on the two countries because of the totalitarian character of their regimes. EEC membership was out of the question for both Spain and Portugal since adherence to democratic values is conditional upon membership. This has not prevented the two countries from pursuing their economic interests by associating themselves with the EEC through other means. Portugal, which participated in EFTA, signed a free trade agreement with the EEC in 1972. The Community denied to Spain an associated membership but endorsed in 1970 a preferential agreement. Spain and Portugal are latecomers to the EC, but while Portugal has kept a low profile, Spain has become an active member and seeks alliances with the leading EU member-states. During meetings of the European Council, Spain has associated itself many times with France and Germany or acted like Italy as a go-between in bridging the different positions of the French–German alliance and Britain. In a relatively short period it managed to build a reputation as a member-state that is strongly committed to the cause of European integration. At the same time, Spain has learned to look after its own interests, acting as the promoter and defender of the interests of the Mediterranean member-states as a whole.

After their entry to the EC in 1986 Spain and Portugal have not only formally accepted the *acquis communautaire*, the whole corpus of treaties and legislations as well as the general policy framework that have been accepted by the member-states over the years and have to be accepted as non-negotiable by new members; they have also acted as loyal members in the integrationist spirit of older member-states. Their record of implementing the EC directives concerning the completion of the Community's single market is, for example, much better than the poor record of Italy and even better than other veteran member-states. In the negotiations of the TEU, Spain and Portugal have again taken a constructive attitude, supporting the mainstream positions as represented by the French–German views. Like the two larger states, they favour changes in the existing institutional balance and the intensification of the CFSP, expressing a clear preference for an evolutionary process rather than radical leaps forward. With respect to the delicate issue of the introduction of qualified majority voting in CFSP matters, for example, Spain and Portugal stick to the unanimity rule but have introduced during the TEU negotiations the possibility of abstention as a way out of deadlocks. Unlike Spain, Portugal had a more reserved attitude with respect to the priority given in the TEU to the West European Union (WEU) over the North Atlantic Treaty Organization (NATO) as the future military arm of the Union, but in spite of these reservations Portugal took up the mainstream attitude among the member-states and accepted the compromise that has been reached.

In this respect Greece, contrary to the three other Mediterranean countries, has a very unstable record. The troublesome relationship between Greece and the other member-states started shortly after the Greek accession to the EC in January 1981. A change of government ten months later also meant a change of attitude towards European integration. While the former government, which negotiated the terms of membership, was eager to join the EC in the hope of ending the country's isolation from European politics as a result of the military dictatorship between 1967 and 1974, the new socialist government took a hostile position towards European integration. The leader of the socialist party (PASOK), Andreas Papandreou, opposed accession and promised during the election campaign to hold a referendum on EC membership. Once in power, Papandreou accepted EC membership and adopted a more pragmatic attitude towards the EC. Instead of holding a referendum or renegotiating Greece's terms of entry, the Greek government asked the EC for a reexamination of the country's accession terms to the EC. Realizing that withdrawal from the Community would harm the economic interests of his country, Papandreou wanted only to minimize the negative effects from accession and to establish a new kind of relationship between Greece and the EC. Papandreou demanded from the Community more financial support and economic help for his country and claimed the right of Greece to conduct an independent foreign policy. In an attempt to accelerate the integration of Greece in the Community, the Commission reacted positively to the first request. It recognized that Greece faced special economic and social problems as a result of the necessity to compete with the more developed northern member-states. The Commission also made several proposals to help the country to overcome these difficulties and to ease the integration of Greece into the EC. After the endorsement of this plan by the Council in 1983, Greece became the second largest beneficiary member-state (after France and with Spain and Portugal still outside the Community) of a special programme for the Mediterranean regions. There was, however, little that the EC could do to encourage the Greek government to stay in line with the common foreign policy of the Community. Since EPC had in fact a voluntary character, the other member-states could not prevent the Greek government from dissenting from the consensus reached by the foreign ministers in EPC meetings or from declaring that it would not be bound to common declarations (cf. Christakis, 1993).

Over the years the Greek socialist government gradually shifted from a hostile position towards a more cooperative one. The Greek socialists realized that Greece needed the financial aid of the Community to improve its difficult economic circumstances and that their independent foreign policy positions had little impact on the Community as a whole. The Greek leaders also learned that they could exploit the desperate economic situation in their country to squeeze extra financial resources from the Community. They removed, for instance, their blocking opposition to the accession of Spain and Portugal after the promise of extra financial help from the Commission to meet the competition from the two newcomers. Greece remained, however, at odds with most of the other member-states, not only on foreign policy matters but also on questions related to the institutional development of the EC. Together with Britain and Denmark, Greece resisted the supranational tendencies in the Union and defended national sovereignty. Greece resisted any proposal to give up the right of a member-state to use the veto and declared itself time and again in favour of the so-called Luxembourg compromise. It opposed any change in the intergovernmental character of EPC, and insisted on the consensus rule, stressing its right to formulate its own foreign policy. The unsteadiness in the overall attitude of Greece towards the EC came up again during the negotiations of the TEU, when another change of government (placing the socialists in the opposition for a while) meant a U-turn once more in the Greek attitude towards European integration. This time the Greek government gave its blessing to the use of qualified majority voting in a large number of policy areas. It was also strongly in favour of strengthening the CFSP identity of the Community and suggested several measures to improve efficiency in common foreign policy making (Laursen and Vanhoonacker, 1992: 79–97). But the original positive attitude towards the introduction of qualified majority voting in CFSP matters faded away as a result of the rising disagreements between Greece and its European partners over the common policies in the Balkan and the future relationship with Turkey. Once again the Greek government was strongly in favour of maintaining the veto power in CFSP issues.

While the four southern EU members have rarely shared a common position regarding the future institutional development of the EU, they have frequently joined forces to safeguard specific southern European interests and to advance the common goal of increased EU support for the economic development of the southern member-states. Since Italy prefers not to be associated with the pursuit of purely Mediterranean interests and favours operating behind the scenes, Spain has become the champion of southern European interests. The bridging of the differences in economic development between the prosperous northern and the poor southern regions of the Union has become one of its main objectives. Its former leader Felipe Gonzalez has made the necessity of closing the economic and social distance between north and south a matter of principle, which concerns not only the southern member-states but the EC as a whole. During the negotiations of the SEA and the TEU, the Mediterranean member-states succeeded in linking the deepening of the institutional development in the Community to a reinforcement of the economic and social cohesion. A so-called cohesion fund has been created and the funds for regional development, of which the southern countries are the main beneficiaries, has been increased. The EU member-states have agreed, for instance, to apply Community funds to regions where economic and social development are below 75 per cent of the EU's average. This involves the whole of Greece and Portugal, as well as significant parts of Spain and Italy. Spain, Portugal and Greece realize, however, that in an enlarged EU they would have to compete over distribution of EU funds with the new members from Central, East and South Europe. This has increased the coherence among the three countries which have already declared that they will agree to an enlargement in the size of the Union only if this will not be at the expense of the current cohesion policy.

The fringe countries: a worry about the loss of sovereignty

Denmark, Ireland, Sweden, Finland and Austria are not only located on the fringe of the European Union, but also all these countries could hardly be considered as the mainstream of European integration. None of these countries has joined the EC or EU out of a deep belief in European integration, but simply because of the economic advantages that the common market offered its members. Moreover, Denmark and Ireland had almost no other choice but to follow the United Kingdom, at that time their major export market and trade partner, when the British left EFTA in 1973 to join the EC. They have committed themselves to the enterprise of European integration, which they have joined in different enlargement rounds, but, with the exception perhaps of Ireland, they clearly do not share all the ideas on European integration and certainly do not share the Benelux obsession with supranationalism. Since membership of the EC implies the risk of dominance by the larger members and the loss of sovereignty, all five countries share, with different levels of intensity, a worry about the loss of national independence.

The Danish attitude towards the EC/EU has always shifted between anxiety about economic loss in the case of non-participation or withdrawal and fears about the loss of its political autonomy in the case of membership. Danish politicians saw the Community essentially as an economic arrangement and have continuously rejected plans for an expansion of the Community into the political domain (Tiilikainen and Petersen, 1993: 81–2). As the Danish accession to the EC coincided with a period of stagnation in the integration process, the Danish had little to worry about. The advantages of the common market and especially the benefits from the CAP were fully exploited, while the EPC was still in its beginning stage. When the process of integration gained renewed momentum in the 1980s following a double track of both economic and political integration, the Danish became aware of the political price they had to pay for continued membership. The agreement on the SEA obliged the Danish to balance the increased advantages of a single market against the disadvantages of some loss of national sovereignty. Moreover, as any revision of the Treaty of Rome had to be sanctioned by Parliament, the government had to overcome the constitutional obstacles to the transfer of national sovereignty to supranational bodies. The Danish constitution stipulates that such a transfer requires the approval of a special law by a five-sixths majority in Parliament or, if such a majority is not feasible, the endorsement by a simple majority in a popular referendum. Not surprisingly, the government argued during the renegotiations in favour of a full implementation of the existing treaties and the revitalization of the competence of the EC institution as laid down in the Treaty of Rome. Consequently Denmark opposed the starting of the formal negotiations on the SEA and, once started, the Danish government favoured the completion of the internal market but opposed the proposed institutional reforms. However, Denmark had to compromise and finally signed the SEA, though not until it had been approved by a referendum after its initial rejection by Parliament.

The discord over the SEA repeated itself during the negotiations of the TEU and the process of ratification. The Danish government once again opposed institutional changes that would increase the decision-making powers of the EU at the expense of the national decision-making capacity. The government advocated only the deepening of integration in the environmental policy area, demanding common policies and qualified majority voting. In the common foreign policy area, on the other hand, unanimous voting had to remain the rule and it had to exclude a common defence policy (cf. Laursen and Vanhoonacker, 1992: 71–7). The government failed, however, to receive the required majority for the ratification of the TEU from Parliament or directly from the Danish people by means of a referendum. This time the Danish people were much more hostile towards the creeping loss of national authority to EC institutions and were determined to secure Denmark's independence by keeping as much control as possible over their national sovereignty.

Since the Danish rejection of the Maastricht Treaty blocked the further implementation of the Treaty, the Danish government and its EC partners were forced to renegotiate informally Denmark's terms of accepting the TEU. The way out was a liberal application of the opt-out formula. Although Denmark participated in the common foreign policy of the Union, it was allowed not to be involved in the decision making on the common defence policy and was not obliged to become a member of the WEU. As the WEU was projected as the future military arm of the Union, member-states that were not yet members of the WEU were encouraged to become so. Denmark, however, preferred to maintain the organization of its national defence policy within the NATO framework. Denmark was also allowed to stay out of the EMU. It kept its right to formulate its national monetary policy, was allowed to keep its national currency and to stay out of the common currency when the other member-states decide to do so. It was also given the option to opt out of cooperation in the field of justice and home affairs, if this cooperation would change its current intergovernmental structure (cf. Tiilikainen and Petersen, 1993: 90–101).

Contrary to Denmark, Ireland does not fear further integration and its government and people express continuously a very supportive attitude towards European integration. Ireland has traditionally been more concerned about British dominance. Like the Benelux countries, it considers a supranational structure as safeguard against the dominance of the larger member-states. But unlike the Benelux countries, Ireland is less inclined to change the existing balance between the Council and the Commission at the expense of the former. To restrain the dominance of the large states in the Council, Ireland backs the wide use of qualified majority voting in the Council. The only reservation is made with respect to the sensitive area of foreign policy where Ireland wants to preserve the consensus rule. As long as decisions on common positions and joint action are taken by a unanimous vote, Ireland can be certain that such decisions do not jeopardize its neutrality. The main concern of successive Irish governments has actually been the question of how to combine full participation in the CFSP of the EU with Ireland's neutrality.

Until the last enlargement Ireland has been the only member-state with a declared neutral foreign and security policy. But being a neutral country has not prevented Ireland from participating fully in the making of the common foreign policy. Formally Ireland still sticks to its neutrality. Its government has thus far avoided a political debate about the question of whether EC or EU membership is compatible with participation in EPC or the CFSP, by making a distinction between political and military neutrality. The Irish government argued, for example, during the ratification process of the SEA that its endorsement of the SEA, which also codified the EPC practice and committed Ireland to the *acquis politique* of the Community, was not in conflict with Irish neutrality. Referring to the distinction made by the member-states between the political and economic aspect of security on the one hand and the military aspects of security on the other, it defended the position that the provisions included in the SEA do not touch upon military security matters. When this was disputed by the Irish Supreme Court, the government had to use a referendum to proceed on the ratification of the SEA. To satisfy the opponents of ratification who argued that a ratification would imply the loss of neutrality, the Irish government attached to its ratification an official declaration which confirms Ireland's long-established policy of military neutrality and says that coordination of positions on the political and economic aspects of security does not include the military aspects of security and does not affect Ireland's right to act or refrain from acting in any way that might affect the country's international status of military neutrality (cited in Nicoll and Trevor, 1994: 235–6).

During the negotiations of the TEU, the Irish government could not ignore the wish of the Franco-German bloc, with the support of many other member-states, to build into the proposed EU a military dimension as well. Ireland had to make a decision either to stay out of the CFSP or to participate in the proposed military cooperation. The Irish government chose to take a pragmatic approach and to embark on this new avenue as well. Since the TEU provisions on a common foreign and security policy stipulated only the 'eventual framing of a common defence policy, which might in time lead to a common defence' (*Treaty on European Union*,

1992: Art. J.4), the government could argue that nothing was decided yet. Moreover, another part in Article J.4 of the TEU which says that the common defence policy of the Union 'shall not prejudice the specific character of the security and defence policy of certain member states' offered, in the view of the Irish government, a sufficient safeguard for Ireland to preserve its neutrality or, in the worse case, to opt out (cf. Laursen and Vanhoonacker, 1992: 136; Nicoll and Salmon, 1994: 237–8). Its opponents at home argued nevertheless that the ratification of the Treaty implied a departure from neutrality since the Irish government has committed the country to a common defence.

For Ireland, the economic benefits of membership far outweigh the loss of autonomy in the conduct of its foreign relations. This is not only because of the dependency on trade with the EC but also because of the significant contributions from the EC to the economic development of certain regions in Ireland which made the country one of the largest beneficiaries of the economic and social cohesion policy of the EC/EU. Given the considerable amount of financial transfers from the Community funds in the Irish budget, withdrawal from the EU because of a loss of sovereignty is conceived by Irish politicians as economic suicide (Nicoll and Trevor, 1994: 235). But this does not mean that the Irish government is not sensitive at all to matters of national sovereignty. The Irish government insisted, for example, on a special protocol attached to the Treaty that confirms the right of Ireland to maintain its prohibition of abortion. Ireland, like Denmark, attaches great value to the preservation of its autonomy in matters that are seen as vital issues, but it has chosen another more pragmatic strategy to pursue this goal. Contrary to Denmark, which gives preference to the radical opt-out option, Ireland has made a deliberate choice to participate in all the EC/EU policy areas and at the same time to advocate the application of the principle of subsidiarity as a safeguard against an excessive intervention of the EC/EU institutions in the national policies of the member-states.

The three new member-states, Sweden, Finland and Austria, still have to adapt their foreign policy to the new environment of the Union and have not yet established a record of activities which may help us to trace a pattern in their behaviour. But so far, it hardly differs from those of the two veteran members Denmark and Ireland. Their attitude towards the EU since their entry reflects, to a great extent, a similar desire to ensure national independence on matters that are considered national interests. Their attitude towards the CFSP is deeply rooted in a foreign policy characteristic that they all have in common: adherence to the principle of neutrality. One might expect that, because of their support for neutrality, they may share and strengthen the traditional Danish worry about the loss of national independence and, like Denmark, opt for an *à la carte* participation in the CFSP. Before its entry to the EU, Sweden's attitude towards the EC has indeed been driven by an aspiration to preserve the country's political independence in the face of European integration, besides an ambition to build a close trade relation with the EC. The Swedish were truly convinced that EC membership would weaken both their external and internal autonomy. The Swedish believed that joining the EU would end their ability to stick to the doctrine of neutrality (which excluded any form of binding political cooperation such as EPC or CFSP) and to maintain the superior Swedish welfare system (Tiilikainen and Petersen, 1993: 25–6). But Sweden as well as Finland and Austria have adjusted to the realities of the CFSP in the same way that Ireland has done with respect to the EPC. During the accession negotiations, all three countries stuck to neutrality. But, like Ireland, they interpreted it in such a way that would allow participation in CFSP. Finland has even gone as far as committing itself politically and legally to the obligations of a common defence, promising that Finland is prepared to contribute in a constructive way to the development of the defence dimension of the EU (Tiilikainen and Petersen, 1993: 73–4). Sweden, for its part, has accepted without reservation the requirements of the CFSP, but also emphasized that formal neutrality will be upheld (cf. Edwards and Pijpers, 1997: 162–3). Austria simply argued that a complete abandonment of neutrality was not proposed by the government and that a neutral status should be maintained until a European security order could replace it (Luif, 1995: 241).

Being located far from the core, the three newcomers clearly try to avoid marginalization by playing an active role in EU politics, seeking informal coalitions with the larger or older members, depending on the issue at stake. But in the debates on the revision of the TEU, the three newcomers did not hesitate to represent views that placed them, like Denmark, in a more isolated position. In line with the political culture in the Nordic states they expressed themselves in favour of measures that will increase the effectiveness and openness of decision making in the EU. At the same time, like Denmark, they demonstrated little enthusiasm for the strengthening of the powers of the Commission or any other revision that would reduce the influence of the member-states or erode the powers of the Council of Ministers as the central decision-making body. In the dogmatic debate about the democratic control of EU decision making, the newcomers clearly side with those members who favour the strengthening of the role of national parliaments at the expense of an increase in the competence of the European Parliament (cf. Edwards and Pijpers, 1997: 174–183).

Chapter 4

Domestic foreign policy styles

Now that we have some understanding of the basic goals, interests and values that shape the general attitude of the EU member-states towards European integration, we may turn in this chapter to a close examination of the diversity of style in foreign policy making in the member-states. We have, however, no intention of dealing with all the factors that account for the national processes of foreign policy making in the different member-states. We will rather focus on the specific way in which the member governments have arranged their national input into EU policy making. To put it in another way, we will explore the differences and similarities in the national procedural decision regime which govern the framing of the national positions for negotiations in the EU. As indicated in Chapter 1, procedural decision regimes refer to a leadership consensus regarding the process of foreign policy making and specify the set of rules by which foreign policy is made. In our description and comparison of the various national modes of decision making, we will concentrate on two questions: first, *who* is involved in the making of the national negotiation positions on EU policies; second, *how* these national negotiation stands are shaped. Although the member-states vary in the way they have organized their input into EU decision making, there are also similarities. In this chapter we will make in this respect a distinction among four types of decision making:

- a centralized/tight style of decision making;
- a decentralized/tight style of decision making;
- a centralized/loose style of decision making;
- a decentralized/loose style of decision making.

Each of these four modes of national decision making will be illustrated by one or more member-states (see Table 4.1).

Table 4.1 National decision-making styles

	Centralized		Decentralized
Tight	France	Britain	Germany
	Netherlands	Denmark	Austria
	Luxembourg	Portugal	
	Sweden	Finland	
Loose	Italy	Spain	Belgium
	Greece	Ireland	

A centralized/tight style of decision making

France and Britain

In France and Britain the making of foreign policy in general, and the framing of national positions for negotiations in the EU in particular, are concentrated in central government. In France foreign (and European) policy making is considered to some extent to be the reserved domain of the president, although it is not his sole responsibility. The French constitution gives the president the responsibility for the independence of the nation, the integrity of its territory, and respect for international and Community agreements. The president is also authorized to negotiate and ratify treaties and must be informed about the negotiations of any international agreement not subject to ratification. But since the French prime minister has the constitutional responsibility to direct the policies of the government, including foreign policy, the president and prime minister have to share in the conduct of France's foreign and European policies. This is less visible when the president and premier are from the same political party and the premier is a personal choice of the president. It becomes more manifest when they represent two opposite political parties and have to experience what the French have called *cohabitation* where one cannot act without the consent of the other. Hence, the freedom of manoeuvre that the president actually has in the management of French foreign and European policy depends on the political composition of the government. Obviously the president has more grip on that policy when he and the government do not oppose each other politically and the president is able to appoint his own foreign minister to whom he entrusts the execution of the president's desired policies. So far, during the periods of *cohabitation*, the president and premier have managed to 'live together' by a division of responsibilities (cf. La Serre, Leruez and Wallace, 1990: 204–9).

In France (as well as in Britain) European policy making is by no means the prerogative of the foreign ministry. A large number of governmental departments are involved in foreign and especially European policy making and almost every department has its own international or European section. The foreign ministry in both countries has therefore to share in policy making with other ministries. It has kept this privilege only in the area of political cooperation within the CFSP, where the foreign ministries still have a monopoly. Although the foreign ministries in both countries have a prominent voice in the decision-making process, the ultimate coordination and control over the European policy-making process is located outside the foreign ministry. As coordination has become the key instrument for effective foreign and European policy making in both Britain and France, the two countries have created a number of similar institutional arrangements to coordinate European policy making and to secure a coherent national negotiation position.

In France the machinery of European coordination is placed in the Secrétariat Général du Comité Interministériel (SGCI) – the General Secretariat of the Interministerial Committee – for matters relating to European economic cooperation, which is subject to the prime minister and is the key coordinating body on EU business. The SGCI was established in 1948 to coordinate the French policies towards the OEEC. With the establishment of the ECSC, EEC and Euratom, the SGCI was authorized to deal with all the matters arising in the relations between France and the new European institutions. It has even survived the tide of governmental reforms introduced by de Gaulle during the transformation from the Fourth to the Fifth Republic.

The SGCI has become the focal point of the relationship between France and the EC/EU. All proposals from the Commission have to be addressed through the French permanent representation to the SGCI, not the foreign office. The SGCI then distributes it to the foreign ministry and the ministry of European affairs as well as the other relevant departments through a network of European correspondents located in the diverse departments and regional authorities. The SGCI also has the sole responsibility for the formulation of a coherent French position in the negotiations on proposals of the Commission or any issue discussed in Council meetings and its numerous working groups sessions. Officials of the SGCI are present during the negotiations in Brussels to ensure that the position expressed on behalf of the French government is consistent with the position defined in Paris. The various policy units of the SGCI deal with almost all sectors of European integration with the exception of CFSP issues which, like the former EPC matters, have remained within the competence of the foreign ministry (Lequesne, 1993: 108–9).

The Treaty of Maastricht (also called the Treaty on European Union) has made the exclusion of CFSP matters controversial. As we will see in the next chapter, under the provisions of the Maastricht Treaty, the EC and CFSP have been brought under one roof, though not yet merged; in the General Affairs Council the foreign ministers deal with EC and CFSP questions, and the national representatives (the so-called COREPER – Committee of Permanent Representatives) who prepare these Council meetings received, in addition to their responsibility for EC issues, the responsibility for CFSP matters. This should have extended the control of the SGCI to the CFSP area as well, in accordance with the reasoning that there should be only one communication line to COREPER and the Council. However, officials from the well-established ministry of foreign affairs still determine the final French negotiation position in CFSP issues. In addition to the SGCI, a special post of Minister for European Affairs was created in 1981, to stimulate the horizontal coordination between the departments. The minister of European affairs plays a very important role in the definition of a coherent French negotiation position and is very much involved in the actual negotiations in Brussels. In case of a disagreement that cannot be settled at the SGCI level, the issue is arbitrated by the prime minister's office or decided by the president (cf. Lequesne, 1993).

Although the constitutional authority of the British prime minister is nowhere defined (since the country has no written constitution), the prime minister is recognized by constitutional conventions as the leading figure in foreign affairs. In accordance with the principle of collective responsibility for the cabinet's policies, of which foreign and European policies are an integral part, the foreign minister is usually fully associated in the making of foreign and European policy as well as other senior cabinet members. But in practice the prime minister exercises full control over the foreign as well as the European policy-making process.

In Britain the coordination of European policy making is also concentrated outside the foreign ministry, in the European secretariat in Cabinet Office, which is one of the three secretariats within Cabinet Office that cover external affairs. Cabinet Office is a very powerful coordination mechanism which works closely with the prime minister and its European secretariat is heavily involved in the shaping of Britain's policies towards the EU. As Clarke has noted, 'where power over the agenda constitutes power over the outcome, the Cabinet Office has an important bearing on the detail of cabinet business' (Clarke, 1992: 92). The Foreign and Commonwealth Office (FCO) has two separate European departments, one responsible for the external EU policies, the other for the internal EU policies, which fulfil a major role in the formulation and coordination of British views on EU matters and share with other departments in the preparation of British negotiation positions. But the European secretariat has nevertheless developed into the decisive policy-making unit in the preparation of British negotiation positions in the various EU Council meetings.

Crucial in the process of drawing up the instructions for the British negotiators in Brussels are the weekly meetings in London chaired by Cabinet Office and participated in by the British permanent representative in the EU and the EC department in the FCO. The European secretariat in the Cabinet Office will then draft the final proposals for the negotiation stands which are finally defined in cabinet or one of its committees. It is at this stage that the minister of foreign affairs or any other senior minister can exercise influence in determining the final outcome. Very significant in this respect could also be the informal role played by the policy unit of the prime minister which is housed in the premier's political office in Number 10 Downing Street, and includes personal advisers for foreign and European affairs (cf. Clarke, 1992: 76–106 and George, 1992: 65–90). The FCO will then communicate the negotiations instructions to the British Permanent Representation in Brussels. Unlike the French SGCI which has also monopolized the communication between the French government and the European institutions, the British FCO has remained the main formal channel of communication to the Permanent Representation.

Denmark and the Netherlands

Denmark ranks among the small member-states as the member-state with the tightest European policy-making process. The Danish foreign ministry supervises all governmental activities at the international level and holds the primary responsibility for overall foreign and European policy coordination. It is placed hierarchically, so to speak, on top of the many other governmental departments that are also involved in international and European politics (cf. Karvonen and Sundelius, 1987: 131). As a consequence of EU membership, the Danish foreign ministry has been divided into two departments: a foreign affairs department concerned with the political aspects of foreign policy, and a foreign economic affairs department which was supposed to deal with matters arising from EC/EU membership. When, shortly after entry, the member-states also started to coordinate their diplomatic activities within the EPC framework, European political cooperation became the responsibility of the foreign affairs department (Hill, 1983: 108).

To make sure that Denmark presents in the Council meetings a strong coherent national position, the foreign ministry functions as the central coordinator of all the relations between the Danish government and the EU and is present at all levels of European policy making in Denmark. Although the Danish foreign ministry has a firm grip on all EU policy making, it has to allow that proposals from the EU are first discussed in the interdepartmental special committees, by officials in the relevant policy sector. Officials from the foreign ministry are present during these discussions but the meetings are chaired by the ministry that is competent in the specific issue area. Many of the Danish positions are actually fixed in these special committees, since the vast majority of proposals from the Commission have a technical or administrative nature. Officials and experts from the more technical ministries participate also in the Council working groups meetings in Brussels, set up by the Council of Ministers to prepare the decision making on a specific issue. Again, at this level many of the dossiers concern technical matters which are settled and passed for final decision making through COREPER to the relevant Council. The foreign ministry, however, chairs the meetings on the next level, that of the EU Committee. This committee of high-ranking officials from the ministries most involved in EU business finalizes all the rather technical and administrative matters and functions as a clearing house for the Cabinet Committee on EU Affairs. This committee, chaired by the minister of foreign affairs and composed of the prime minister and a number of other ministers, prepares the proposed negotiation position in the Council of Ministers. It becomes, however, the official negotiation mandate only after its approval by Parliament's European Committee (cf. Rometsch and Wessels, 1996: 199–203; Pappas, 1995: 114–22).

This parliamentarian European Committee controls, almost completely, Danish participation in the Council negotiations as all the negotiation instructions given by the government have to be sanctioned by this committee. Representatives of the foreign ministry are present at the meetings in Parliament, although the proposed negotiation position is presented by the minister who participates in the Council meeting. Danish ministers cannot bind Denmark to decisions of the Council of Ministers if the negotiation mandate was not discussed and accepted in advance by a majority of the parliamentary committee. In practice the government takes the expected views into account when it defines its negotiation position. According to Peter Nedergaard, 95 per cent of all government proposals for the negotiation instructions in recent years were endorsed by the parliamentary committee without any change (Pappas, 1995: 125). To prevent a weakening of the Danish negotiation position in the Council, the negotiation instructions of the government are presented in the parliamentary European Committee behind closed doors and the government may ask the committee members to keep discussions in the committee confidential. In any case, the government has to report to the parliamentary committee after the Council meeting in Brussels, where Danish negotiators have to follow the fixed mandate. It makes the Danish position less flexible and sometimes isolated as Denmark could always be outvoted on issues where a qualified majority voting procedure is applicable (cf. Pappas, 1995: 122–31).

The Dutch way of dealing with proposals from the EC and the preparation of a national negotiation position resembles, to some extent, the Danish system. The technical ministries enjoy, however, much more autonomy in their dealing with EU matters and Parliament usually does not intervene during the preparatory stage of the negotiations by a fixed negotiation mandate. Dutch foreign and European policy making is grounded on two principles: departmental autonomy and collective decision making in Cabinet. As a result, the ministry of foreign affairs has no responsibility for the first stage of decision making, where the proposals of the EU, after a formal assessment by an interministerial working group, are dealt with by the most relevant ministry. All this may happen in consultation with other ministries, including the foreign ministry, or in *ad hoc* interdepartmental committees, chaired (as in Denmark) by the most concerned ministry. Officials from the same ministry will also participate in the working groups meetings of the Council where, as mentioned above, many of the deals among the member-states on these technical and administrative dossiers are informally concluded. In this respect the technical ministries can act independently of the ministry of foreign affairs, as they all have their own person on the spot, usually as a member of the Permanent Representation of the Netherlands at the EU.

It is, however, the task of COREPER and the Council of Ministers to sanction these outcomes and to deal with the more politically sensitive items still left. This is where the foreign ministry enters the decision-making process and takes responsibility for interdepartmental coordination and the drawing up of the negotiation instructions to the Permanent Representative, as well as the drafting of a negotiations position in the Council of Ministers. The instructions are issued by a so-called COREPER instruction meeting, chaired by a high-ranking foreign ministry official and attended by officials from the other ministries. But in accordance with the principle of departmental autonomy, the first draft for the negotiation instructions to the Permanent Representative are formulated in the competent ministry or in close consultation with the relevant ministries. Only CFSP issues are considered to be the main responsibility of the ministry of foreign affairs, which has, however, to cooperate closely with the ministry of defence in matters of security policy.

The preparation of the Dutch negotiation position in the various meetings of the Council of Ministers takes place under the chairmanship of the state secretary for European affairs in the Coordination Committee for European Integration, the so-called Co-Co meetings. This has not always been the case as the ministry of economic affairs was, until 1972, charged with the coordination of Dutch policies in the EEC. Because of competence problems between the economics ministry and the foreign ministry, the ultimate responsibility for the coordination was put in the hands of the foreign ministry. However, the economics ministry still holds a dominant position within the Co-Co meetings, where it is represented by the minister of economic affairs or, in his absence, one of his high-ranking officials. The Co-Co proposals are finally discussed in the Cabinet which also defines the definitive negotiation instructions for the minister participating in a Council meeting.

It is here in Cabinet where the ministerial autonomy is balanced by a collective responsibility for governmental decision making. The Dutch Cabinet decides collectively on all important matters of foreign and European policy. It has to approve each commitment entered into by a Dutch representative in international or European organizations and to endorse each international treaty or agreement concluded by a Dutch representative. For this reason, Cabinet has the ultimate responsibility for the formulation of the instructions to Dutch negotiators in international forums including the Council of Ministers. Hence, the Dutch Cabinet may be considered as the ultimate coordinator of foreign and European policy making and its chairman, the prime minister, as a super-coordinator of that policy. In a special subcommittee of the Cabinet, under the chairmanship of the prime minister, a selective group of ministers discusses international and European affairs and prepares the Dutch position for the meeting of the European Councils. It is evident that, because of his participation in the European Council, the Dutch prime minister has increased his involvement in foreign affairs and fulfils an active role in European politics. As a result he has gained more influence on foreign and European policy making at the expense of the minister of foreign affairs.

Unlike the Danish Parliament, the Dutch Parliament controls the performance of the Dutch government in the Council of Ministers mainly after the decision making in the Council has already been concluded, although it may exercise its power to control the government before the Council meetings if it wishes to do so. It has become routine that Parliament discusses with the prime minister and foreign minister in advance the meetings of the European Council of heads of state or government, which are also debated in Parliament after the meetings have taken place. According to a new procedure, Members of Parliament have also the possibility of exchanging views with the relevant ministers on the Dutch position for the Council meetings of the coming week. This new practice offers Dutch Parliament members an opportunity to exercise better control over the performance of Dutch ministers in Council meetings, but it is not as effective as in Denmark since this involvement is not binding. The final Dutch negotiation position is still decided in Cabinet.

Luxembourg and Portugal

The making of foreign and European policy in Luxembourg is also characterized by a relatively tight method of decision making. As a result of the small size of government in Luxembourg, very few officials are involved in the formulation of foreign policy and the preparation of the country's negotiation position. In Luxembourg as well, the technical ministries are involved in the preparation of the technical dossiers and attend the technical Councils that fall under their competence. They are, however, accompanied to these gatherings by officials from the foreign ministry (or Permanent Representation), who also have the exclusive responsibility for the coordination of the preparation of all Council meetings. The European Council conferences and other important Council meetings are prepared, again under the responsibility of the foreign ministry, in the Coordination Committee on the European Union and discussed in Cabinet (cf. Pappas, 1995: 359–68).

In Portugal, policy making on EU matters and the preparation of the national negotiation position also follows a centralized mode of decision making. A tight structure at both the political and administrative levels stipulates the responsibilities for the coordination of European policy making. So the overall coordination of the political aspects of the European policies is examined in the Government Commission for Community Affairs (CGAC), under the chairmanship of the minister of foreign affairs, who also coordinates the preparation of the Portuguese negotiation position in the Council of Ministers. The ultimate decisions are taken in Cabinet by the Council of Ministers for Community Affairs (CMCA) which is the highest decision-making body at the political level and is chaired by the prime minister. Interministerial technical coordination at the administrative level takes place within the Interministerial Commission for the European Community (CICE). The task of this interministerial coordinating body is to monitor all EU dossiers and to advance the formulation of coherent and consistent negotiation positions on the technical issues considered in the working groups of the Council of Ministers. Participants in this interministerial commission are, besides the state secretary for European integration who chairs this body, the director for European integration in the ministry of foreign affairs and the Permanent Representative as well as officials representing the relevant technical ministries and the autonomous regions of the Azores and Madeira. The state secretary for European affairs, who is answerable to the minister of foreign affairs, forms the link between the political and the administrative levels since he is also a member of the CGAC and sits on the Council of Ministers for EU Affairs (cf. Pappas, 1995: 443–5).

Sweden and Finland

The two Scandinavian newcomers to EU business, Sweden and Finland, are still in a process of adapting to the realities of EU decision making and negotiation. As in other member-states, the two countries have to cope with the increasing involvement of the domestic ministries in European policy making at the expense of the foreign ministry. Whereas the foreign ministry considers the formulation of a national position for the negotiations in Brussels and the conduct of these negotiations as its prerogative, the sectoral ministries regard the involvement in European policy making, when it touches upon their domestic authority, as an extension of that responsibility. This is very similar to the problem that the ministries of foreign affairs in these countries had in adapting to the rising international interdependence in recent decades (cf. Karvonen and Sundelius, 1987). So far we notice that sectoral ministries on the basis of their autonomy indeed gain new responsibility for the European policies that are related to their domestic responsibility. But at the same time the ministries of foreign affairs in these countries maintain their present function as the central coordinator of European policy making. Besides the foreign ministry responsibility for CFSP matters, they also control the coordination of the preparation of the national input into EU decision making. The foreign ministry is the official link between the EU institutions and the Swedish government and it chairs the main body for the coordination of EU policy making, the Coordinating Group for EU relations. This high-level coordinating committee is composed of the state secretary for European affairs in the foreign ministry (who chairs the meeting) and the state secretaries of the Cabinet Office, the ministry for justice and the ministry for finance. It resolves interministerial disagreement over EU matters which were not settled by the committee of EU coordinators (representing the different ministries) which issues the negotiations instructions for the COREPER and Council meetings. All final decisions regarding the EU are formally taken collectively by the Cabinet (Hanf and Soetendorp, 1998: 136–8).

From the beginning the Swedish government has secured a prominent role for Parliament in the shaping of its negotiation position for negotiations in the EU. Following the Danish example, the involvement of Parliament precedes decision making in the Council, through weekly briefings of the parliamentary Advisory Committee on European Affairs about upcoming Council meetings. There is, however, one important difference between the Danish and the Swedish case. Contrary to the Danish government, the Swedish government has no legal obligation to follow the advice of the parliamentary committee during the exchange of views.

A decentralized/tight style of decision making

Germany

In Germany, due to the practice in the early postwar period when Adenauer had to act as prime minister as well as his own foreign minister, the chancellor is recognized as the principal person in the shaping of Germany's foreign and European policies. The German constitution gives the chancellor a so-called guidelines competence (*Richtlinienkompetenz*) which has, however, to be combined with respect for the principle of departmental autonomy (*Resortprinzip*). Both principles are highly respected standards in German politics and are clearly laid down in the constitution which stipulates: 'The Chancellor determines and bears responsibility for the guidelines of policy. Within these guidelines each Federal Minister conducts his department independently and under his own responsibility' (Paterson and Southern, 1991: 90). This has given the German prime minister the potentiality to exercise individual leadership but has also set limits to his ability to control the enforcement of his policies.

Compared to France and Britain, Germany arrives at the negotiations in Brussels less organized. The coordination of European policy is hindered in Germany by two factors: ministerial autonomy and federalism. Germany has no dominant central organization, like the SGCI or the European secretariat in Cabinet Office, which is responsible for the coordination of European policy making and the preparation of a coherent national negotiation position. The foreign relations unit within the office of the chancellor, which has developed into a powerful centre of governmental decision making that plays an important role in foreign and defence policy (including CFSP and bilateral relations with EU partners), has taken some responsibility for the coordination and planning of European policy. It is also able to observe the activities of the federal ministries which have to inform the chancellor of 'matters significant for the determination of the guidelines of policy and the conduct of the business of the Federal government' (Paterson and Southern, 1991: 95–6). But as a consequence of the principle of departmental autonomy, the major actual responsibility for the making of European policy remains with the ministry of foreign affairs and the ministry of economic affairs.

The two ministries have to share in this task as a result of the fact that the ministry of foreign affairs is a relative latecomer to EC business. Whereas the ministry of economic affairs was already responsible for ECSC matters from the early 1950s, the foreign ministry became involved in Community business only in 1957 and had to agree that the economics ministry would keep its responsibility for day-to-day European policy. The foreign ministry has been charged only with integration policy, dealing with the general aspects of European integration (Bulmer and Paterson, 1987: 31). The development of EPC enabled the foreign ministry to widen its scope and to add the responsibility for political cooperation to its tasks. But the creation of the common market and the extension of EC policy making to new policy areas has not only deepened the interference of the economics ministry with EC matters, it has also involved more and more ministries in European policy making. In accordance with the principle of ministerial autonomy, all these newcomers are jealously guarding their competence in the additional policy areas.

To make things even more complicated, the governments of the *Länder*, which possess their own legislative powers, also claimed their share in the making of European policy. Because of the federal structure of Germany, which implies the sharing of competence between the governments of the *Länder* and the federal government, the *Länder* have been involved from the beginning of European integration in the implementation of European policies. As some of their policy responsibilities were allocated by the federal government during the negotiations on the SEA and the TEU to the EC/EU level, they started to demand more involvement in European policy making and participation in the Council negotiations. During the ratification process of the SEA and TEU, the *Länder* used their power in the *Bundesrat*, their representative body at the federal level, to make the endorsement of the treaties by the *Bundesrat* conditional upon some concessions from the federal government. The *Länder* received a formal consultation procedure which has been laid down in the German constitution. According to these new rules, the observer of the *Länder* at the EU has to be informed of all communications between the German government and the EU institutions. The *Bundesrat* has also to be involved in the determination of the German voting in the Council in cases where EU policies touch upon internal matters for which the *Länder* are responsible. This consultation procedure makes the preparation of the German negotiation position more complex and less unified when this may result in disagreement between the federal government and the governments of the *Länder* or the inability of the *Länder* to reach a consensus among themselves. It may lead to situations where Germany would be unable to agree on a national position and would have to withhold its support for a European policy because of the opposition of the *Länder*. This makes it necessary for the government to take into account the views of the governments of the *Länder* already at an early stage of the decision-making process. To have better access to EU policy making independently of the federal government, the governments of the *Länder* have also established their own joint representation in Brussels (Bulmer and Paterson, 1988: 249–52 and Pappas, 1995: 146–7).

The sectorial and federal nature of Germany's European policy making has made the coordination of EU policy making a complicated task. Germany faces, as it were, a problem of horizontal coordination and a problem of vertical coordination. Although the economics ministry and the foreign ministry have to share the responsibility for the preparation of a coherent German negotiation position in Brussels, the economics ministry fulfils a pivotal role as it chairs the interministerial committees on EU affairs and commands the coordination of routine EU business at the federal level. It also functions as the only communication channel between the German government and the European institutions and issues the negotiations instructions to the Permanent Representation and the negotiators in Brussels. This structure has led to the peculiar situation, as noted by Bulmer and Paterson, where 'the Permanent Representative in Brussels is a Foreign Office diplomat who receives instructions from the Economics Ministry!' (Bulmer and Paterson, 1987: 34).

Interministerial coordination is also sought in other interdepartmental forums of which the Committee of State Secretaries for European Affairs, under the chairmanship of a foreign office minister of state, is the most authoritative body to solve interministerial disagreements before such disputes reach Cabinet. But in practice, even at this high level, sectorial loyalties prevail. Trade-offs and package deals can primarily be arranged at the Cabinet level or directly between ministers. As Bulmer and Paterson have argued: 'The various forms of co-ordination within the Federal Government still leave a loose and sectorial European policy. In fact, effective co-ordination comes mainly from crisis-management in the Cabinet' (Bulmer and Paterson, 1987: 40–1). The lack of an effective centre of coordination for centralized preparation of a coherent national negotiation position places, in the view of Bulmer and Paterson, a serious constraint on Germany's ability to play a leadership role in the Community. It is, in their view, one of the crucial reasons that Germany, which dominates Europe economically, is not as influential as France in dominating EU politics (1987: 240, 251; 1988: 261; and 1989: 115).

Austria

As a newcomer to the EU, Austria has still to organize its participation in EU decision making. So far, its federal structure of government and its informal consensus-oriented political system have determined the style of European policy making and the way that the government has arranged its input into EU decision making. As a rule, the negotiation position for the Council meetings in Brussels and its working groups are prepared by the competent federal ministry. Since European issues usually touch upon the authority of more than one ministry and the powers of the provinces, the responsible ministry arranges interministerial meetings involving officials from the other relevant ministries, from the provinces and social partners. During such informal meetings the responsible ministry tries to reach a consensus on a desired negotiation position. Only the European Councils of heads of state and government and the meetings of the Permanent Representatives in Brussels (the so-called COREPER) are prepared by the federal chancellery and the foreign ministry. The Cabinet also discusses EU matters in an attempt to improve coordination among competing ministries. Both the provinces and Parliament exercise an effective control over the positions taken by the responsible Austrian minister in the Council. The provinces and Parliament, which are informed about all EU matters, can take a view on any proposed position, from which the minister can deviate only in the case of compelling reasons concerning foreign or integration policy. Although a minister is not bounded by the position of the provinces or Parliament, he will take their views seriously into account, as Parliament and the provinces have the powers (under certain conditions) to put him on trial before the constitutional court or to force his resignation (Hanf and Soetendorp, 1998: 119–24). Whether this tight control over the voting behaviour of the Austrian representative in the Council of Ministers will survive the realities of decision making in the Council, where a small country like Austria can easily be outvoted, remains to be seen.

A centralized/loose style of decision making

Spain and Italy

Spain has a less structured system of foreign and European policy making than the countries discussed so far. It has, nonetheless, a strong central institution in the person of the prime minister who provides the necessary leadership in the foreign policy field and the area of European decision making. As Katlyn Saba has argued, the Spanish prime minister has actually the status of president (1986: 27). He occupies a powerful position and is placed hierarchically above his ministers. The Spanish premier issues the guidelines for foreign and European policies and has the ultimate responsibility for the execution of these policies. He commands a small staff who helps him to control the making of foreign policy and fulfils a vital function in the coordination of that policy. In practice the premier shares decision making in this area with the minister of foreign affairs. The foreign minister is entrusted with the concrete realization of foreign and European policies, but the extent to which the latter is involved in policy making depends on his relationship with the premier and his political weight. Much of the general policy making is initiated during the frequent meetings between the premier and the foreign minister, whereupon it is adopted formally by Cabinet.

No ministry in Spain has exclusive responsibility for EU matters. European policy making is supervised by the Secretariat of State for the European Community (SECE), which is placed at the foreign ministry. It takes the lead in the coordination of all EU matters through two subunits, of which one deals with the technical matters and the other with the legal and institutional issues. Questions related to the CFSP are dealt with in a separate unit within the foreign ministry. As in the other member-states, the foreign ministry does not possess the expertise to deal with the many technical matters of the EU proposals and needs the active participation of the other ministries in the decision-making process. As a consequence, many national positions are usually taken by the sectoral ministries. The interministerial contacts have been institutionalized in the Interministerial Committee for Economic Affairs Relating to the European Communities, which is chaired by the state secretary for European affairs. It manages the day-to-day EU business and coordinates the positions taken by Spanish negotiators on the many technical matters discussed in the Council of Ministers. Some of this consultation is nevertheless done informally through personal contacts. The Cabinet remains, however, the central place where the ultimate coordination of foreign and European policies takes place. It is here that competing views are presented, consensus is built and, if necessary, the premier makes the final decision (Saba, 1986: 27–31; Pappas, 1995: 201–4; Hanf and Soetendorp, 1998: 102–4).

Italy represents a very loose system of foreign and European policy making. The loose nature of central government in Italy is not balanced by a centralized system of foreign and European policy coordination or strong centralized leadership. As David Hine has noted, policy coordination is a central concern for Italian government. As in many other member-states, policy making in Italy is segmented, with policy communities taking decisions in relative isolation from one another. But sectorization of the policy-making process in Italy suffers, according to Hine, 'from a chronically low level of policy coordination compared to most of Western Europe' (Hine, 1993: 197). The principle of individual ministerial responsibility is authorized by the constitution which makes it difficult for the Italian prime minister to comply with his responsibility for the general policy of the government and to use the Cabinet as an instrument for policy coordination, as in the Netherlands. Moreover, the Italian fascist experience during the Second World War made the Italians more cautious towards strong leadership. It has become a custom in Italian politics to see the premier not as a dominant leader of the government but as a member of a team who exercises collegial rather than individual leadership. A prime minister in one Cabinet may be a minister in another Cabinet. This is in contrast to Germany where, in spite of the experience with strong fascist leadership, the chancellor was given some powers to balance the strong departmental autonomy, and where the chancellor is recognized as the political leader of his party (cf. Hine, 1993: 198–224). The principle of departmental autonomy combined with a preference for weak prime ministerial leadership and the absence of a coordinating machinery at the centre of government, makes the task of policy coordination almost an impossible assignment.

The complexity of the preparation of a coherent Italian negotiation position in Brussels is even more difficult as a result of the great fragmentation in Italian government and the large administrative diversity. It is common that the responsibility for one policy sector is divided among several ministries and that governmental tasks are executed by special (autonomous) state agencies. This makes the formation of European policy in Italy a serious problem as nearly each European policy touches upon the responsibilities of a number of ministries. From the early days of Italian EC membership, the ministry of foreign affairs had the major competence in EU affairs. By means of the Permanent Representation, the ministry of foreign affairs is the official link between Brussels and Rome and acts in practice on the administrative level as the major coordinator of EU policies. At the ministry of foreign affairs, the responsibility for European integration is divided between two directorates general, one for economic affairs and another for political affairs. However, as EU issues have become more technical, the ministry of foreign affairs has not only to share its competence with other ministries but it also needs the expertise of other ministries. Although the ministry of foreign affairs managed to keep its virtual monopoly over the external relations of Italian government with the EU institutions, it had to allow other ministries to participate actively in the shaping of EU policies. The only challenge to its position was posed by the new Department for the Coordination of European Community Policies which was established in the 1980s. In an attempt to improve the Italian management of EU matters, the new department was supposed to coordinate the making and implementation of EU policies throughout Italian government. It is not an independent ministry even though it is headed by a minister for the coordination of European affairs, who is responsible to the prime minister. But so far the department has been unable to establish itself as an authoritative coordinating mechanism or to challenge the central role still played by the ministry of foreign affairs in the preparation of the Italian negotiation positions in Brussels. The limited coordination capabilities of the foreign ministry has led, however, to a situation that Italian ministers are present in the Council meeting without an official negotiation position except their own views (cf. Ronzitti, 1987; Agostini, 1990b; Hine, 1993: 290–7; Rometsch and Wessels, 1996: 114–16).

Italy and Spain recognize the existence of local autonomy, but this has little impact on foreign policy making since the autonomous regions have only domestic competence. In Spain, all the powers in the area of foreign and defence policies (as well as the field of macroeconomics) are concentrated and put in the hands of central government. The Spanish central government has only the obligation to provide the autonomous regional authorities with information about international treaties and to consult them on the provisions that concern their competence before the conclusion of such international agreements (Saba, 1986: 24). As in Spain, the Italian government also has only to communicate to the regions the proposals for regulations, recommendations and directives from the EU. The regions may then submit their observations. However, they very rarely make use of this privilege as they realize that it is unlikely that they will influence governmental policy making (Agostini, 1990a: 88). In both countries consultation mechanisms are in progress which are charged with improving the cooperation between central government and the autonomous communities in EU matters, to enhance the participation of the autonomous communities in the preparatory stage of EU decision making.

Ireland and Greece

Ireland has a loose system of foreign and European policy making but at the same time a strong involvement of the prime minister in the making of foreign and European policies. In Ireland, which also lacks a central coordination machinery, the prime minister sets out the guidelines for the conduct of the country's foreign and European policies and actually takes the major decisions in this area. As Brigid Laffan has argued, the Irish system of policy formation on EU issues is much less institutionalized than in most other member-states (Laffan, 1991: 193). The overall strategy towards the EU and important negotiation positions are determined at the political level in Cabinet under the guidance of the prime minister who is responsible for the coordination of all the government's policies. This applies especially to the foreign and European policies wherein the stakes for Ireland are sometimes very high. The Irish prime minister is, according to Brian Farrel, not only head of government but also the ultimate authority. He is simultaneously chief executive, government chairman, party leader, national spokesman, principal legislator, electoral champion and media focus (Blondel and Müller-Rommel, 1988: 44). In his task as the chief coordinator of Ireland's policies towards the EU, the prime minister is assisted by a minister of state in his department who is also responsible for the coordination of EU policies at the administrative level. Because of the high degree of departmental autonomy, each ministry deals with the specific EU activities that fall within its domain. Interdepartmental cooperation and the preparation of the national negotiation position is carried out within the EU Committee, chaired by the minister of state in the prime minister's office and composed of assistant secretaries from the ministries most involved in EU policies. Although the chairmanship of the EU Committee has been transferred in 1987 to the minister of state responsible for the coordination of EU policy at the department of the prime minister, the ministry of foreign affairs still exercises an overall control of the actual positions presented by Ireland in the various Council meetings. Through the Permanent Representation the foreign ministry is the main channel of communication between Ireland and the EU's institutions and has a prominent voice in the determination of national negotiation positions (cf. Laffan, 1991: 191–4).

In Greece the responsibility for EU affairs is divided between the ministry of foreign affairs and the ministry for national economy. While the former tries to act as the main gatekeeper of the external relations between the Greek government and the EU institutions, the latter is responsible for the domestic interministerial coordination, especially with respect to the implementation of EU policies. The ministry of foreign affairs is supposed to represent Greece in the EU and to co-ordinate the overall policy of the Greek government towards the EU at all levels. But in practice it is hindered in the effective exercise of its coordinating function by the autonomy of the functional ministries. The existence of European affairs services within each ministry, which have actually maintained their original involvement in the management of the relevant EU dossiers at the European level, has reinforced that autonomy. The initial negotiation positions are in fact determined by the relevant technical ministry, independently of the foreign ministry. The foreign ministry is only involved in the drafting of the instructions for the COREPER meetings. It is also no exception that the minister who represents Greece in the Council (usually from the department most concerned) does not inform the foreign ministry about the position he defends. Moreover, disagreements between ministries can be settled only at the political level, namely in Cabinet (cf. Pappas, 1995: 163–73).

A decentralized/loose style of decision making

Belgium

Belgium ceased to exist in 1993 as a unitary state and has been transformed officially into a federal state. As a result of this state reform many governmental tasks were transformed from the federal government to the regional governments. This has, as we will see, significant consequences for the way that Belgium formulates its input into EU decision making. Even though the Belgian federal government is still responsible for the foreign policy of the country, the regional governments share in the making of foreign and European policies more than in any other member-state. Belgium is formally composed of two main regions and three linguistic communities each with its own competence, its own government, its own legislative and its own administrative bodies. But because of the overlap between the Flemish region and the Flemish community (which have a single government and a single Parliament) the country is actually divided into two separate entities: a Flemish state composed of the Flemish region and the Dutch-speaking Flemish community; and a Walloon state composed of the Walloon region and the French- and German-speaking communities. Because of the dualistic composition of its population, the Brussels region has a special status. There is no hierarchy between the federal and the regional governments or communities; each has its own exclusive powers and is not allowed to intervene in the competence of the other.

The federal Belgian government still represents Belgium in its foreign relations with other countries and its external relations with the EU, but the far-reaching autonomy of the regional states includes the power to conclude international treaties concerning matters that are within their jurisdiction. This right is, however, subjected to a number of conditions to ensure a coherent Belgium's international and European performance. The regional governments are also allowed to engage in international activities in their area of competence. Whereas the federal government, for instance, is responsible for an overall foreign trade policy, the authority over the conduct of export and import relations has been transferred almost completely from the federal level to the regional level. As a consequence of the change from a unitary state to a federal state, the former system of foreign and European policy coordination has been transformed into a more complex system of decision making. The federal government, and more specifically the ministry of foreign affairs, is still entrusted with the preparation of a unified Belgian position (not a national position), but this position has to be based on a consensus between the federal government and the regional governments. The federal government is required by law to consult the governments of the regional states in the making of foreign and

European policies in areas where the latter have exclusive competence or where both have a mixed competence.

To compensate for this far-reaching federalization, some decision-making bodies have been created at the federal level to help the federal government to have some grip on the regional governments and to make sure that Belgium will continue to speak to its European partners with one voice and present in the various international and European forums a coherent and unified view. Most important in this respect is the Interministerial Conference for Foreign Policy. This interministerial committee has evolved into the key forum where the federal government consults the regional government on EU policies and where the federal foreign ministers (and the eventual federal minister(s) or state secretaries for trade and European affairs) have to reach agreement with the regional ministers for external relations, on a common Belgian position. Decision making is done by consensus which gives each of the parties concerned a veto power and could have led to disastrous deadlocks. But in practice the federal government and the regional governments have learned to give and take. Similar coordination of views and policies between the federal government and the regional governments on more technical matters, which may touch upon EC policies like the CAP, takes place in a number of other consultation committees or interministerial conferences wherein matters have also to be arranged sensibly so that each gains advantages or suffers disadvantage to the same extent. The actual coordination of the Belgian negotiation position is still carried out by the foreign ministry. It consults other federal ministries and is obliged to involve the regional governments in the preparation of the Belgian negotiation position and the drafting of the instructions for the Belgian negotiators, whenever this concerns the regional government's competence. Since only national governments are allowed to represent member-states in the Council of Ministers, the federal government represents Belgium in the Council meeting. The regional governments, which are also represented in the Belgian Permanent Representation at the EU, usually participate in the Belgian delegation during Council meetings. In cases where the discussions in the Council concern items that are the sole responsibility of the regional governments, a regional minister may even chair the Belgian delegation.

Our comparison of the styles of foreign and European policy making in the different member-states and the discussion of the way that the member governments have organized their national input into EU decision making may be summarized by several characteristics that the member-states have in common, and a number of features in which they differ. First, in many member-states the head of state or government plays, directly or indirectly, a central role in the formulation of the country's foreign and European policies. In countries where his role is less prominent, he has become much more involved in the shaping of his country's foreign and European policies, because of his participation in the European Council of Heads of State and Government.

Second, in the three large member-states the ministries of foreign affairs can only play a secondary part in this respect, due to pressures from both the prime minister's office as well as other powerful competing ministries like economic affairs and finance, and (in the case of France and Britain) the building of a very effective organization for the coordination of their European policies and the pre-paration of their national negotiation positions, subjected directly or indirectly to the premier. There is, however, a significant difference between the larger and the smaller member-states. Notable is the absence in all the smaller members of a cent-ral organ like the SGCI or the European Secretariat in Cabinet Office to coordinate European policy making and to prepare a coherent national negotiation position. As a matter of fact, we may conclude that the ministries of foreign affairs in almost all the small states have managed to maintain a prominent place among the many domestic actors involved in European policy making. Contrary to their counterparts in the larger member-states, they have kept their role as gatekeeper between their country and the EU institutions and avoided becoming simply a central postbox.

In this connection it is also important to note that in all the member-states the regulation and supervision of external economic issues is separated from the man-agement of CFSP matters, not only in the countries where the responsibilities for these questions have been divided among more than one ministry but also in those member-states where the foreign ministry is responsible for all EU policy making. With such a broad range of national attitudes towards European integration and so many different styles in foreign and especially European policy making, what sort of foreign policy decision regime has emerged on the European level? This is the subject of the next chapter.

Chapter 5

The common foreign policy decision regime

To gain insight into the complexities of foreign policy making at the European level we will describe in this chapter the institutionalized arrangements created by the member-states of the European Union (EU) and the former European Communities (EC) to organize their cooperation in the traditional sectors of foreign policy: diplomacy, defence, external trade and international development cooperation. Just as in the former chapters we will concentrate our analysis of the decision rules that shape the EU's foreign policy behaviour in these distinct areas, around three questions: *who* makes these decisions; *how* are the foreign policy decisions of the EU made; and *what* are the general basic goals, interests or values on which these decisions are based? As mentioned in Chapter 1, I will use for this purpose Kegley's notion of decision regime, and his distinction between procedural and substantial rules in particular, to construct the European foreign policy decision regime. In addition, a differentiation will be made between the written rules that the member-states agreed formally to accept and the unwritten rules that the member-states informally observe.

Two separate decision regimes

The EU institutional framework in the various foreign policy sectors, as it exists in its present form, is part of a continuing process of European integration in the broad area of foreign policy. The founders of the EC were in fact only concerned with the external implications of the creation of a common market. Consequently, the original Treaty of Rome treated exclusively the way that the new entity should deal with its external trade relations and handle its relationship with the member-states, overseas countries and territories. It deals with the EC diplomatic activities only when it involves the management of the external trade policy, known as the Common Commerce Policy (CCP), the treatment of overseas countries and territories, and the conclusion of trade agreements and association treaties with third countries. The Treaty of Rome made no reference to a common foreign or security policy. The political dimension of the Community's foreign policy developed therefore outside the formal EC institutional structure.

Table 5.1 The common foreign policy decision regime

Decision regime / Decision rules	CFSP decision regime	External economic relations decision regime
Who decides	European Council General Affairs Council Presidency	General Affairs Council European Commission European Parliament
How is decided	Unanimous vote (qualified majority)	Qualified majority voting (unanimous vote)

As a result, integration at the EC level in the particular foreign policy sectors developed along different routes and at different speeds. Whereas cooperation in the external trade sector has evolved within the institutional framework established by the Treaty of Rome, the political cooperation has developed outside the institutional structure laid down in that treaty. This differentiation created two methods of operation in the area of foreign policy: first, a so-called community method of policy making which refers to a mode of decision that involves all the four major EC institutions (the Council of Ministers, the Commission, the Parliament and the Court of Justice), and is based on a separation of powers between these institutions; second, an intergovernmental mode of policy making that preserves the authority of the member-states over the EU institutions. In the governmental method, the balance between the different EU institutions is clearly in favour of the Council of Ministers (representing the member-states' interests) at the expense of the other institutions. The European Commission and the European Parliament (representing the supranational interest) play a very limited part in shaping the EU's policies, whereas the European Court is entirely excluded from the decision-making process. This distinction has been institutionalized in the Treaty of Maastricht, whose official title is the Treaty on European Union (TEU). Within the overall institutional structure of the EU, the external economic policies (the CCP and development cooperation policy) and the CFSP have been organized in separate institutional frameworks, the so-called 'pillars'.

In the analysis of the foreign policy decision regime we will consequently follow the distinction in decision methods made by the member-states. We will first discuss the CFSP decision regime which covers the joint diplomatic activities and the common defence policy of the EU, as institutionalized in the second pillar of the EU. We will then move to deal with the external economic relations decision regime of the EU which comprises the CCP and the development cooperation policy of the EU, as institutionalized in the first pillar (see Table 5.1).

The CFSP decision regime

In our description and analysis of the CFSP decision regime we will start with the CFSP procedural decision regime. As mentioned in the introduction, procedural decision regimes condition the process of foreign policy making. The procedural rules in the European foreign policy decision regimes determine how an issue may enter the decision-making process, who can become involved, who must be consulted, who will decide, how the decision will be made and who will implement it. This collection of procedural rules, as indicated earlier, is composed of formal and informal rules. The formal procedures for the management of the common diplomacy evolved over the years as part of the organizational framework that was set up in the early 1970s to implement the European Political Cooperation (EPC). They were seen by the member-states more as conventions or norms for conduct than legally binding rules, but were nevertheless formalized in the Luxembourg Report (1970), the Copenhagen Report (1973), the London Report (1981) and the Solemn Declaration on European Union (1983), which were formally endorsed by the heads of state and government during their summits. Many of these procedural rules were included in the Single European Act (SEA) of 1987, which gave the EPC practice, for the first time, a legal basis. They were finally codified under the new heading of CFSP in the TEU, which has been in force since 1993. Any further change in the CFSP formal rules is now part of the continuous process of intergovernmental negotiations on institutional innovations and changes in the decision rules in the EU. The first amendments of the TEU provisions concerning the CFSP are set out in the Treaty of Amsterdam (1997).

In this connection it is important to emphasize that although the TEU has incorporated the CFSP provisions in the Union's *acquis communutaire*, it has not made the CFSP part of the judicial system of the EC. Whereas the CFSP is clearly linked to the overall institutional structure of the EU and has even some linkages to the EC institutional framework, the decision making regarding the CFSP has been deliberately organized in a separate institutional framework. In that way the CFSP as such has been placed outside the jurisdiction of the EC Treaty, and is not subject to judicial review by the European Court of Justice. Moreover, as we will see in more detail later, within the CFSP pillar the procedural rules do not apply to much of the actual decision making over security matters. NATO and the West European Union (WEU), the two main organizational settings wherein most of the member-states have organized their cooperation in the field of security, do have decision-making institutions and procedural rules of their own. As a matter of fact, much of the decision making in the security field is still guided by informal rules that are rooted in the practice of decision making, and may develop into formal rules. After all, many of the informal rules in the foreign policy field on which the member-states reached agreement within the EPC framework have finally been incorporated into the TEU.

Who makes CFSP decisions?

The European Council has clearly emerged as the highest decision-making forum of the EU in the field of foreign policy. At the same time, the Council of Ministers has become the supreme manager of the EU's foreign policy. The European Commission and the European Parliament, on the other hand, play a marginal role in the management of matters that fall under the CFSP. Thus, the European Council and the Council of Ministers may be pictured as the EU's ultimate decision-making unit, which has the ability to make a decision that cannot be readily reversed (cf. Hermann and Hermann, 1989: 362).

The European Council

Officially, the creation of the European Council in 1975 meant simply the institution-alization of the summit meetings of heads of government (with the exception of France which is represented by both its president and prime minister). But in practice, since the participants embody the highest authority in the member-states, the establishment of the European Council gave the Community a centre of author-ity which neither the Commission nor the Council of Ministers was able to provide. The European Council received for the first time a treaty-based status, though still a very loose legal standing, in the SEA. The European Council's actual role as the directing body of the Union has been formalized in the TEU, although the decisions made by the heads of government still enjoy a very vague legal basis and can there-fore rather be seen as essentially political decisions (TEU, Article D). As members of the European Council, the national leaders (joined by the president of the Com-mission) function as a collective leadership which provides the general political direction for the internal development of the Union. They take the necessary initia-tives and possess the political power to make irreversible decisions, to reach com-promises or to cut the Gordian knot when necessary. Moreover, through the joint declarations on major international affairs issued at the end of their summit meetings, the European Council has become the most visible personification of the interna-tional identity of the Union.

In the specific area of foreign policy the European Council authorizes, in fact, any significant foreign policy act that the EU takes. By means of the guiding function of the European Council, the political leaders of the member-states control the overall framing of the CFSP as well as the adoption of more concrete joint actions. As specified in Article J.3 of the Amsterdam Treaty, the European Council defines the principles of and general guidelines for the CFSP, including matters with defence implications. The European Council also decides on common strat-egies, to be implemented by the Union in areas where the member-states have important interests in common.

The Council of Ministers and Presidency

The Council of Ministers, in this case the General Affairs Council composed of the member-states' foreign ministers, figures as the decision-making body which implements CFSP on the basis of the general guidelines defined by the European Council. It is the Council of Ministers (hereafter called the Council) that recom-mends the common strategies to the European Council and realizes these common strategies by adopting joint actions and common positions. Thus the Council decides on the goals and the scope, the means, the duration and the conditions for imple-mentation of such an operational action, and defines the common approach to a particular foreign matter (Treaty of Amsterdam, Articles J.3 (3), J.4 (1) and J.5).

The member-state holding the rotating Council presidency has the responsibility for the day-to-day management of the CFSP. The president-in-office chairs all the EU's meetings, from the European Council and the Council of Ministers down to the working groups (including agenda setting and the drafting of compromises). The country holding the presidency also represents the EU internationally and acts as spokesman for the member-states in international conferences and international organizations (Treaty of Amsterdam, Article J.8). To deal with the problem of changing the presidency (which lasts for only six months), the current Presidency fulfils its tasks in close cooperation with its immediate successor and a member of the Commission.

In addition to this so-called 'troika' formula, continuity from one Presidency to another has been reinforced by the creation of a new function of High Representative for the CFSP, to be fulfilled by the secretary-general of the Council of Ministers. The High Representative operates in the first place as a CFSP coordinator to ensure greater coherence and effectiveness in the Union's foreign policy and is placed under the authority of the Union's foreign ministers and the Presidency in particular. As the Amsterdam Treaty stipulates, the High Representative assists the Presidency and the Council in CFSP matters through contribution to the formulation, preparation and implementation of policy decisions. On behalf of the Council and at the request of the Presidency, the High Representative is also allowed to conduct political dialogue with third parties (Treaty of Amsterdam Articles J.8(3) and J.16). The decision on whether the first appointed High Representative should actually be a senior civil servant who is an integral part of the existing decision-making structure of the EU or a heavyweight politician in line with the original French idea of a so-called 'Mr or Mrs CFSP' has been delayed. What the French still have in mind is a recognizable high-profile political figure who would give the CFSP a human face and would make the EU a serious foreign policy player. This would mark a large leap forward compared to the present practice of the Council to appoint a special representative (from outside the Union's machinery) with a mandate in relation to a particular foreign policy issue (Article J.8(5)). So far 'special envoys' have been designated to act as representatives of the EU in specific crisis zones such as former Yugoslavia, the Middle East, Cyprus and Central Africa. They function as the foreign ministers' eyes and ears in the troubled spots of the world, and present the EU with a voice and a face in these regions (cf. *European Voice*, 20–6 February 1997; Peterson and Sjursen, 1998: 57).

Despite the introduction of the new figure of High Representative for CFSP, the actual management of the CFSP administrative burden is still carried by the national foreign ministry of the country that holds the presidency. There is, however, a tendency to share some tasks with officials from the Council's general secretariat, which also brings some continuity to the day-to-day diplomatic activities of the Union. So each Presidency is assisted, in the preparation of the Council meetings and the implementation of the decisions taken, by a separate unit which deals exclusively with CFSP issues and is part of the Directorate-General for External Relations within the Council's general secretariat. This rather small unit, which acts as some kind of a collective memory for the rotating presidencies, is staffed by

European civil servants and an equal number of national officials on secondment to the CFSP unit. However, the extent to which the CFSP unit is involved in real policy making rather than just an administrative preparation of the Council meetings depends on the country holding the presidency. Smaller countries and newcomers are much more inclined to use the know-how of the Council's officials.

The still modest role of the Council secretariat in the running of CFSP matters has further been intensified by another institutional innovation introduced by the Treaty of Amsterdam. In an attempt to strengthen and improve the collective planning and analysis capabilities of the Union in the CFSP field and to make the foreign policy choices independent of the foreign policy preferences of the country holding the presidency, the member-states created (in addition to the CFSP unit) a new policy planning and early warning unit. It will be placed in the general secretariat of the Council under the responsibility of the new High Representative for the CFSP. The tasks of this policy planning unit are, first of all, to monitor and analyse developments in areas relevant to CFSP. It provides assessments of the Union's foreign and security policy interests, identifies areas where the CFSP could focus in future and gives timely assessments and early warning of events or situations that may have significant repercussions for the Union's foreign and security policy, including political crises. The policy planning and early warning unit produces, at the request of either the Council or the Presidency or on its own initiative, argued policy options papers to be presented under the responsibility of the Presidency as a contribution to policy formulation in the Council, and which may contain analyses, recommendations and strategies for the CFSP. The staff is recruited from the member-states, again on secondment to the general secretariat, complemented by officials from the Council's general secretariat, the Commission and the WEU (Declaration No. 6 annexed to the Treaty of Amsterdam). We have still to wait and see whether the new unit will indeed become the focal point of independent definition of foreign policy options, or just another administrative unit at the disposal of the Council to improve foreign policy making throughout the shifting presidencies.

COREPER and the Political Committee

The groundwork for the Council's decision making with respect to CFSP issues is done within two separate bodies. The Committee of the Permanent Representatives of the member-states to the EU (known by its French abbreviation of COREPER) has the formal responsibility for the preparation of the Council's decision making. This includes the decisions concerning the CFSP. However, its actual role is very limited. The key actor in preparing the discussions in the Council and the drafting of the common positions and the joint actions taken by the foreign ministers is actually the Political Committee, which consists of the political directors of the national foreign ministries (who are in many countries the direct chiefs of the Permanent Representatives). This high-ranking committee, which already existed under the EPC, still plays an essential role in the shaping of the CFSP. The Treaty of Amsterdam clearly points out that the Political Committee monitors the international situation in the areas covered by the CFSP and makes, in principal, all the policy proposals to the Council at the request of the Council or on its own initiative. It also observes the implementation of agreed policies (Treaty of Amsterdam, Article J.15). Since the Political Committee has in fact the principal responsibility for preparing the CFSP items on the agenda of the General Affairs Council, the main task of COREPER in CFSP matters is to ensure that the opinions and conclusions of the Political Committee are forwarded to the Council. COREPER may attach to these proposals its own comments and recommendations, but usually COREPER does not change proposals forwarded by the Political Committee.

Much of the work of the Political Committee is prepared in specialized working groups composed of national officials from the Permanent Representations or the national foreign ministries, who meet usually in Brussels. The TEU has led to the merger of the former EPC working groups and the equivalent Council's external relations working parties as a consequence of the removal of the distinction between the economic and the political aspects of the EU's external relations at the working-party level. But, according to David Galloway, 'it is still commonplace for the agendas of "merged" working parties to be divided into two sections, one covering primary "Community" matters and the other covering CFSP questions . . . This distinction has often meant one group having two chairmen for different portions of its agenda' (cited in Westlake, 1995: 216). The day-to-day coordination of the involvement of the national foreign ministries in the preparation and implementation of the CFSP is conducted through a separate group of national officials from the foreign ministries of the member-states, the so-called European Correspondents network (also known by their French abbreviation COREU), which already existed under the EPC.

The European Commission

In the early days of EPC, the European Commission was almost excluded from the decision making on EPC matters. The establishment of the EU has modified the Commission's role in the making of the CFSP, as the Commission is fully associated with the work carried out in the CFSP field. This relates to the implementation of CFSP decisions as well as the representation of the EU in CFSP matters (Treaty of Amsterdam, Articles J.17 and J.8(4)). In practice this means that the Commission participates in the meetings at all levels and is a member of the troika, but that it has no special management tasks in the area of the CFSP. In theory, the involvement of the Commission in the preparation and execution of the CFSP could guarantee some continuity among the changing presidencies. But as we have seen above, the member-states preferred to create some continuity through the troika formula, the EPC/CFSP administrative unit, the High Representative for the CFSP and the CFSP planning and early warning unit, which have limited the involvement of the Commission in EPC/CFSP affairs to a minimum.

To move the institutional balance in favour of the Commission, the former president of the Commission Jacques Delors tried to create a quasi foreign office within the Commission by the appointment in 1993 of a special commissioner with responsibility for external political relations. At the same time the previous Directorate-General for External Relations was split into a Directorate-General for External

Economic Relations and a Directorate-General for External Political Relations in the hope that the latter would develop into the Union's single ministry of foreign affairs. Such an ambition was actually undermined two years later by the next president of the Commission, Jacques Santer, who had to satisfy the need to find employment for another three commissioners representing the three new member-states. In the new Commission the responsibility for the external relations of the EU were divided between four members of the Commission, each in charge of the economic as well as the political relations with countries in specific geographical regions in the world or certain international organizations. One of these commissioners is still in charge of CFSP (which he shares with the president of the Commission) and acts as the liaison between the Commission and the Council. In the new proposed organization of the Commission these tasks are entrusted to the new vice-president for external relations.

The European Parliament

In the making of the CFSP the European Parliament (EP) is an almost negligible factor. Although the Presidency is required to inform the EP regularly on developments of the EU's CFSP, to consult the EP on the main aspects and basic choices of the CFSP and to take the EP's views into consideration, there is no mechanism that enables the EP to enforce its views on the Council or the Presidency. However, this may change slightly as a result of the new arrangements for financing the CFSP. In addition to the already existing arrangement regarding the administrative expenditures involved in the CFSP, in the future also the CFSP operational expenditure, with the exception of expenses arising from military and defence operations, will be charged to the budget of the EC (Treaty of Amsterdam, Article J.18). Given the record of the EP in the effective use of its budgetary powers, the EP may gain some foothold in the CFSP through the new agreement.

The WEU and NATO

During the intergovernmental negotiations on the TEU and the Amsterdam Treaty, the member-states agreed that the CFSP would deal with issues related to the security of the Union and opened the prospects for the framing of a common defence policy with respect to humanitarian and rescue tasks, peacekeeping tasks and tasks of combat forces in crisis management, including peacekeeping. But neither the EU's policy-making institutions nor the CFSP decision-making mechanism handle defence matters. Such questions are still treated outside the Union in two separate organizations: the WEU and NATO. So far the member-states have not reached a final agreement on the question of how to organize their common defence and whether the WEU or NATO should be the most important organization in this respect. On the one hand, the TEU has established the WEU as the EU's decision-making body in the area of defence policy and expresses the willingness of the member-states to strengthen the role of the WEU as the defence component of the Union. As the Amsterdam Treaty restates, the WEU is an integral part of the development of the Union, providing it with access to an operational capability to fulfil the tasks mentioned above. The Union shall accordingly foster closer institutional relations with the WEU with a view to the possibility of the integration of the WEU into the Union, should the European council so decide. On the other hand, however, both treaties recognize that certain member-states see their common defence realized in NATO. It emphasizes therefore that the security policy of the Union should respect the obligations that certain member-states do have within NATO and should take into account the common security and defence policy established within NATO (Treaty of Amsterdam, Article J.7).

In fact, the member-states compromised by keeping both options open and postponing a final choice to a later date. As a result there is no single decision-making body that deals with the overall defence policy of the Union. In the meantime, in separate declarations annexed to the TEU and the Amsterdam Treaty, the member-states encourage the development of closer defence cooperation between the two defence organizations and stress that the WEU should also function as a means to develop and strengthen the European pillar of the Atlantic Alliance, the so-called European Security and Defence Identity (ESDI). As a matter of fact, the member-states recognize that such an ESDI can be realized through close cooperation with NATO. Such close cooperation is also dictated by the day-to-day realities and the experience gained in recent peacekeeping and peace enforcement operations.

In spite of repeated declarations about the intention to strengthen the operational role of the WEU, it still has a very limited operational capacity compared to NATO. The WEU has no integrated military command and does not have at its disposal an electronic command and communication system to conduct large-scale military peacekeeping and peace enforcement operations. Given the limited financial resources that the WEU members are ready to invest in such an operational infrastructure, the WEU has no other choice but to use the NATO infrastructure. This has led to a contradictory situation. While the TEU openly promotes the idea of establishing the WEU as the military organization of the Union, in practice the WEU is not yet an alternative to NATO as the EU's military arm, and NATO remains indispensable for the implementation of major joint military actions. No wonder that the EU member governments emphasize the need for operational links between WEU and NATO, in the planning, preparation and conduct of operations using NATO assets and capabilities, under the political control and strategic direction of the WEU. In other words, the member-states can use the military resources and capabilities of NATO to conduct WEU operations, as long as the political and strategic responsibility rests with the WEU. This condition makes the likelihood of a WEU operation conducted with NATO resources quite rare, since the use of NATO machinery and military equipment depends on American approval.

On the basis of this discussion regarding the question of who makes the CFSP decisions, we may summarize the procedural decision rules as follows:

- The European Council defines the overall principles of the CFSP and specifies the general guidelines for the common positions and the joint actions.
- The Council of Ministers takes the actual decisions necessary for the adoption and implementation of the common positions and the joint actions.

- The Presidency, assisted by the High Representative for CFSP, acts as the executive in the area of CFSP and represents the Union in issues that fall under the CFSP.
- The EU as such does not deal with defence matters. The WEU functions as the military organization designated to carry out the defence policy of the EU.

To this set of formal decision rules we may add two informal decision rules:

- The Political Committee is still responsible for the preparation and implementation of the Council's decisions on CFSP matters.
- Because of the WEU's limited military resources and capabilities, NATO remains the essential military organization for major crisis management and peacekeeping operations.

Hence, it is clear that the national governments, through the presidency, continue to operate as the central managers of the CFSP. When collective administrative capabilities are created, they are placed within the Council Secretariat. That way the member-states maintain their predominance over the Community institutions and make sure that they hold control over any development towards some kind of a European foreign ministry. However, neither the creation of the function of High Representative for CFSP, nor the establishment of the policy planning and early warning unit in addition to the existing CFSP unit, indicates a willingness on the part of the member-states to move the authority in foreign policy making from the national ministries to an evolving European foreign ministry located in the Council of Ministers. It is just another manifestation of the growing tendency among member-states to choose Brussels instead of the national capitals as the main venue for European foreign policy making, a trend that some observers of European policy making call the 'Brusselization' of European foreign policy making (cf. *European Voice*, 4–10 September 1997; Peterson and Sjursen, 1998: 56–8). The Commission, sometimes considered as the executive of the Union, has in fact lost any hope of being charged with the management of CFSP affairs.

How are CFSP decisions made?

During the EPC period the member-states have already developed and institutionalized a habit of cooperation in their diplomatic activities which has been coined as a 'coordination reflex' and has been codified in the SEA and the TEU (Soetendorp, 1994: 118). In the Amsterdam Treaty the member-states affirmed their willingness to support the Union's foreign policy actively and unreservedly in a spirit of loyalty and mutual solidarity. They have also declared that they are willing to work together to enhance and develop their mutual political solidarity, and to refrain from any action that is contrary to the interests of the Union or likely to impair its effectiveness as a cohesive force in international relations (Treaty of Amsterdam J.1(2)). But how are these general commitments put into practice?

CFSP instruments

The member-states have agreed on five policy instruments to pursue a common foreign and security policy. The first two instruments are quite vague and simply refer to the definition of the general principles and guidelines for the CFSP, and the decision on common strategies (which set out the objectives, duration and the means to be made available by the Union and the member-states). The other three instruments are much more specific and relate to the adoption of joint actions, the adoption of common positions and the systematic cooperation between member-states. Joint actions address specific situations where operational action by the Union is considered to be required. They specify the objectives, scope, and the means to be made available to the Union. If necessary the joint actions also mention their duration and the conditions for their implementation. Common positions define the approach of the Union to a particular matter. The member-states are committed to the joint actions in the positions they adopt and in the conduct of their activity. They have also the obligation to ensure that their national policies conform to the common positions (Treaty of Amsterdam, Article J.3, J.4 and J.5).

As a rule, the member-states inform and consult one another on any matter of foreign and security policy of general interest, so that the EU presents itself as a unified actor on the international scene and employs its combined influence as effectively as possible. Since adherence to this commitment still depends on the members' goodwill, they have also agreed on some procedural rules to strengthen the cooperation between member-states in the conduct of policy and to make sure that member-states behave in accordance with agreed policies. Member-states are required to coordinate their action in international organizations and at international conferences where they are obliged to uphold common positions. If not all the member-states participate in such fora, those that take part are required to support the common positions. They also have the obligation to keep the other member-states informed of any matter of common interest. This duty applies also to those member-states who are members of the United Nations Security Council. The two EU member-states that are permanent members of the Security Council, France and the United Kingdom, are asked to ensure the defence of the positions and the interests of the Union. Finally, the diplomatic missions of the member-states and the Commission delegations in third countries as well as their representation to international organizations and international conferences have to cooperate by exchanging information and carrying out joint assessments, to ensure that the joint decisions are complied with and implemented (Treaty of Amsterdam, Articles J.6, J.9 and J.10).

Agenda setting and voting procedures

Usually the agenda of the European Council and the Council of Ministers is set up by the Presidency. Regarding the CFSP items, both the member-states and the Commission may initiate proposals to the Council and place any question related to the CFSP on the Council's agenda. In crisis situations, the Presidency, on its own initiative or at the request of the member-state or the Commission, can convene a Council meeting within 48 hours or within a shorter period (Treaty of Amsterdam, Article J.12).

Generally speaking, decision making on CFSP matters still requires a unanimous vote. At the same time the member-states have opened, under certain conditions, the possibility of decision making on non-military CFSP questions by qualified majority voting and have allowed the adoption of CFSP decisions even if some countries abstain during a vote. Joint actions, common positions or any other decisions that are based on a common strategy that was adopted unanimously by the European Council can be decided by a qualified majority of the Council of Ministers. At present a qualified majority requires at least 62 votes in favour, cast by at least 10 members. Any decision implementing an agreed joint action or a common position can also be taken by a qualified majority of the member-states. To make decision making in CFSP matters more effective, the member-states also agreed to avoid deadlocks with respect to Council decisions on CFSP requiring unanimity, or, as the Amsterdam Treaty says, abstention by member-states shall not prevent the adoption of CFSP decisions. However, such a decision cannot be adopted in the event that the votes of those members who abstain represent more than one-third of the weighted votes of the members of the Council. Under the provisions of this form of so-called 'constructive abstention' the member governments that have abstained are not obliged to apply the decision, but shall accept that the decision commits the Union. The concerned governments also refrain from any action that is likely to conflict with actions of the EU based on that decision. The novelties with respect to the rule of unanimity in CFSP decision making do not apply to decisions with military or defence implications which still need unanimous agreement. Furthermore, the member-states still have the possibility of vetoing the holding of a vote. The member-states agreed that a vote is not taken in case a member of the Council declares that, for important and stated reasons of national policy, it intends to oppose the adoption of a decision to be taken by qualified majority. In such an event the Council of Ministers can decide, by a qualified majority, to refer the matter to the European Council for decision by unanimity (Treaty of Amsterdam, Article J.13). This looks very much like the formal institutionalization of an informal ground rule that guides the participants in EU decision making in general, based on the so-called Luxembourg compromise, which we will discuss in another section.

Thus the fundamental procedural decision rules regarding the question of how the CFSP should be conducted clearly point out the following:

- Agreed common strategies, joint actions and common positions commit member-states in the foreign policy positions they adopt and in the conduct of their international activity.
- The member-states are obliged to refrain from any action that may damage the effectiveness of the Union as a cohesive force in international affairs and inform and consult one another on any matter of foreign and security policy.
- Decisions are taken by the Council of Ministers unanimously. However, decisions that follow from a common strategy as well as decisions that implement joint actions and common positions can be decided by a qualified majority.
- The foreign ministers are allowed to take a decision while some members abstain from a decision (comprising up to one-third of the weighted vote).
- Any member-state can veto the holding of a vote if it claims that a special national interest is threatened.

What are the CFSP goals and interests?

The European decision regime is more than a set of rules that deals merely with the process of European foreign policy making. It also handles the basic goals, interests and values on which those decisions are based. To begin with, the objectives of the common foreign policy of the EC member-states were limited and formulated in vague terms. The Treaty of Rome, which established the EEC in 1958, referred in its preamble only to the wish of the member-states to contribute to the progressive abolition of restrictions on international trade by means of a common commercial policy; the intention to ensure the development of the prosperity of the overseas countries (which at that time still belonged to the member-states); and their determination to preserve and strengthen peace and liberty through the pooling of their resources. In the formulations of the concrete common policies we find no further reference to this last statement. With respect to the external relations of the Community, the Treaty of Rome includes only a few provisions dealing almost entirely with the setting up of a common commercial policy to complement the customs union on which the EEC was to be based, as well as some articles dedicated to the EEC relationship with the member-states' overseas countries. As I have argued in Chapter 1, the fear of the member-states to lose control over the conduct of their foreign policy has conditioned from the very beginning the willingness of member-states to pool their national sovereignty.

The first concrete steps towards European cooperation in the field of foreign policy was taken only in the early 1970s with the adoption of two reports by the EEC member-states, the so-called Luxembourg Report and Copenhagen Report. The objectives of European Political Cooperation (EPC) as stated in these first building blocks for future foreign policy cooperation were still modest, but they reveal already the double function of EPC: to provide the member-states with ways and means of harmonizing their views in the field of international politics, and to demonstrate to all that Europe has a political vocation (*Bulletin of the European Communities*, 1970, no. 11: 9–14, and 1973, no. 9: 14–21). Indeed, as I have argued elsewhere, the rise in the economic power of the EC and the changing status it has acquired in the minds of the outside world has generated the necessity to improve control over the economic effects of foreign policy decisions of individual member-states. As a matter of fact, EPC received its initial major impulse from the need to coordinate the various national policies during the Middle East War in 1973, when the Arab selective use of the oil weapon demonstrated the vulnerability of the Community to external events (Soetendorp, 1994: 115).

The provisions stipulating the general goals of the common foreign policy in the TEU contain, in comparison to the Treaty of Rome, much more rhetoric. However, the TEU, even in its latest amendment by the Treaty of Amsterdam, remains quite tentative. The member-states have stated that the overall foreign policy objective of the EU is to create a more effective international presence of the Union, or, as the TEU says, to assert its identity on the international scene, in particular through the implementation of a common foreign and security policy. The more concrete political ambitions of the CFSP are set out in more detail in the provisions on a common foreign and security policy and defined as follows: to safeguard the common values, fundamental interests, independence and integrity of the Union; to strengthen the security of the Union in all ways; to preserve peace and strengthen international security; to promote international cooperation; and to develop and consolidate democracy and the rule of law, and respect for human rights and fundamental freedoms (Article B and Title V, Article J.1, Treaty of Amsterdam).

These rather ambitious objectives are put into perspective by the decisions of the European heads of government during the post-Maastricht European Councils to narrow the scope for their joint activities. They decided that, instead of making the entire world potential for joint action, priority will be given in the application of joint actions to a limited number of areas and issues where member-states have important interests in common. The purpose is to reach consensus among member-states on objectives in a particular area and to facilitate rapid and coherent reaction to events when they occur. The main rule for deciding whether a certain area or issue will be subject to joint action is geographic closeness, that is to say, member-states deal first with issues and interests arising in the immediate neighbourhood. Besides geographical proximity, the other criteria are the extent to which the Union has an important interest in the political and economic stability of a region or a country and the existence of threats for the security interests of the Union. On the basis of these criteria the European Council identified the following geographical regions for the implementation of joint action: countries in Central and Eastern Europe (including Russia and the other members of the Commonwealth of Independent States, as well as the Balkan states), the Mediterranean countries (especially the Maghreb states) and the Middle East (cf. Buchan, 1993: 46–7).

The European Council has also indicated the issues for which joint action towards the selected individual countries or groups of countries may be helpful. With respect to Central and East European countries, the member-states and the Union will promote political and economic stability in these countries and contribute to the creation of political and economic frameworks for regional cooperation, and will stimulate the relations between these countries and the EU or other European organizations and frameworks for cooperation like the Conference on Security and Cooperation in Europe (CSCE), now the Organization for Security and Cooperation in Europe (OSCE). They will also reinforce the democratic process in those countries, encourage respect for human rights and the rights of minorities and support the settlement of the conflict in former Yugoslavia. Regarding the Middle East, the Union will support and play an active role in the Middle East peace process, take measures to move Israel to change its policies with respect to the settlements in the occupied territories, induce the Arabs to end their economic boycott of Israel and back attempts towards regional integration. After the political transformation in South Africa which ended the apartheid regime, cooperation with a democratic South Africa has been added to the list of issues open to joint action (cf. Piening, 1997: 41).

In the TEU the member-states expressed for the first time their explicit goal to include in the common foreign policy also a common defence policy. The TEU (as amended by the Treaty of Amsterdam) spelled out that the CFSP shall include all questions relating to the security of the Union, including the progressive framing of a common defence policy, which might lead to a common defence, should the European Council of heads of state so decide (Treaty of Amsterdam, Article J.7).

As the phrasing of this goal indicates, it contains more a promise than a definite determination to set up a common military capacity. So far the European Council has managed to identify a number of issues for joint action in the specific field of security. But these issues in fact concern areas wherein the Community already has an established practice within the former EPC framework, namely: the CSCE process; disarmament and arms control in Europe; and non-proliferation of nuclear weapons and economic aspects of security, in particular with regard to the control of transfers of arms technology to non-member countries and controls on the export of weapons. A more innovative substantive element in the common defence policy is a common understanding on the vital security interests of the EU which has been reached by an *ad hoc* working group on security set up by the Council. In very general terms, the working group states that the promotion of European interests will encompass the reduction of risks and uncertainties that might otherwise prove damaging to the territorial integrity and political independence, economic stability, ecological basis and the democratic fabric of the Union and its member-states.

The external economic relations decision regime

In spite of the differences in the member-states' external trade relations and the conflicting interests within the EU between 'free traders' and 'protectionists', the Common Commerce Policy (CCP) is one of the most integrated policy areas and widely accepted by the member-states. As one observer of the EU has remarked: 'Europe may not be able to command a single army, or run a joint embassy, but in the heady world of international commerce it is a formidable power' (*European Voice*, 26 February–4 March 1998). Michael Smith has even gone as far as arguing that external economic relations and external economic policies are the core of EU foreign policy (Peterson and Sjursen, 1998: 78). The history of the CCP goes back to the creation of the EEC, when it was necessary to complement the custom union, which regulated internal trade relations, by a common external trade policy to manage the member-states' trading relations with the rest of the world including their overseas countries and territories. The original formal rules concerning the basic questions of who makes the common decisions in the CCP, how the decisions are made and what are the goals on which these decisions are based, were already laid down in the Treaty of Rome. Since then the basic decision rules have hardly been changed, although the member-states have tightened, during the succeeding intergovernmental negotiations on the TEU and the Amsterdam Treaty, their control over the handling of the external economic relations of the EU.

The development cooperation policy as such is of a more recent date. The Treaty of Rome dealt with the economic relations of the EEC with the members' overseas countries and territories. Moreover, the EC has always been a generous provider of development grants to the developing countries, in addition to the development cooperation programmes of the member-states. But the formal competence of the EC to formulate a common development cooperation policy received a treaty base only in the TEU. There is another important difference between the two policy areas. While the CCP replaced the national trade policies, the common development cooperation policy complements the national development cooperation policies. The EC has, for example, the exclusive competence to determine the common tariff on trade with countries outside the EU, whereas the member-states are allowed to conclude development cooperation agreements with third countries (cf. Church and Phinnemore, 1994: 184). As we will see below, this distinction is reflected in the procedural decision rules concerning both common policies.

Who makes the external economic policies?

As mentioned earlier, contrary to the common foreign and security policy-making process, decision making on external economic policies follows the 'community method'. Consequently, the EU institutions, the Commission in particular, are more involved in the framing of the external economic policies than in the shaping of the CFSP.

The Council/Commission tandem

The roles and tasks of each participant in the formulation and the implementation of a CCP, as well as the conclusion of external agreements, are well defined. It is the General Affairs Council of Ministers that decides on all aspects of the CCP. Development cooperation issues and policies are decided by the Council of Development Cooperation Ministers. All decisions are based on recommendations made to the Council by the Commission. External trade agreements and development cooperation agreements, like any other agreement between the EC and non-member countries or international organizations, are concluded by the Council. The Commission puts proposals for the opening of such negotiations to the Council and negotiates on behalf of the Community as a whole. But the Council authorizes the Commission to start the negotiations and it decides how the Commission may proceed with the negotiations. A special restriction applies to trade negotiations in services and intellectual property. Here the Commission is allowed to conduct negotiations only after the Council has decided unanimously to give the Commission the authority to negotiate on issues of services and intellectual property (TEU and Treaty of Amsterdam, Articles 113 and 228). In all negotiations the Commission has to work within the mandate laid down by the Council and to conduct the negotiations in consultation with special committees, appointed by the Council to assist the Commission in the negotiations. They act as the member-states' watchdog during the negotiations and reinforce the predominance of the Council over the Commission. In the external trade agreement this is the so-called Article 113 Committee, which is composed of senior national officials responsible for the member-states' external trade policy.

It is important to note in this connection that while many of the development cooperation agreements are negotiated and concluded in accordance with these procedural decision rules, the member-states maintain the competence to negotiate and conclude international development cooperation agreements on their own (TEU, Article 130y). In addition, member-states are also allowed to impose protective measures on imports from countries outside the EU, although such measures need authorization from the Commission (TEU, Article 115).

The Commission and Parliament

Contrary to the CFSP, the conduct of the day-to-day common external economic policies is entrusted to the Commission. Within the Commission itself the competence for external relations is spread over four commissioners and organized in three different Directorates-General for External Relations and one Directorate for Development Cooperation. One commissioner has the responsibility for external relations with the European countries of Central Europe, Russia and the other newly independent states in eastern Europe as well as Turkey, Cyprus and Malta. This commissioner deals in fact with the issue of enlargement. The same commissioner is also in charge of all the external missions and, as mentioned above, is responsible for the Commission's involvement with the CFSP. A second commissioner has the responsibility for external relations with North America, the Far Eastern countries (including Japan), Australia and New Zealand, as well as the CCP and the relations with the Organization for Economic Cooperation and Development (OECD) and the World Trade Organization (WTO). This commissioner acts as the European counterpart of the American and Japanese trade negotiators within the WTO. The management of external relations with southern Mediterranean countries, the Middle East, Latin America and Southeast Asia has been entrusted to a third commissioner, while the conduct of external relations with Africa, Caribbean and Pacific countries and South Africa, including development aid, are entrusted to a fourth commissioner. This division of labour between the four commissioners for external affairs, based on geographical instead of functional responsibilities, ended the artificial distinction between the economic and political aspects of the EU's external relations, but it has not contributed to the unity of external policy making within the Commission. Since the commissioner responsible for humanitarian aid and the commissioner in charge of economic and financial affairs are also involved in the external economic relations of the EU, the responsibilities for the economic external relations of the Commission are actually shared by six commissioners. To these six commissioners one has to add the president of the Commission whose policy portfolio includes CFSP questions.

To gain some control over the activities of the different commissioners, Santer established an External Relations Working Group (Relex), chaired by himself and including all six commissioners. Its task is to coordinate action in external affairs, including the setting of priorities and strategic planning, to ensure consistency on questions likely to affect Commission action in the various geographic areas for which members of the Commission are responsible. The working group is also responsible for the preparation of meetings in which more than one member of the Commission has an interest and it decides on representation at such meetings. Where necessary, the working group coordinates the position of the members of the Commission responsible for external relations on matters within their jurisdiction which must be put to the full Commission. To increase the effectiveness of the Commission with respect to its external relations, the Commission has worked out two reorganization schemes, one on the level of the commissioners, the other on the level of the directorates. The first plan draws upon the positive experience with the Relex Group. It gives the future president of the Commission the final responsibility for the coordination of external policies. He is assisted by two vice-presidents: one is fully responsible for external policies, the other is responsible for economic and monetary policies. The other reorganization which has already been put into motion makes a distinction among the officials in all the external directorates between policy makers and policy implementers. Those who qualify as policy makers remain within the existing directorates, while all the other officials who qualify as implementers have been placed in a new common external relations service. The new service carries the responsibility for the management of all the economic projects and financial aid programmes to countries outside the EU. It will contribute to a harmonization of the various procedures and lead to more coherence and effectiveness.

Although the 'community method' is employed in external economic policies, since the powers of the European Parliament (EP) in the external economic relations field are still limited, its role is also quite restricted. The external common trade agreements negotiated under Article 113 are excluded from any control by the EP. The Council has in most cases actually only an obligation to consult the EP. An exception is made for a limited number of agreements such as cooperation and association agreement, when it is necessary to acquire the EP's approval before the conclusion of the external accord (TEU, Article 228). The European Court of Justice may also get involved in the external economic relations if the Council, the Commission or a member-state wishes to obtain the opinion of the Court as to whether a foreseen agreement is agreeable with the stipulation of the TEU.

Hence, the formal procedural decision rules regarding the question of who makes the external economic policies are the following:

- The Council of Ministers decides on questions regarding common external relations policies but the Commission has the responsibility for the preparation and implementation of the CCP and the common development cooperation policy.
- The European Commission (not the Presidency) represents the member-states in negotiations with third parties where external relations agreements with one or more states or international organization need to be negotiated.

How are the external economic policies made?

External economic policy instruments

The EU uses in the implementation of its external economic policies a number of relevant policy instruments. Changes in tariff rates, the conclusion of tariff and trade agreements, trade liberalization, export policy and anti-dumping measures and subsidies are the most important CCP instruments (TEU, Article 113). These general policy instruments are, however, bounded by the trade rules agreed upon within the frameworks of the General Agreement on Tariffs and Trade (GATT) and the current World Trade Organization (WTO). Many of the trade concessions agreements that create free trade areas or custom unions between the Union and other countries or regions are regulated through the large number of association agreements or trade and economic cooperation agreements, which the EC has concluded over the years with individual countries or groups of developed and less developed countries throughout the world. To the list of external economic policy instruments we should add the foreign economic policy instrument of economic sanctions (defined as an action to interrupt or to reduce, in part or completely, economic relations with one or more third countries), although they are usually utilized in a joint action under the CFSP (TEU, Article 228a).

The common development and cooperation policy instruments usually take the form of multiannual programmes and joint actions (TEU, Article 130w and 130x). It includes the granting of trade concessions and preferential access to the EU market such as non-reciprocal trade preferences, financial support to compensate for losses in export earnings, the purchase of goods at a guaranteed price, emergency humanitarian and relief aid, food support, infrastructural development training and technical assistance. As we have mentioned earlier, the common development cooperation policies are considered as complementary to the national development cooperation policies. The member-states agreed therefore to coordinate their policies on development cooperation and to consult each other on their aid programmes, since they are allowed to cooperate with third countries and with international organizations independently of the Community.

Agenda setting and voting

In the CCP area and the development cooperation policy the Commission has the exclusive right to submit proposals to the Council. It is, however, the Council that decides by a qualified majority vote to authorize the Commission to open the necessary negotiations, to issue the directives for the negotiations and to conclude the negotiated agreements. An extension of the Commission's mandate to trade negotiations in services and intellectual property has, however, to be decided unanimously by the Council. A unanimous vote is also necessary for the conclusion of Association agreements (TEU and Treaty of Amsterdam, Articles 113 and 228). In cases where the CFSP and the external economic policies intermingle, the applied decision-making procedures depend on the nature of the joint action. The imposition of economic sanctions under the CFSP, for example, is decided in the Council by a qualified majority on a proposal from the Commission.

It is in this connection important to note that, notwithstanding the formal voting rules, in practice the member-states prefer to achieve consensual agreement and always make an effort to proceed on the basis of unanimity. The explanation for this informal rule has been the practice established since 1966 as a result of the Luxembourg compromise which ended the French boycott of the EEC decision making. According to this compromise, the member-states have agreed that when issues are at stake that one or more countries considers very important, the members of the Council will try to reach solutions that can be adopted by all member-states and takes into account their mutual interests and that of the Community. France also established the informal procedural rule that whenever this is the case, discussions must be continued until unanimous agreement is reached (Dinan, 1994: 58). The SEA and the TEU, which have established qualified majority voting as a mode of decision making in a number of issue areas including CCP matters and development cooperation questions, have made voting less rare. The use of the Luxembourg compromise has actually become a weapon of last resort, to uphold the taking of a vote whenever a country feels that their interests are jeopardized. France, for instance, threatened to block the ratification of an agreement between the EU and the United States during the Uruguay round of trade negotiations in 1994 (Hayes-Renshaw and Wallace, 1997: 49, 262).

The revitalization of the qualified majority voting procedure in external economic policies has also changed the nature of the bargaining process. In the past, like in the present CFSP, decisions were taken on the basis of unanimous agreement, which gave each member-state a veto power and placed each member government in a position to create a deadlock. Member-states were therefore forced to compromise in their final common decisions on the lowest common denominator or to continue the debate until agreement is reached. Now that voting by qualified majority is applied in most cases, participants can be outvoted and are therefore more inclined to compromise on a common decision that does not coincide wholly with their national views. In external economic policies, even in issues where member-states decide unanimously, they use their veto power more as a negotiation tactic. A country blocks agreement on one issue where the veto power applies, in an attempt to obtain concessions on another issue where qualified majority voting is exercised. The former president of the European Commission Jacques Delors has called this practice 'to take hostages'. Spain used this tactic, for example, in December 1994, when it threatened to block the entry of Austria, Finland, Sweden and Norway to the EU unless Spanish fishermen were allowed to fish in British and Irish waters (*The Economist*, 18 February 1995).

As one state's gain is another state's loss, member-states are willing to compromise and accept to end up as satisfiers rather than optimizers. This makes the preparatory work for the Council meetings crucial for the reaching of compromises. The preparatory work and the search for a compromise consists of bilateral pre-negotiations outside the conference rooms as well as multilateral negotiations inside the conference rooms. It involves officials in the capitals of the member-states, delegates from the Permanent Representation in Brussels, representatives of the Commission and officials of the Council's Secretariat General. Very important in this respect are the meetings of the 'working groups' in Brussels, where the Commission proposals are actually first discussed, under the chairmanship of the country holding the presidency which examines the proposal and explores the extent of agreement or disagreement among the member-states. It is there that member-states' officials and Commission representatives try to reach a common understanding of whether the proposal can be accepted, and if not, what changes might make it acceptable and to see whether the Commission is ready to modify its proposal. If the 'working group' reaches a consensus, then the proposal will be passed to COREPER and endorsed by the Council of Ministers. In case the proposal remains disputed, the search for compromise continues within COREPER and if it is not settled there, discussed in the Council. As Nicoll and Salmon have noted, it is not always necessary to take a vote even if the issue could be decided by a qualified majority. A chair can conclude from discussions that agreement exists without polling the delegates and if this conclusion is not challenged, the proposal is accepted

(Nicoll and Trevor, 1994: 69–71). In an attempt to reach a consensus or a qualified majority the Commission can agree during the process of negotiations to change its original proposal if such a modification will obtain a consensus or the necessary qualified majority. Agreements on compromises are also worked out by creating a linkage between issues and putting together package deals.

The structure of multilateral negotiations makes the requirement of coalition building conditional to the exercise of influence on Community decisions (Wallace, 1990: 213–14). In the external economic policies sector where qualified majority voting is the rule, the proponent of a certain option or course of action has to build a coalition around either a winning majority or a blocking minority. With the exception of the Franco-German coalition, no recognizable pattern of permanent coalitions have emerged. Most of the coalitions are formed on an *ad hoc* basis and differ according to the issue at stake. The experience of the last two decades has nevertheless illustrated that the building of a winning coalition is conditional on the support of at least two of the larger member-states, while a blocking coalition needs the support of one of the larger countries. As Helen Wallace has argued, it is obvious that the weight of the larger states matters, and that nothing very substantial can be decided against the will of one of the large members (Wallace, 1990: 114).

From this brief discussion we may derive the following formal and informal procedural decision rules with respect to the question of how external economic policies are made:

- The CCP and most external relations agreements concerning development cooperation policies are decided in the Council by a qualified majority. (Only association agreements require a unanimous decision of the Council and the assent of the European Parliament.)
- Irrespective of the formal voting rules, participants usually make an effort to accommodate national interests and to proceed on the basis of consensual agreement.
- Coalition building is the key to desired outcomes. A winning coalition usually requires the participation of at least two large member-states.

What are the external economic policy goals and interests?

The EU's common external trade policy goals, which were already spelled out in Article 110 of the Treaty of Rome, are in fact reiterated in the TEU. The member-states and the Union still give priority to the elimination of all barriers to free trade and the lowering of all customs barriers. They aim to contribute to the harmonious development of world trade, the progressive abolition of restrictions on international trade and the lowering of customs barriers. The TEU places explicit limitations on the possibility of member-states taking protective measures beyond the common external tariff. Purely defensive acts need the authorization of the Commission (TEU, Article 115).

But the implementation of the principle of free trade does not exclude protectionist measures. In the area of the common trade policy, parochial national loyalties actually still predominate, which makes the EU at times rather protectionist. The practice of the CCP shows that narrow sectoral or national interests may influence the decision making on the common external trade policy of the EU, which is sometimes just the continuation of domestic politics as the deliberations in the EU about the Uruguay Round accord illustrate. On certain occasions in the past, several members resisted not only the lifting of protection measures in certain sectors (such as agriculture or the car industry), but also favoured protection measures to create an advantageous market for the launching of new products (for instance in the electronic industry). Thus, in spite of the member-states' adherence to the principle of free trade and the strong belief that acting together in the external trade area is more advantageous than unilateral actions, in the view of many member-states there is no such thing as a community interest – there are only competitive and interdependent interests of the member-states.

Before the TEU came into force in 1993 the common international development and cooperation policy was essentially conducted under the provisions of the Treaty of Rome which included special stipulations for the association of the member-states' overseas countries and territories with the Community. The purpose was to establish close economic relations between them and the EC, which will promote their economic and social development and extend the benefits of the Community to these countries and territories (cf. Church and Phinnemore, 1994: 241). These goals are reinforced in the TEU which determines, for example, that these countries will have an equal trade status to member-states and abolishes custom duties on imports from these countries and territories (TEU, Articles 132 and 133).

The TEU has also broadened the scope of the common development cooperation policies beyond the former overseas countries and territories, to cover economic and social development in all developing countries. The objectives of the common development and cooperation policy are to promote the sustainable economic and social development of the developing countries and more particularly the most disadvantaged countries among them; to advance the integration of these countries into the world economy; and to campaign against poverty in the disadvantaged countries of the world (TEU, Article 130u).

In this overview of the two separate decision regimes that the EU members have created to deal with the CFSP and the external economic relations of the EU, a final word should be said about the attempts made so far to bridge the two decision regimes. The member-states have recognized over the years the necessity to link the foreign policy activities in the particular foreign policy sectors. The TEU, for example, stipulates that the Union shall be served by a single institutional framework and determines that the Council of Ministers shares with the Commission the task of ensuring the consistency of the Union's external activities as a whole in the context of its foreign relations, security, economic and development policies – each in accordance with its respective powers, however (TEU, Article C). In the Amsterdam Treaty, Article C was sharpened further, saying that the Council and the Commission have the duty to cooperate, to ensure consistency in the EU's overall foreign policy. During the intergovernmental negotiations over the TEU, the member-states have indeed made some progress towards the creation of a single institutional framework. Under the provisions of the TEU, the General Affairs Council, consisting of the ministers of foreign affairs of the member-states, decides on both CFSP and external economic relations issues. But as we have seen above, the creation of a single institutional framework at the level of the Council of Foreign Ministers with an overall responsibility for the conduct of the EU's foreign policy has not yet improved efficiency in the decision-making procedures regarding the overall foreign policy of the Union. A distinction is still made in the procedural decision rules with respect to the CFSP and external economic relations.

In conclusion then, progress in the institutional arrangements for the formulation and implementation of a European common foreign policy in which the EU member-states have been engaged over the last two decades, has been achieved through a continuing process of institutional adaptation. The pattern of institutional change is very much in line with what Ernst Haas has called adaptation through incremental growth (Haas, 1990: 97–108). In such a process the organization (in this case the EPC framework) is created by states which decided that their separate interests cannot be adequately met without some mechanism for collaborative, programmed or joint action. The initial task of the organization is, Haas explains, the elaboration of a programme and a set of rules of conduct to bring about such joint action. Adaptation by increments is, according to Haas, usually informal. Only later are formal rules and procedures brought in conformity with the actual changes (Haas, 1990: 97, 99). The European political cooperation in the foreign policy area indeed started outside the legal framework of the EC. The informal EPC practice was given a formal treaty basis much later, first by means of the SEA and later through the TEU. However, even then the formal rules and procedures of the EPC were not yet incorporated into the legal structure of the EC, but kept in a separate part of the TEU, giving the economically based external relations of the EU (in the first pillar) and the politically based external relations (in the second pillar) a different and separate set of formal rules. A formal merger of the first and the second pillars has therefore to be achieved first in an informal manner, by means of a growing practice of decision making and institutional interaction whereby the distinction between the two policy areas fades away.

Part II

Foreign policy practice

Chapter 6

Dealing with the Middle East conflict and peace process: building a visible international identity

The formulation of a common policy of the EC member-states towards the Middle East and especially the Arab–Israeli conflict was one of the first items on the agenda of the European Political Cooperation (EPC) when it started in the early 1970s. It was, however, not before the October War in 1973 and the oil crisis of that same year that the member-states were able to frame their first common statement on the Middle East conflict. In spite of the original different views among the member-states with respect to the Arab–Israeli conflict, the EC member-states managed during several years to bridge their differences and to compromise on a common foreign policy towards the Arab–Israeli conflict and the preferred course of action to solve this conflict. Moreover, this common policy was a deliberate effort to follow an independent course towards the Arab–Israeli conflict and the resolution of that conflict, by which the EC as such distinguished itself from the other major Western player in the Middle East, the United States (US). The common foreign policy towards the Arab–Israeli conflict and the Middle East peace process illustrates how the member-states, through the EC/EU, managed to build a visible international identity. This has always been one of the main goals of their cooperation in the foreign policy field. In this chapter we will examine how this common policy has developed and consider the way that it has been determined by the relevant national views. Two European countries, France and Britain, have played an important role in the way the EC/EU has dealt with the Arab–Israeli conflict. We will start therefore with a brief review of their diplomatic record in the Middle East up to the 1970s, when the EC member-states through EPC began to frame their common policy towards the region. Throughout this chapter, the European policies towards the Middle East conflict and the Middle East peace process will be compared with that of the US to illustrate the separate and independent character of the European position.

The French and British historical legacy

Among the West European countries, Britain and France have the longest history of involvement in the Middle East and the Arab countries of the Mediterranean.

But while Britain's foreign policy towards the Middle East was dominated by the strategic importance of the region as a link between Europe and the former British colonies in Asia and East Africa and the significance of the oil reserves in the region, France was much more concerned about the control over its Mediterranean backyard, even though the French recognized the magnitude of the oil resources in the Middle East. With the collapse of the Ottoman Empire in the First World War, the two imperial European powers divided the region into a British and a French sphere of influence. Britain, which already held control over Egypt and the Persian Gulf region, managed to establish its authority over Iraq, Jordan and Palestine, whereas France gained control over the Lebanon and Syria in addition to its rule over the Maghreb countries: Tunisia, Algeria, and Morocco. As a result, the involvement of France and Britain in the political developments in the region, and in Arab–Israeli conflict in particular, was governed by completely different interests. Britain tried to maintain its influence in the oil-producing Arab countries in the Persian Gulf and to secure its position in Iraq, Jordan and Egypt, which controlled the Suez Canal. France was much more concerned about its influence in the Arab Mediterranean countries. Contrary to Britain, which has been deeply involved in the genesis and evolution of the Arab–Israeli conflict, France (with the exception of one brief period of very close relations between France and Israel) had almost no direct interference in the Arab–Israeli dispute.

For many years the Arab leaders held Britain responsible for the coming into existence of the state of Israel, an entity that they refused to recognize until recently and were determined to eliminate by military and economic means. It was indeed the British failure to reconcile the conflicting demands of the Jewish and Arab inhabitants of Palestine for an independent state that led to the United Nations partition plan of 1947 which divided Palestine into an Arab state and a Jewish state. While the Arab leaders in Palestine and throughout the Arab world refused to accept any idea of partition and pressed Britain to stop the entry of Jewish immigrants to Palestine, Britain was under considerable pressure from the American government to let the Jewish survivors of the holocaust emigrate to Palestine and subsequently to allow the establishment of an independent Jewish state in some parts of Palestine. Caught in the crossfire of the Arab–Jewish dispute, Britain decided to withdraw from Palestine, leaving behind two fighting parties. Britain expected, however, that the Arab community, with the support of the Arab armies which invaded Palestine the moment Britain left the country, would manage to get large parts of the country under their control. But with the exception of the Jordanian army, British trained and operating under British command, the Arab armies failed to overrun the Jewish community. While Jordan got hold over some parts of the West Bank and the eastern part of Jerusalem, the militarily poorly equipped Jewish community was nevertheless able to defend its own territory and to proclaim an independent state.

The Arab loss in Palestine was a bitter blow for British prestige in the Middle East, as the Arabs did not blame themselves but the British (and the Western countries) for the humiliating defeat in Palestine and the enormous refugee problem that it has created. However, this would be only the first of successive setbacks in the position of Britain in the Middle East as a consequence of the coming to power of Gamal Abdel Nasser in Egypt in the early 1950s. Nasser became the charismatic leader of a radical pan-Arabic movement which combined Arab nationalism with a special blend of Arab socialism and a strong anti-Western sentiment. One of Nasser's first targets was the Suez Canal company of which the British government and individual French citizens were the main shareholders and thus the beneficiaries from the tolls paid by the vessels using the canal. The decision of the Egyptian leader in 1956 to nationalize the Suez Canal company so that the revenues from the Suez Canal could be exploited by Egypt to finance the economic modernization of the country, became the trigger for a military confrontation between Egypt on the one hand and Britain and France on the other. Yet the political and military clash over the Suez Canal had to do more with declining British influence in the region and Egyptian support for the rebellion in Algeria than the loss of British and French profits from the Suez Canal. The British government considered Nasser to be the major source of political instability in the region and a severe threat to its position in Iraq and Jordan, two traditional British strongholds in the region. The French government regarded Nasser as the motor behind the armed rebellion of the Muslim community in Algeria against the French attempt to keep Algeria under French rule, in accordance with the wish of the large French community in that country (in 1946 France had already ended its rule over Lebanon and Syria and a decade later it transferred its power to the local leadership of Tunisia and Morocco). The aim of the joint British–French military operation in the Suez Canal zone was therefore actually to bring about a political destabilization of Egypt that would cause the downfall of Nasser.

Thanks to American (and Russian) pressure on Britain and France to stop their joint military operation, Nasser managed not only to stay in power but also to present the forced retreat of the British and French military from Egypt as a major political success. Nasser turned into an Arab hero who successfully stood up against the West and became a source of inspiration to a massive pan-Arabic movement called Nasserism. It would lead to successful political and social revolutions in Iraq and Libya, provoke political instability in Lebanon, induce several military coups in Syria, prompt an abortive attempt to overthrow King Hussein in Jordan and cause a civil war in Yemen. Nasser also helped the Soviet Union (SU) to penetrate into the Middle East, in exchange for weapon supplies and other military assistance. This made the Middle East a major theatre of the rivalry between the two superpowers. While the SU became the political and military patron of Nasser and the other radical Arab regimes, the US became the sponsor and defender of the remaining conservative and pro-Western Arab regimes, which happened also to be the major oil-producing countries in the region. Although Britain kept its traditional ties with Jordan and the Gulf states, the US actually replaced Britain as the guardian of Western interests in the Middle East. The change of guard had important consequences for the resolution of the Arab–Israeli conflict.

Contrary to the British and French, which treated the conflict between Israel and its Arab neighbours as a local dispute, the American policy makers perceived the Arab–Israeli conflict as a potential source of military confrontation between the two nuclear superpowers, since a military intervention of the SU on behalf of its Arab clients would require an American military response. A final settlement of the

Arab–Israeli conflict was therefore seen as the best way to avoid such an encounter. In their search for a final resolution of the complex Arab–Israeli conflict, the Americans tried to win the trust of both sides by making choices that would not be seen in terms of pro-Israeli or pro-Arab. The starting point for such an effort was Resolution 242 of the United Nation's Security Council which was accepted after the June war in 1967 by the major belligerent, Israel, Egypt and Jordan, as a basis for a settlement. It established the basic principle of trading territory for peace. Israel had to withdraw from Arab territories occupied in the June war in exchange for an Arab recognition of Israel's sovereignty and right to live in peace within secured and recognized boundaries. Whether the call for an Israeli withdrawal from occupied territories meant a full withdrawal from all the occupied territories or that it allowed some territorial adjustments, was left deliberately vague. A difference between the English version of Resolution 242 and the French version of the same resolution, whereby the latter could be interpreted as requiring a full Israeli withdrawal, made the intentional ambiguity even more complicated (cf. Quandt, 1977: 64–5; Soetendorp, 1982/83: 113–18). Hence, before the major oil crisis in 1973 the management of the superpower competition in the Middle East and the resolution of the Arab–Israeli conflict were the primary factors in the American policy considerations towards the region. Since the US did not depend on oil supplies from the Middle East, the oil factor was of only secondary significance in the formulation of policies, even though the American policy makers recognized the importance of securing a stable flow of Middle East oil to Europe and Japan.

This was in sharp contrast to the policies of France and Britain. Access to Middle East oil and friendly relationships with the Arab leaders were their principal policy concerns already before the oil crisis of 1973. The British and French were much more troubled than the Americans by their increasing dependency on oil imports from the Arab oil-producing countries, as a result of a steady growth in the consumption of oil and the predominance of oil as an energy source for West European industries. They also realized that the Arab oil-producing countries were becoming aware of this dependency and were ready to use their newly acquired leverage. The oil companies had to cope more and more with the economic consequences of the continuous demands from the Arab oil producers for a growing participation in the exploitation of their oil resources, a larger share in the oil revenues and a higher price for their oil. They had little choice but to accept these demands since the alternative was a complete takeover of the oil industry by the Arab governments, which was already the case in Libya, Algeria and Iraq which nationalized large parts of their oil industry (cf. Maull, 1980). In anticipation of political demands concerning the Arab–Israeli conflict, British and French leaders made public statements in favour of Arab positions. The British were also opposed to Israel's insistence on direct peace talks between Israel and the Arabs. Speaking in 1970 over the Palestinians' legitimate aspirations and their desire for a means of self-expression, the British foreign minister went beyond the text of Resolution 242 which simply refers to the necessity to achieve a just settlement of the refugee problem. More important from Israel's point of view was the decision not to sell Chieftain tanks to Israel to replace the ageing British Centurion tanks (Licklider, 1988: 67–8). But all in all, the British, who in 1967 played an active role in the drafting of Security

Council Resolution 242, were careful not to antagonize the American effort to achieve an overall settlement of the Arab–Israeli dispute along the framework of Resolution 242. In this respect France followed a much more radical policy.

After the June war of 1967, France ended, in a demonstrative manner, a period of very close relations with Israel. France not only became, after the Suez crisis, the main source of arms supplies for Israel, but it also cooperated with Israel in a nuclear research programme. As a matter of fact, Israel helped France to build its own bomb and France delivered to Israel the necessary components for the construction of an Israeli nuclear reactor. With the coming to power of President de Gaulle, France stopped its participation in the building of the nuclear facility in the early 1960s. By then the French bomb was ready so that de Gaulle could easily suspend the French–Israeli nuclear connection. He continued, however, the cooperation in the development of missiles for the delivery of such a bomb, a joint project from which France still had something to gain (Aronson, 1992: 61–2, 86). De Gaulle also managed to settle the Algerian problem and wanted thereafter to bring the French relationship with the Arab world onto a new footing, especially with the oil producers in Arab Mediterranean – Algeria and Libya.

Recognizing France's dependency on imported oil, de Gaulle seized practically every opportunity to get hold of new oil concessions in the oil-producing Arab countries. During the crisis preceding the June war, de Gaulle was therefore much more worried about good relations with the Arab countries than a good relationship with Israel. De Gaulle asked Israel to refrain from any military action and suggested that France, together with Britain, the US and the SU, would try to resolve the crisis (Aronson, 1978: 68). To underline the French neutral position in the conflict, the French president imposed an embargo on the supply of French arms to the Middle East, which actually affected only Israel since almost all the Israeli aircraft at that time were of French origin. Although Israel had already paid in advance for the weapons it had ordered before the June war, or, as in the case of the missiles, had participated in the design and funding of the embargoed weapon systems, de Gaulle decided to prolong the French embargo after the June war as a retaliation for Israel's preemptive strike against the Arab armies at the beginning of the June war, contrary to his advice. This was not without significance as it compelled Israel to rely more on its own military industries and to switch to the US as its major source for arms supplies which, however, made Israel more vulnerable to American pressure.

As from 1967 France in fact embraced the Arab position. Instead of selling arms to Israel, it became a major arms supplier to Arab countries, selling to Libya aircraft that had originally been earmarked for Israel. Being less troubled than Britain about American irritations over an independent French course towards the Middle East conflict, France adopted, right from the beginning of the controversy over the interpretation of Resolution 242, the French version, demanding from Israel a complete retreat from all the occupied territories. In an attempt to put Israel under international pressure to withdraw from the territories occupied during the June war, in 1969 de Gaulle proposed four-power talks on the Middle East involving France, Britain, the US and the SU. As Henry Kissinger (at that time the national security adviser of the American President Nixon) has noted, the Americans did not like the negotiating forum suggested by the French president. The Americans doubted whether such a forum could produce any result that the Israelis would accept, given the French and Soviet biases towards the Arab viewpoint. They were afraid that such a four-power forum could lead to a lineup against the US which would have to deliver Israeli agreement. Kissinger also realized that, in the case of success, the other parties would enjoy the credit for having pressed the settlement and would be able to saddle the US with the blame if the talks resulted in a failure (Kissinger, 1979: 349–51).

Notwithstanding these considerations, the US agreed to start four-power consultations at the UN over the Middle East, but simultaneously conducted serious talks with the SU which took central stage (Quandt, 1977: 84). However, neither the four-powers deliberations nor the bilateral US–SU talks was able to produce any results. An American unilateral diplomatic initiative aimed at the full implementation of Resolution 242 which was launched at the end of 1969 was also rejected by the SU and the Arabs as well as the Israeli government. Israel regarded it as an attempt to appease the Arabs and impose on Israel a forced solution at the expense of Israeli security interests. Soon after this abortive attempt the American policy makers were nevertheless forced to launch another diplomatic initiative as a result of the intensification of the so-called war of attrition that broke out in the Suez Canal area between Egypt and Israel in April 1969. This second American effort was less ambitious than the former and was simply meant to bring about an end to the fighting which entered a dangerous stage when Soviet military personnel became directly involved in the air defence of Egypt against Israeli attacks. An air battle between Israeli and Soviet pilots in the Canal zone, in which four Soviet jets were shot down, created another escalation and a situation where the two superpowers could be drawn into a confrontation that neither of them wanted. Both Egypt and Israel were ready to accept the American proposal for a ceasefire, but Israel did not do so until the American president had made several significant and fundamental commitments. The American government gave Israel written assurances that the US would not insist that Israel should retreat from all the occupied territories; that the US would not ask Israel to withdraw its troops until a peace agreement has been achieved; and that the US would not force Israel to accept a settlement of the refugee problem which would basically change the Jewish nature of the state or endanger its security (Quandt, 1977: 102).

The American commitments highlighted the disparity between the French position and the American position on a Middle East settlement, a difference that would become even more evident after the October war in 1973, as we will discuss in the next section. But in addition to the divergence in positions, a decisive distinction in the nature of the involvement of France and Britain on the one hand and that of the US on the other, is already apparent before the Arab use of the oil weapon in 1973. While France and Britain (as well as western Europe as a whole) lack the potency to help or hurt the Arabs or Israel in any critical way, the US had the potential to do so. Besides its ability to use the weapon supplies to Israel as both a carrot and a stick, the US was also the only superpower that could deliver Israeli concessions to the Arab states. As Adam Garfinkle has argued: 'West Europeans can be hurt by the disputes in the Middle East, but there is little they can do directly to reduce their vulnerabilities' (Beling, 1986: 116). It is also obvious that while Frar regarded themselves as neutral in the Arab–Israeli conflict, Israel jud attitude as hostile and was very suspicious of the British stance Israel considered the US to be the only acceptable mediator. In the view ᴏ. – Israeli leadership, the two West European countries have in fact disqualified themselves as honest broker (cf. Beling, 1986: 117).

The common policy

When the member-states of the EC started to coordinate their views on certain foreign policy issues in 1970, as we have mentioned earlier, the Arab–Israeli conflict was one of the first and most prominent items on the agenda. The French were not only the initiators of the European Political Cooperation (EPC), they were also resolved to use the EPC framework to promote their own foreign policy goals. As Nutall has noted, the Middle East was discussed for the simple reason that the French wanted it. France was determined to bring its partners closer to the French position and to strengthen European support for the Arab cause, which would in addition express European independence of American foreign policy (Nuttall, 1992: 56). No wonder then that when France occupied the EC presidency in the first six months of 1971, the French foreign minister used that opportunity to produce a first draft paper that outlined the joint position on the Middle East. Initially the positions of the then six member-states clashed but finally the foreign ministers of the six member-states were able to agree on a joint document. The reconciliation among the different views of the Six produced, however, a moderate report in the sense that it was consistent with Security Council Resolution 242 and it still referred to the Palestinians as refugees. But despite the modest language of the document, Germany and the Netherlands were ready to approve it only on the condition that it would not be made public. When it nevertheless leaked to the German press and the West German foreign minister came under firm domestic critic for his willingness to adopt the French document, he played down the significance of the document, saying that it was simply a working paper to serve as a basis for discussion (cf. Greilsammer and Weiler, 1984: 132–3; Ifestos, 1987: 420–1; Nuttall, 1992: 68).

Before the oil crisis of 1973 the German Federal Republic and the Netherlands were indeed not yet ready to play the French card fully with respect to the Arab–Israeli conflict. Contrary to France, which chose the Arab side after the June war of 1967, the Federal Republic and the Netherlands refused to take sides in the Arab–Israeli conflict and wanted to maintain a good relationship with Israel and preserve friendly relations with the Arab countries. But the German and Dutch foreign policy makers were not completely blind to the consequences of the increasing dependency of western Europe on oil supplies from the Middle East. West Germany had already started in the early 1970s to move away from their unqualified support for Israel in the preceding years, when West Germany's policy towards the Jewish state was predominated by the German moral guilt towards the victims of Nazi Germany, and to pay more attention to the restoration of the Federal Republic's relationship with the Arab countries. The relations with Israel were still defined as special relations, but the interpretation of these special relations in the sense of a privileged status was denied (Büren, 1978: 59).

Also the Netherlands began to shift towards the Arab position before its boycott by the oil-producing Arab countries in 1973. At the end of the June war, the Dutch government took up a straightforward position on the issue of the territories occupied during the war, saying that Israel should not annex these territories unilaterally. Notwithstanding the sympathy of the Dutch political leaders for Israel's striving for security, they stated very clearly that this could not be achieved through territorial expansion. The Dutch did not oppose minor border corrections, but these were only allowed with the consent of the Arab countries, in the context of a peace agreement. The disapproval of territorial expansion by means of war had nothing to do with pro-Arab or anti-Israeli sentiments, but was simply a prompt interpretation of Resolution 242. Of more significance, therefore, was the Dutch move on the Palestinian issue which was obviously influenced by the EPC deliberations on the Middle East conflict. Up to the 1970s the Dutch government treated the Palestinian problem as just a refugee problem, emphasizing its humanitarian character. But in 1970 the Netherlands joined its European partners in recognizing the political dimension of the Palestinian question as well. In the end of 1972 the Netherlands even closed ranks with the other two Benelux countries, France, Italy and Britain, and voted for the first time in the United Nations in favour of a resolution that maintained that recognition of Palestinian rights was an indispensable element of any peace settlement. Explaining the Dutch voting behaviour in the United Nations, the Dutch foreign minister admitted that this was indeed a result of the consultations among the EC member-states, in an attempt to present in the United Nations General Assembly a common position towards the Arab–Israeli conflict (Soetendorp, 1984: 39–40).

Such voting behaviour in the United Nations General Assembly on issues related to the Middle East conflict was, until the October war of 1973, rather an exception. The EC member-states did not actually make much progress on a joint policy towards the Arab–Israeli conflict and the real breakthrough came only as a result of the Arab use of the oil weapon during this war. By then Britain, which, like France, was more inclined to support the Arab positions rather than the Israeli views, had joined the EC.

From Copenhagen to Venice

The goal of the oil-exporting Arab countries in utilizing their oil power during the October war of 1973 was to change the political attitude of the US and some countries in western Europe towards the Arab–Israeli conflict. To complement the military offensive of Egypt and Syria against Israel, the Arab oil producers wanted to persuade the international community, and the US in particular, to force Israel to retreat from the occupied territories. In the past, Arab attempts to employ their oil as an economic weapon against West Europe actually failed. Since the oil imports from the Middle East to western Europe during the Suez crisis of 1956 and the June war of 1967 were relatively small, imports from other sources could easily compensate the shortages caused by cuts in oil supplies from the Middle East. However, this time the Arab oil producers, organized in the Organization of Arab Petroleum Exporting Countries (OAPEC), had a much better starting position because of the increased dependency of the West European oil consumers on Middle Eastern oil. To use their oil weapon in an effective manner, the Arab oil producers divided the oil consumers into different categories depending on their positions *vis-à-vis* the Arab–Israeli conflict. Only countries that were ranked as friendly could enjoy a continuing free supply of oil. The other countries were exposed to various production cutbacks, with the exception of countries that were classified as enemies and therefore subjected to a total oil embargo. France and Britain were included in the first category while most of the other EC member-states were placed in the second group. The only exception was the Netherlands which was fully embargoed (cf. Licklider, 1988: 11–13; Treverton, 1980: 7–8).

The initial reaction of the EC member-states to the outbreak of the Middle East war on 5 October 1973 was rather fragmented and varied considerably. While the French expressed some understanding for the Arab attack on Israel, the Netherlands held Egypt and Syria responsible for the beginning of the fighting. A meeting of the nine foreign ministers, almost a week after the outbreak of the war, was at first unable to agree on a common position. However, the French and British pressed the other members to endorse a joint statement which was finally issued on 13 October but included just a general call for a ceasefire and negotiations on the basis of Resolution 242. The Nine were able to come forward with a more explicit position on the Middle East conflict only after the Arab oil producers started to use the oil weapon on 17 October 1973. The political pressure generated by the selective employment of the oil embargo persuaded the EC member-states to consider and accept a joint political declaration. It was based on a French–British text and satisfied the Arab political demands. This joint declaration of November 1973 reaffirmed some of the views that the member-states had expressed before, but it also included an important new element. In this way the inadmissibility of the acquisition of territory by force and the necessity for Israel to end the territorial occupation which it has maintained since the June war of 1967 was confirmed. It also repeated the right of each state in the region to live in peace within secure and recognized boundaries. This was already laid down in Security Council Resolution 242, but for the first time the nine member-states recognized in a collective statement that, in the establishment of a just and lasting peace, account must be taken of the legitimate rights of the Palestinians (cf. Lukacs, 1992: 13–14). The common declaration, which was confirmed the next month by the EC heads of state and government during their summit in Copenhagen, was still vague about the rights of the Palestinians as it did not specify what these rights are. It was, nonetheless, a turning point in the way that some member-states had approached the Palestinian issue thus far. The reward followed soon. In a meeting of the Arab oil producers on 19 November, they decided to stop the 5 per cent cutback to the EC, with the exception again of the Netherlands which remained under a full oil embargo. The damage to the Netherlands from the oil embargo was, however, limited, thanks to the major oil companies which managed the international oil distribution system in such a way that the pain was more or less evenly spread among all the EC members including France and Britain.

Despite the economic ineffectiveness of the oil weapon, its political impact was quite significant. The Arab oil producers forced those member-states that thus far had pursued more or less a neutral course with respect to the complicated Palestinian question to take sides on this issue, or at least to be more careful about Arab sensitivities. This made countries like West Germany, the Netherlands and Denmark much more receptive to France's views which were far ahead of its European partners. Already in 1974 the French expressed their understanding for the Palestinian aspiration to have a homeland or, as the French President Giscard d'Estaing formulated it at that time: 'Once the international community has recognized the existence of a Palestinian people, what is the natural aspiration of that people? It is to have a homeland' (Soetendorp, 1982/83: 160). Italy adopted almost the same position but the other member-states embraced the French definition of the Palestinian rights step by step. In 1974 the Nine started to refer in their common statements to the Palestinians as the Palestinian people. A year later the Nine stated in the United Nations General Assembly that a Middle East settlement should include a recognition of the right of the Palestinian people to the expression of their national identity. What the Nine meant by a Palestinian national identity was made clear when the Nine declared, the next year and in the same forum, that the exercise of the right of the Palestinian people to the effective expression of their national identity could involve a territorial base. The next year the Nine finally endorsed the French opinion that the Palestinians have the right to have their own homeland (Soetendorp, 1982/83: 161; Nuttall, 1992: 101).

In a meeting of the European Council in June 1977 the Nine adopted a declaration prepared by the British Presidency which said that the Nine believe that a solution to the conflict in the Middle East will be possible only if the legitimate right of the Palestinian people to give effective expression to their national identity is translated into a homeland for the Palestinian people (cf. Ifestos, 1987: 612). The declaration also stated that the Palestinian people should participate in the negotiations on an overall settlement. But contrary to the Arab demand to recognize the Palestinian Liberation Organization (PLO) as the representative of the Palestinians in such negotiations, no reference was yet made to the PLO. Although in 1974 the Arab leaders recognized the PLO as the sole and legitimate representative of the Palestinian people, some member-states still identified the PLO with the terrorist actions carried out by PLO members. It would therefore take some time before the EC member-states would settle among themselves the question of whether the PLO should be involved in negotiations on a peace settlement and follow the French lead also in this matter.

France was actually the only member-state that did not vote in 1974 against the invitation to the PLO to participate in the United Nations General Assembly debate on the Palestinian question in the capacity of an observer. French diplomacy was also the first to recognize the political and even legal legitimacy of the PLO to act as a representative of the Palestinians. During a visit of the French president to the Middle East in January 1979, Giscard d'Estaing went as far as calling for Palestinian self-determination and the participation of the PLO in Middle East negotiations. By then the other member-states also began to modify their reserved attitude towards the PLO, as the meeting between the German leader Willy Brandt and the PLO leader Yasser Arafat in 1978 in Vienna illustrates (cf. Ifestos, 1987: 448–9).

The British and the French even began to play with the idea of putting forward an amendment of Security Council Resolution 242 or replacing that resolution with a new one. The intention was to make an explicit reference to the Palestinian right to self-determination as an integral part of any peace settlement. Due to an American threat to veto any modification of Resolution 242, the British–French revision of Resolution 242 never materialized. Instead, the Nine produced another common declaration that marked the most fundamental and most far-reaching common policy statement on the Arab–Israeli dispute for many years. During a meeting of the European Council in Venice in June 1980, the heads of government stated that the Palestinians are entitled to exercise fully their right to self-determination besides the right of Israel to existence and to security. They also declared for the first time that the PLO has to be associated with the negotiations on a peace settlement, even though they stopped short of recognizing the PLO as the sole representative of the Palestinian people (cf. Lukacs, 1992: 17–19). Thus, within ten years France managed to push its views on the content of the common EPC declarations regarding the Middle East conflict. The EC as a whole endorsed the French belief that the recognition of the rights of the Palestinians is the key to a Middle East peace settlement.

A European Middle East peace initiative

The French success was more than just harmonizing the positions of the other member-states in this respect along the French view. Its EC partners were also willing to propose, for the first time, a concrete peace plan which would reflect the European policy preferences. To determine the shape that such a European peace initiative could take, the member-states decided to make the necessary contacts with all the parties concerned. Thus far, the EC as such or any of its larger member-states – France, Britain or West Germany – were absent from Middle East peace diplomacy. The only external power that played an active diplomatic role in trying to resolve the Arab–Israeli dispute was the US.

After the abortive American attempt to bring about the implementation of Resolution 242 in the late 1960s, the American peace efforts gained new momentum after the October war. The use of the oil weapon against the US and the indirect confrontation between the US and the SU during the October war forced the American government to place the settlement of the Arab–Israeli conflict high on its foreign policy agenda again. Henry Kissinger (who had become in the meantime the US foreign minister under President Nixon) would be the architect of a completely new American strategy towards the settling of the Arab–Israeli conflict, adopting a gradualist step-by-step tactic instead of an overall approach. Kissinger had actually no peace plan that dealt with the principal issues of the Middle East conflict. His strategy was much more pragmatic. As Quandt has pointed out, since the key demands of the Arabs and Israel were phrased in totally incompatible terms, Kissinger moved towards practical agreements rather than an agreement that would realize the ultimate goals of peace and security for Israel and territories and justice for the Arabs (Quandt, 1977: 153). Kissinger had only a short-term goal: to bring about an Israeli withdrawal from the territories that it had occupied in 1967 and 1973. He believed that the accomplishment of this goal would help the US to secure its other two objectives: to reduce the Soviet influence in the region and to avoid another Arab oil embargo. Kissinger was quite successful in his diplomatic effort, which became known as 'shuttle diplomacy'. Through deep involvement in the negotiations between Israel and Egypt, substantial offers of economic aid to both parties and the winning of Israel's confidence by means of arms shipments, Kissinger managed to start a process of Israeli withdrawal from Arab territories in exchange for security guarantees. In two successive disengagement agreements, which Egypt and Israel concluded in 1974 and 1975, Egypt regained control over the Suez Canal and Israel withdrew beyond the strategically important Mitla and Giddi passes in the Sinai (Quandt, 1977; Kissinger, 1982).

An important side effect of Kissinger's effective diplomacy was the confidence building between the leadership of Egypt and Israel, which would lead in 1977 to the visit of the Egyptian President Anwar Sadat to Jerusalem. The timing of this breakthrough in the relations between the two countries was no coincidence. It had to do with the change of strategy in the American search for a Middle East settlement when a new American administration under President Jimmy Carter took over the management of the peace process in 1977. Instead of partial solutions the Carter administration wanted to achieve comprehensive peace agreements which would be negotiated at a peace conference. Moreover, while Kissinger tried to circumvent the Palestinian issue, Carter was willing to accept the creation of a Palestinian entity and was prepared to deal with the PLO if this organization accepted Resolution 242 (cf. Brzezinski, 1983: 101–2).

The projected peace conference was still in the stage of procedural debates, when Egypt and Israel blew up the idea of such a conference. The two countries had actually nothing to gain from a huge peace conference that would involve a great number of parties. The American attempt to make another bilateral Egyptian–Israeli agreement part of a comprehensive Middle East peace agreement and to integrate the Palestinians in a single Arab delegation, offered Egypt little perspective for any result as Syria and the Palestinians were expected to come up with demands that Israel would consider to be unacceptable. The proposed negotiations between joint Arab delegations and Israel gave Syria, in Egyptian eyes, in fact the power to veto a separate Egyptian–Israeli deal or any other outcome they dislike. Israel, for its part, was ready to discuss with Egypt a further withdrawal from the Sinai but had no intention of negotiating with Syria or Jordan a retreat from the other occupied territories, or to deal with the Arab demands for Palestinian self-determination. Anticipating an American peace plan that the US would try to impose on it, Israel preferred direct negotiations with Egypt without American involvement. In secret bilateral talks, Egypt and Israel had already reached an informal understanding on the principle of a full Israeli withdrawal from the Sinai in exchange for a concrete peace agreement. As far as Egypt and Israel were concerned, a peace conference could only serve as an umbrella for the conduct of direct bilateral negotiation or, to put it more bluntly, a decorum for the signing of bilateral peace agreements.

The direct negotiations between Egypt and Israel, following Sadat's visit to Israel, compelled the US policy makers to adjust their approach on Middle East peace negotiation to the changing reality. If they wanted to keep an American involvement in the peace negotiations, they had to fall back on the former strategy of partial agreements and their role of mediator, leaving the primary burden of the negotiations to the parties themselves. As Quandt has indicated, the US was willing to support anything upon which the parties themselves could agree. The US would be drawn into the negotiations only in its capacity as mediator, suggesting ways to resolve the differences as they arise (Beling, 1986: 73). The Egyptian leader indeed called upon the support of the US when Egypt tried, in the negotiations with Israel, to achieve more than just a bilateral peace agreement. Sadat wanted to avoid the impression that he was prepared to make a separate peace with Israel at the expense of an overall peace settlement. To prove that he was not abandoning the Arab cause, the Egyptian leader insisted on a broader framework for an Egyptian–Israeli peace treaty. It also had to include an Israeli agreement in principle to withdraw from Arab territories occupied in 1967, and an Israeli commitment to a solution of the Palestinian problem. This created a deep gap between the Egyptian and Israeli positions as Israel was ready to withdraw in stages from the Sinai to its international border with Egypt. Israel was not willing to commit itself to a further withdrawal and it was only prepared to propose Palestinian home rule in Gaza and the occupied West Bank as part of a final settlement.

By then the American conception of Middle East peace had been reduced to the idea of supporting a first step between Egypt and Israel, with a vaguely defined transitional period for the West Bank and Gaza (Quandt, 1986: 169). Taking this limited conception as their starting point, the Americans tried to help the two sides to bridge the gap in lengthy discussions and many meetings with Egyptian and Israeli leaders. Since the American effort produced almost no result, President Carter decided to break the impasse by means of a three-party summit in Camp David in September 1978. The result was the Camp David accords which consisted of two separate agreements: a general framework of peace in the Middle East and a framework for the conclusion of a peace treaty between Egypt and Israel. The Camp David agreements were a compromise between the Egyptian and Israeli positions. Applying the withdrawal-for-peace principle, Egypt secured an Israeli withdrawal from the Sinai in return for a demilitarization of substantial parts in the Sinai and the normalization of all relations between Egypt and Israel. Israel, however, made no commitment to withdraw from Gaza and the West Bank. On the delicate question of the Palestinian issue, the three parties in fact reshaped the Israeli idea of Palestinian autonomy, making it not a final solution to the Palestinian problem but a transitional measure for a limited period of five years. The final status of the West Bank and Gaza would be decided by the end of the transitional period through negotiations involving Egypt, Israel, Jordan and the representatives of the inhabitants of the West Bank and Gaza. In March 1979 the Camp David accords were followed up by the signing of an Egyptian–Israeli peace treaty which has been fully implemented. The initial negotiations between Egypt and Israel over

the implementation of the other part of the accords, which concerned the establishment of a Palestinian self-governing authority, soon reached an impasse. The
Americans were, however, less inclined to make a great effort to break the deadlock over the West Bank and Gaza, as the chances of making headway on the
realization of a Palestinian autonomy on the West Bank and Gaza were very gloomy,
given the rigid attitude of the Israeli government in this respect and the unwillingness of Jordan and the Palestinians to cooperate (cf. Quandt, 1986; Sobel, 1980:
228–30).

In this setting, the EC member-states tried to get involved in the Middle East
peace process. The Arab frustration over the separate peace between Egypt and
Israel and the stalemate concerning the Palestinian issue encouraged the EC members to try to push the peace process further towards a comprehensive peace settlement. The French leaders have always regretted Europe's failure to launch its own
Middle East peace plan. Such a European undertaking could, in the French view,
serve European interests in the Arab world and contribute to the European ambition
to develop an independent European identity. But thus far the EC member-states
got almost no chance to play an active role in the Middle East peace diplomacy.
Kissinger excluded the Europeans from the negotiation process that he had started
after the October war. His step-by-step strategy was also contrary to the comprehensive approach that France preferred and which has been endorsed by the other EC
members. In the European view such an overall approach was the only way to settle
the Arab–Israeli dispute.

But as long as Kissinger's diplomacy was successful, the British and West Germans in particular had no intention of interfering in the American efforts to bring
about a peaceful settlement. Only when President Carter launched his initial plans
for a peace conference in Geneva did Britain and France see an opportunity to get
indirectly involved in the peace diplomacy, in their capacity as permanent members
of the Security Council. Moreover, statements of the American president in favour
of a resolution of the Palestinian problem, saying that the solution must recognize
the legitimate rights of the Palestinians and enable them to participate in the
determination of their future, were much closer to the European views than those of
Kissinger, and opened the possibility of American–European collaboration on the
Palestinian issue. But this prospect also faded when the Americans decided, after
Sadat's visit to Jerusalem, to end their preparations for a peace conference and to
set the Middle East peace process back on the track of partial agreements instead of
a complete settlement.

The initial reaction of the EC as a whole to the historic breakthrough in the
Egyptian–Israeli relationship was therefore quite reserved, questioning the objectives and methods of the step-by-step process. The EC member-states expressed their
admiration for the brave initiative of Sadat, but at the same time the Nine voiced
their hope that the Egyptian–Israeli dialogue would open the way for comprehensive negotiations, leading to an overall Middle East peace settlement that would
take into account the rights and concerns of all the parties involved, including the
Palestinians. The Nine also expressed their hope that it would be possible in the
near future to convene the Geneva peace conference (Nuttall, 1992: 158–9; Ifestos,
1987: 443–4). Besides the disappointment over the cancelling of the proposed peace

conference, the rather cool reaction of the Nine to the rapprochement between Egypt and Israel had also to do with the enormous disapproval of Sadat's unilateral step in the Arab world. The member-states did not want to antagonize the Arab countries which almost unanimously criticized Sadat's visit to Jerusalem as an attempt to reach a separate peace agreement with Israel.

When Egypt and Israel indeed managed to conclude, with American help, a bilateral agreement on the principles that would guide a comprehensive peace in the Middle East in general and a peace treaty between the two countries in particular, the EC member-states issued a declaration in support of the Camp David agreements. The Nine hoped that this agreement would be another major step towards a comprehensive peace and that the other parties would join the peace process. Notwithstanding this favourable reaction, the member-states were internally divided over the course they should follow under the new circumstances. While Britain, West Germany and some other members were inclined to support the Camp David peace process, France was more sensitive to the Arab rejection of the accords (cf. Nuttall, 1992: 161). As a consequence, the EC as a whole actually adopted a wait-and-see approach to the ongoing Middle East peace negotiations between Egypt and Israel. On the occasion of the signing of the Egyptian–Israeli peace treaty, the EC member-states took an equivocal position. On the one hand they declared their appreciation for the effort that the three parties had made to achieve such a result. On the other hand, they stated that the establishment of a Middle East peace can only take place within the framework of a comprehensive settlement which must implement the right of the Palestinians to a homeland.

The member-states were able to agree on a clear-cut common position only at the Venice summit when it became evident that the negotiations between Egypt and Israel over the implementation of the Camp David accords had produced a final peace treaty between Egypt and Israel but offered no prospect for similar progress on the other fronts and failed to generate any result on the Palestinian issue. The uncompromising attitude of Israel in the negotiations on the creation of a Palestinian self-governing authority in the West Bank and Gaza, in accordance with the Camp David accords, and the Israeli refusal to freeze the establishment of new Israeli settlements in the occupied West Bank, turned the balance in the continuous deliberations among the Nine over their attitude towards the so-called Camp David peace process against Israel. Besides, now that the American peace diplomacy had come to a standstill, not only France but also Britain and West Germany found the time ripe to give a European peace initiative a chance, even if the Americans, and certainly Israel, would perceive such a step as European interference in the Camp David peace process. As the EC members had indicated in the Venice declaration, the traditional ties and common interests which link Europe to the Middle East oblige them to play a special role and to work in a more concrete way towards peace in the region (Lukacs, 1992: 18). To soften an American opposition to such a European step, the British foreign minister, who was a crucial player in the EPC decision making which led to the Venice declaration, presented the European peace initiative as complementary to the American peace effort, not as an independent European undertaking. According to Lord Carrington, 'none of us is labouring under the illusion that Europe is capable of producing a settlement on its own. Full United

States involvement is vital to the chances of peace. Cooperation, not competition is uppermost in our minds' (Ifestos, 1987: 462).

The EC members failed, however, to understand that, because of the Venice declaration, such a European peace initiative was a non-starter from the beginning. As the EC member-states were soon to learn from their fact-finding mission to the Middle East, the Venice declaration closed the gap between the West Europeans and the Arabs but deepened the breach between the West Europeans and Israel which regarded the Venice declaration as a European commitment to a Middle East peace settlement on Arab terms. European willingness to involve the PLO in the peace negotiations particularly stirred up Israel's anger. Contrary to the EC, the Israeli government considered the PLO to be a terrorist organization whose only goal is to liquidate the existing Jewish state and for this reason should be excluded from any participation in future peace negotiations between Israel and the Arabs. The EC position, as it was laid down in the declaration of Venice, emphasized in Israeli eyes the European bias towards the Arabs, which disqualified the EC as an honest broker in the Middle East conflict. The Israeli government in fact denied the EC any role in the Middle East peace process and had therefore no intention of cooperating with the EC in its search for common ground among the various parties. But even some Arab governments and the PLO in particular were not fully content with the European failure to propose an amendment of Resolution 242 and to recognize in the Venice declaration the PLO as the sole representative of the Palestinian people. The EC had created before Venice some expectations in the Arab world that at least such a recognition would be the centrepiece of the Venice declaration. In the eyes of the PLO, this failure was due to American pressure and proved that Europe was still not able to follow its own course, independently of the US. Many Arabs drew the conclusion that since this was the case, they would do better to deal directly with the Americans, and to use the EC peace initiative only as a means to put some pressure on the US to keep its active involvement in the Middle East peace diplomacy.

During the two major European fact-finding missions, the EC representatives found no indication that would justify a further search for comprehensive negotiations involving all parties. The EC member-states had little choice other than to conclude that an independent European initiative would almost certainly bear no fruit. As one observer of the West European peace diplomacy had pointed out, the emperor had no clothes (Beling, 1986: 116). The European attempt to launch its own peace initiative was finally given a death blow by a change of government in France in 1981 which led to a more positive attitude towards the Camp David peace process and a reconsideration of the need for a European peace initiative. According to the newly elected French President François Mitterrand, Middle East peace could only be reached through a number of partial agreements which together could make up a comprehensive settlement. The new French foreign minister acknowledged that the European initiative had reached a dead end, since no European initiative could be taken except upon the demand of the parties involved in the conflict. As far as the new French government was concerned, there was no French peace plan and there would be no European peace plan or a European peace initiative (cf. Greilsammer and Weiler, 1984: 154). Thus, after two years there was little left of the ambition of the EC as a whole to leave its finger prints on the Middle East peace process. As Nuttall has rightly said, the Venice declaration remained the point of reference for the EC member-states in their subsequent statements on the Middle East, but it failed to open a new way towards a settlement of the Arab–Israeli conflict (Nuttall, 1992: 168).

Promoting a Palestinian state

Throughout the decade following their abortive attempt to play a special role in the Middle East peace process, the EC as a whole was again on the sidelines of the Middle East process. On an individual basis, France, together with Britain, Italy and the Netherlands, contributed to the implementation of the Egyptian–Israeli peace treaty through the participation of their military in the multinational force which had to be placed in the Sinai as a buffer between Israel and Egypt in 1982. But the EC as such had to limit itself to the making of joint declarations which did not contain new elements. For many years the Venice declaration would in fact remain the most far-reaching declaration regarding the member-states' common position towards the Middle East conflict. In their joint reactions to developments in the region, the member-states gave their opinion on actual events such as the Israeli invasion in Lebanon or the Israeli bombardment of a nuclear reactor in Iraq, expressed their convictions concerning the Palestinian rights, demonstrated their support for the various peace plans launched by the US and the Arabs, and voiced their readiness to contribute to the peace effort initiated by others. One of the few exceptions to this passive attitude was the suggestion of the twelve EC member-states in February 1987 to convene an international peace conference under the auspices of the United Nations. The Twelve stated that they were prepared to make an active contribution, both through the president-in-office and individually, to bring the positions of the parties concerned closer to one another (Lukacs, 1992: 27). At the same time Israel and Jordan also discussed secretly the possibility of an international conference that would serve as an umbrella for separate bilateral talks between Israel and its neighbours. Both ideas never materialized due to the Iran–Iraq war and the later Gulf War which moved the Palestinian issue for a while from the Middle East agenda of the regional as well as the external actors (Makovsky, 1996: 7).

Besides this declaratory common diplomacy within the EPC framework, the EC used other instruments as well to induce Israel to change its policy towards the Palestinians in general and the Palestinian inhabitants of the West Bank and Gaza in particular. During the military intervention of Israel in Lebanon in 1982 which was aimed at the destruction of the PLO infrastructure in that country, the EC refrained from taking economic sanctions against Israel, but endorsed a decision not to sign a financial protocol between the EC and Israel. The EC as such initiated in 1987 a direct aid programme to the Palestinian inhabitants of the occupied territories, in addition to its vast contributions to the United Nations Relief and Works Agency for Palestinian Refugees. The EC Commission and Parliament did not hesitate to clash with Israel in 1988 over the right of Palestinian farmers in the occupied territories to export their products directly to the EC without the intervention of the Israeli agricultural export authority. The European Commission also suspended in 1989 an EC–Israeli scientific cooperation agreement to protest against Israel's closure of universities in the occupied territories (Buchan, 1993: 115–16).

France, which has been the motor behind the common Middle East policy, tried to convince the other member-states to move beyond the Venice declaration by referring in a new declaration directly to a Palestinian state, but was unable to reach the necessary consensus among its European partners. Mitterrand persisted nevertheless in his ambition to make progress on the Palestinian issue by bringing about a mutual Israeli–Palestinian recognition. In his public statements Mitterrand made no secret of his conviction that the Palestinians should have their own independent state, a belief that almost all the other member-states shared but were not yet ready to express in a formal declaration. But Mitterrand also made a real effort to win back Israel's confidence and was ready to that purpose to distance himself to some extent from the Venice declaration. The unilateral French diplomatic activities were intensified during the war in Lebanon in 1982, when France interfered in the crisis directly. It helped the US to end the fighting between Israel and the Palestinians and to secure the evacuation of PLO troops from Beirut. Within the EPC framework, France advocated the use of economic sanctions against Israel or the embracement of an unequivocal statement in favour of a Palestinian state, but failed again to convince its European partners to adopt such a firm policy towards Israel.

The common diplomacy of the EC member-states gained, nonetheless, new impulses in 1991 when the US organized, in cooperation with the SU, a Middle East peace conference in Madrid. The American powerful international position after its successful performance in the resolution of the crisis over Iraq's invasion of Kuwait, and the unique coalition of Western and Arab countries, created in American eyes an exceptional political opportunity to advance the resolution of the Arab–Israeli dispute as well. The US collaborated not only with Britain and France but also with Egypt and Syria which fought side by side against another Arab country. This caused a reshuffling of the existing inter-Arab relations. Egypt was back on centre stage of Middle East politics after its compulsory isolation during more than a decade as a consequence of Sadat's visit to Israel in 1977. Syria was again in the camp of the moderate Arab regimes, and the PLO, which chose the side of the Iraqi leader Sadam Hussein, was in a very vulnerable position as its major financiers, Saudi Arabia and the Gulf states, stopped their financial aid. Israel, still under the impact of American assistance during the Gulf War, could hardly resist the American pressure to participate in the peace conference. It placed only two conditions: the Palestinian participants should be part of the Jordanian delegation and inhabitants of the West Bank or Gaza. The PLO, which had already accepted in 1988 Security Council Resolution 242 and was eager to participate in the conference, approved these Israeli demands.

Thus for the first time since 1973, all the obstacles that had so far hindered the organization of a Middle East peace conference were removed. The European wish to solve the Arab–Israeli conflict at such a forum was all at once reality. Although the EU had not become a co-chairman of the peace conference, it became nonetheless deeply involved in the conduct of the conference which, after the ceremonial open-ing of the peace conference in Madrid, was adjourned. The actual talks between the participants continued in separate bilateral negotiations between Israel and Syria, Lebanon and a joint Jordanian–Palestinian delegation, as well as in a number of working groups where much of the work was actually done. The EU became a member of the steering committee which was supposed to coordinate the bilateral talks and the multilateral talks in the various working groups, The EU itself chaired the important working group on regional economic development and was co-chair of the other four working groups that dealt with the problems of water resources, environment, disarmament and the issue of the Palestinian refugees (cf. Buchan, 1993: 117–18).

The bilateral negotiations between Israel, Syria, Lebanon and the joint Jordanian–Palestinian delegation soon reached a deadlock as the Israeli Likud government refused to discuss Palestinian self-government or territorial concessions in the occupied territories. More fruitful were the secret negotiations between Israel and the Palestinians which started in 1992 with the coming to power of a new Israeli government which was more motivated to make peace with the Palestinians and its Arab neighbours. The secret negotiations led within a year to the mutual recogni-tion between Israel and the PLO and the signing of a declaration of principles by Israel and the PLO in September 1993, which included an Israeli commitment to set up Palestinian self-government and to withdraw in several stages from Gaza and large parts of the occupied territories on the West Bank. These so-called Oslo agreements paved the way for a peace treaty between Israel and Jordan which was signed soon thereafter. The EU reacted to this breakthrough not only with verbal support but also with tangible help. The EU member-states were determined to achieve the goal of which some countries made no secret but which was never declared in public in the form of a joint declaration: the creation of a Palestinian state next to Israel.

The European Council of heads of government decided in April 1994 to launch a joint action in support of the Middle East peace process. This was one of the first joint actions within the new common framework of the CFSP which replaced the EPC after the agreement on the TEU. The joint action refers to some general actions such as contributing to redefining the relations between the countries of the region, monitoring Israeli settlements in the occupied territories and working to lift the Arab boycott of Israel. The joint action also specifies a number of specific instruments such as support for the establishment of a Palestinian police force, help in organizing and monitoring elections in Gaza and the West Bank and participa-tion in the temporary international presence in the occupied territories if needed. To reward Israel for its agreement with the PLO, the joint action also provides sup-port for the organization of an international economic conference on infrastructure projects in the region and the conclusion of a new association agreement with Israel. Another concrete measure, which has been decided during the same Council meeting, concerned a commitment to contribute, for the five years from 1994 to 1998, aid for the development of the occupied territories involving ECU 500 million, half in grants and half in loans (*General Report on the Activities of the European Union 1994*, 1995: 260, 303).

The EU has been in recent years by far the biggest donor to the occupied territories. This has made the EU quite visible in the Middle East peace process and more assertive in its effort to play a more active role in the peace process. The member-states made no secret of their intention to help the Palestinians in Gaza and the West Bank to form their own state. Through huge financial support and various development projects the EU contributes directly and indirectly to the Palestinian Authority effort to establish Palestinian self-government in the former territories from which Israel has withdrawn. The EU, for instance, has equipped the Palestinian police and pays its salaries. It helped to build in Gaza an airport and a harbour. Anticipating an independent Palestinian state, the EU treats the Palestinian Authority in the former occupied territories as a state in being. The EU, for example, formalized in 1977 its political and economic ties with the Palestinian Authority by means of a Euro-Mediterranean association agreement similar to those the EU has with Israel and other Mediterranean countries. Since the Palestinian Authority is not allowed to conclude formal international agreements until it has negotiated its final status with Israel, the EU signed the association agreement with the PLO instead of the Palestinian Authority. It was signed, however, by Arafat, chairman of the PLO and at the same time president of the Palestinian Authority (*European Voice*, 27 February–5 March 1997). When the peace process lost momentum as a consequence of the different attitude of the Likud government (which returned to power in 1996) towards the implementation of the Oslo agreements, the EU took a firm position in support of the Palestinians. The member-states adopted several declarations which called on the Israeli Likud government to stop the building and expansion of settlements in the occupied territories which was regarded as an important obstacle to peace. They also demanded that the Israeli government stick to the principle of land for peace which guided the approach of the previous government towards peace.

To increase the EU's political involvement in the Middle East peace process the member-states nominated in 1996 a special envoy to the Middle East. Some member-states hoped that the special envoy would be able to reinforce the EU's role in the peace process, exploiting the political leverage the EU has gained by means of its generous economic aid and financial assistance to the region. But his presence in the Middle East has not prevented the US from playing the leading role in the efforts to resolve the continuous deadlocks in the negotiations between the Israelis and the Palestinians or the Israelis and the Syrians. Israel still denies the EU any significant role in the peace process, arguing that the peace negotiations should be direct negotiations between the parties concerned without foreign participation, except at their request. Under these circumstances, the EU has to limit its role to that of facilitator instead of mediator, and it had to complement rather than compete with the American diplomatic effort. However, American recognition of the EU's positive inputs, such as its readiness to act as the most prominent paymaster of the peace process, has helped the EU to play in the peace process a role of growing importance.

Reflecting on three decades of European common foreign policy towards the Arab–Israeli conflict and the Middle East peace process, we may conclude that, despite the initial internal division and different views regarding the settlement of the Arab–Israeli conflict, the member-states of the EC/EU were able to develop through the EPC and CFSP framework over the last three decades a strong consensus on their policy towards the Arab–Israeli conflict, and their preferred common course of action in the Middle East peace process. This common policy has not prevented some member-states, and France in particular, to practice their own diplomacy in the region when their national views reached beyond the common denominator. The EU has not realized its ambition to participate in the Middle East peace process on an equal footing with the US, but the EU has nevertheless made itself clearly visible on the Middle East stage, presenting a distinguished international identity.

Chapter 7

Steering the transformation in eastern Europe: playing the leading regional power

The ending of the cold war and the political and economic transformation in former Communist countries in eastern Europe has made heavy demands on the EU member-states and the EU itself. Western Europe had to help the central and eastern European countries to build their democratic systems and market economies almost from scratch. Since 1989 the EU has indeed become the main source of economic and financial aid in the central and eastern European countries and the central regional player in the political and economic reordering of the former Communist countries. In their reaction to the transformation in eastern Europe, the EU member-states were pushed towards a collective response. This was not only because of the German conviction that the EC as a whole should generate and handle the substantial financial aid to help the central and eastern European countries to overcome the transitional economic and social difficulties. The EU member-states also had little other choice since only the EU itself, being the sole representative of the member-states in trade matters, could negotiate with the central and eastern European countries over the necessary agreements on trade and cooperation and the later association agreements, or deal with the desire of the central and eastern European states to integrate into the EU.

In this chapter we will discuss how the EU member-states have responded collectively to the transformation in eastern Europe and consider the way this response has been determined by the relevant national views. To understand how the collective *Ostpolitik* of the EC/EU has been shaped, it is necessary to look first at the foreign policy towards eastern Europe of the pivotal country in this respect: Germany. The focus will be on Germany, since its *Ostpolitik* has been a major breakthrough in the relations between West and East Europe. It was also primarily Germany that was quick to react to the political and economic changes in the Soviet Union (SU) and the other East European states and which has taken the lead in the formulation of a common response to the transformation in eastern Europe. Because of its historic ties with eastern Europe, Germany considers eastern Europe as its special sphere of influence, similar to the way that France addresses its relations with the Arab Mediterranean countries.

The German *Ostpolitik*

The West German foreign policy towards the SU and the other states in eastern Europe has become known as *Ostpolitik*. The main goal of the *Ostpolitik* was to create an understanding with the SU and the other eastern bloc states that would allow the reunification of Germany. While it was clear to all postwar West German politicians that the realization of German unity needed the support of the US, it was obvious to them that the SU held the key to German reunification as any change in the postwar settlement with respect to the division of Germany was dependent upon the consent of the SU. Moreover, the West German leaders believed that if the Russian and American leaders could reach an accord over German reunification, other European states, including France and Britain, could hardly prevent it. Although *Ostpolitik* is closely associated with Chancellor Willy Brandt, who laid down the main lines of this policy in the late 1960s and the early 1970s, it has its root in the 1950s.

The West German *Ostpolitik* started actually with the normalization of the relations between the Federal Republic of Germany (FRG) and the SU in 1955, shortly after the Federal Republic had recovered its sovereignty. Following Chancellor Adenauer's visit to Moscow in September 1955, the two countries established diplomatic relations and started to develop a tolerable relationship (Ash, 1993: 50–2). But Adenauer formulated his own terms for the FRG's *Ostpolitik*. Since Adenauer claimed that only the FRG's government could be the truly legitimate spokesman for all Germans, the West German government refused to recognize the German Democratic Republic (GDR) or to deal officially with the East German government. To underline this policy the West German government pronounced in 1955 the so-called Hallstein doctrine, wherein it declared that the FRG would no longer maintain diplomatic relations with the states recognizing the GDR. Only the SU was allowed to maintain diplomatic relations with the two German states. In that way Adenauer tried to isolate the GDR internationally and to deny the East German government any legitimacy. Adenauer also considered the present frontiers of the FRG as provisional borders and, as a consequence, refused to recognize the Oder-Neisse as the permanent border between Poland and the GDR. Although the Federal Republic distanced itself from the Nazi regime, the FRG claimed for itself, nevertheless, the legal status of successor and sought the restoration of the Germany within the borders of 1937, thus rejecting the postwar territorial *status quo* in central Europe as the final political arrangement (cf. Hanrieder, 1989: ch. 5).

Adenauer's successor, Ludwig Erhard, took a more flexible attitude towards eastern Europe which led to the establishment of trade relations between the FRG and almost all the countries of eastern Europe. But the new way of dealing with eastern Europe was not matched by a more realistic approach towards the political reality in eastern Europe, as the FRG continued to reject the European territorial *status quo* as the final postwar settlement. A major reversal of the Federal Republic's *Ostpolitik* took place only with the coming to power in 1969 of a new coalition government of the Social Democratic Party (SPD) and the Free Democratic Party (FDP), who argued in favour of such a reorientation in the FRG foreign policy towards the East.

However, small beginnings of the new *Ostpolitik* were already visible during the coalition government of Christian democrats and social democrats which was formed in 1966 with the Christian democrat Kurt-Georg Kiesinger as chancellor and the social democrat Willy Brandt as foreign minister and vice-chancellor. The government suggested that it was prepared to accept the East German government *de facto* and expressed its desire for a fundamental reconciliation with Poland. But the coalition government of Christian democrats and social democrats was unable to make a real opening to the East. While the socialists wanted to end the West German ignorance of East Germany and to change the uneasy relations with the East European countries, especially Poland, the Christian democrats were still not willing to recognize a second German state or to renounce the Federal Republic's policy on the question of the German–Polish frontier. Such a fundamental revision of the Federal Republic's policies in these matters was possible only after the forming of the new social–liberal coalition government in 1969 under the leadership of Willy Brandt as chancellor and Walter Scheel as foreign minister (cf. Hanrieder, 1989).

The new social–liberal government not only pursued a new approach towards the East, but it also brought the Federal Republic's relations with the East European countries onto a completely new footing. Chancellor Brandt was convinced that the time had come to reach an accommodation with the East and to introduce a new sense of realism into the Federal Republic's foreign policy. As Hanrieder has noted: 'Brandt believed that for moral as well as political reasons West Germany should face up to the consequences of the Second World War and the Cold War, and adjust the style as well as the content of its foreign policy to the realities of the 1970s' (Hanrieder, 1989: 197). Brandt's *Ostpolitik* consisted of two key elements: reconciliation and normalization. The realization of a historic reconciliation with the East European countries, especially Poland, has been a real motive of Brandt's *Ostpolitik*. Prominent intellectuals and religious leaders advocated for moral reasons such a reconciliation since the early 1960s, but Brandt succeeded in translating morality into policy. As Ash rightly says, for many people around the world *Ostpolitik* is the symbolic event of Willy Brandt falling to his knees before the monument to the heroes of the Warsaw ghetto uprising against the Germans during the Second World War (Ash, 1993: 298).

The normalization of the relations between the FRG and its neighbours to the east was expressed through the signing of a number of treaties with the eastern European countries, wherein the FRG expressed its recognition of the existing territorial *status quo* in Europe. All the bilateral treaties were considered by the FRG and the SU as a single whole. The West German leadership realized very well that any improvement in the bilateral relations between the FRG and Poland, Hungary or any other East European country required the approval of the SU and had therefore to coincide with an advancement in the relations between the FRG and the SU. In Brandt's view: 'Ostpolitik could not merely be a series of bilateral relations but had to be based on an overall concept of a systematic, synchronised approach to West–East relations' (Ash, 1993: 104). No wonder that the first and fundamental treaty in this package was signed with the SU in August 1970. The FRG explicitly declared in this treaty its acceptance of the Oder-Neisse line as the permanent frontier between Poland and East Germany and stated its commitment to respect the border between the FRG and GDR. This treaty paved the way for the conclusion of a treaty between the FRG and Poland in the same year, which sanctioned the Oder-Neisse line as Poland's western frontier. Shortly after the signing of the treaty, negotiations also began between the governments of the two German states which led, two years later, to the so-called West German–East German basic treaty of 1972 which became the general framework for the normalization of intra-German relations and the recognition of the GDR by the FRG as an equal partner.

The signing of this treaty did not imply that Brandt gave up the goal of German reunification. During the negotiations on the West German–Soviet treaty, the Soviet foreign minister himself opened the door to the possibility of peaceful voluntary changes of frontiers. Moreover, by the acceptance of the geopolitical reality in central and eastern Europe, Brandt wanted to use the SU's leverage with the East German government to achieve a transformation in the relationship between the two German states, which in the conception of both the FRG and the GDR were parts of one German nation (cf. Hanrieder, 1989: 202–9; Ash, 1993: 74–7). The fourth treaty in the package was signed the next year with Czechoslovakia, where the West German government stated that the Munich agreement of 1938 is of no value. The political significance of the signing of these treaties went far beyond the improvement in the diplomatic and economic relationship between the Federal Republic and the countries in eastern Europe. It created a new psychological atmosphere in the relations between East and West which has set the stage for a Conference on Security and Cooperation in Europe (CSCE) and the beginning of talks on Mutual Balanced Force Reductions (MBFR).

Reconciliation and normalization

The major pattern of Brandt's *Ostpolitik* has not changed after his resignation in 1974. Brandt's successors, Schmidt and Kohl, have made the reconciliation and normalization policy towards the eastern countries an important goal of the FRG's foreign policy and were willing to pay the price of such a normalization: a readiness to accept the loss of the former German territories beyond the Oder-Neisse. Helmut Schmidt, his social democratic successor as chancellor, consolidated the eastern policy he had inherited from Brandt. He was already deeply involved in the framing of Brandt's *Ostpolitik*, when he served as parliamentary leader of the SPD in the 1960s. Like Brandt, Schmidt considered the cultivation of a good relationship with the SU as the centrepiece of *Ostpolitik*. In his view, *détente* at both the superpower and European levels was a necessary condition for the unification of the two Germanies (Ash, 1993: 89). For this reason West Germany had a special interest in the continuation of the *détente* process and was, not surprisingly, highly critical of the American hammering on more respect for human rights in the SU and in other eastern European countries. The American sanctions against the SU and its boycott of the Olympic games in Moscow, in reaction to the SU invasion of Afghanistan in December 1979, were seen by Schmidt as a serious threat to the process of *détente*. The FRG joined the American boycott of the Moscow Olympics in 1980, but it refused a year later to join the US-led sanctions against Poland and the SU as response to the imposition of martial law in Poland in an attempt to limit the damage to *détente*. West Germany also broke ranks with the US (just like the other West Europeans) when it refused to stop the participation of German firms in the building of a natural gas pipeline to deliver gas from Siberia to western Europe. It was asked to do so by the American government which wanted to deny the SU access to advanced Western technology. The pipeline was a symbol of the German–Soviet cooperation and of vital interest to the FRG, since the delivery of natural gas from the SU helped West Germany to diversify its energy sources and to decrease its dependency on oil supplies from the Middle East.

To avoid harmful effects on its relationship with the SU as a consequence of the NATO decision in 1979 to reinforce its nuclear deterrence against the SU by means of the stationing of intermediate missiles in western Europe, Schmidt insisted on a 'double-track' decision. This made the deployment conditional on the outcome of negotiations with the SU on intermediate nuclear forces reductions. To induce the SU to reach such an agreement with the US, the NATO members agreed not to place the American intermediate nuclear weapons in Europe before 1983, and only in the case that these negotiations failed. West Germany was also very quick to endorse the proposal of the SU in the early 1970s to initiate a CSCE. The conference would deal with four areas: security in Europe and the Mediterranean; economic cooperation in the fields of economics, science, technology and the environment; human rights; and multilateral cooperation. The first result was the Helsinki accords, signed in 1975. Important in this connection was the recognition of the existing frontiers in Europe (including the borders separating the two Germanies) by all the 35 participants (Evans and Newnham, 1990: 154). The Federal Republic regarded the CSCE from the start as a vital forum for the activation of a process of *détente* on the European level, and would become a key player in the second area dealing with economic cooperation. It believed that success in building economic cooperation would lead to arms control and ultimately to freedom of movement of people throughout Europe (cf. Ash, 1993: 264).

One of Schmidt's most important instruments to secure *détente* in Europe and consequently to advance his *Ostpolitik* was West Germany's economic power. Brandt was already able to exploit the Russian hope to modernize its economy with German help, for his successful opening to the East. But Schmidt made economic cooperation with the SU a cornerstone of German–Soviet relations. By the end of his term as chancellor in 1982, West Germany would be the SU's most important trading partner. However, as Ash argues, although some sectors in the German industry benefited from expanding export to the East, the West German economy was not very dependent on trade with the SU and the other eastern European countries. On the contrary, 'West German dependency on eastern trade fades into insignificance beside the growing real dependency of Eastern Europe on West Germany . . . virtually all the European members of Comecon looked increasingly to the West for trade, technology, finance and know-how, and their leading partner in the West was the Federal Republic' (Ash, 1993: 247). Schmidt and his successor Kohl used this leverage as a carrot rather than a stick. Whereas the American presidents (Carter and Reagan) tried to change the Soviet policies in Afghanistan and Poland through the imposing of sanctions, the West German leaders tried to create incentives for the SU and the East European regimes to change their policies. As we will see in the next section, the EC/EU would follow the same strategy in its common policy towards the transformation in eastern Europe. To increase the long-term interest of the SU in a good relationship with West Germany, in 1978 the FRG, for instance, signed with the SU a long-term agreement on economic and industrial cooperation. Economic statecraft was also the name of the game in Schmidt's relations with the other East European countries. In exchange for a considerable loan at a very low interest Schmidt managed, for example, to persuade the Polish authorities in 1975 to let a large number of the German minority in that country to leave the country, even though the Polish government had denied five years earlier that Germans still live in Poland (Ash, 1993: 237).

Another important element in Schmidt's *Ostpolitik* was his conviction that West Germany's eastern policies have to be part of a multilateral effort. Being aware of the concerns that West Germany's economic power may arise in the perception of other states and the negative effects this may have on *Ostpolitik*, the FRG had to operate not nationally and independently but in the framework of the EC and NATO, or, as Schmidt phrased it, to cover West Germany's actions multilaterally (Ash, 1993: 86). The Federal Republic has indeed exploited the EPC framework as an important platform for its *Ostpolitik*. The coordination of the national positions of the EC member-states at the CSCE was one of the first items on the EPC agenda and remained so throughout the CSCE process (cf. Hill, 1983: 46).

A clear sense of direction

When the Christian democrats returned to power in 1982 under the leadership of Helmut Kohl, the new government adhered to the general framework of the *Ostpolitik* that it had inherited from former socialist-led governments. Although he added his own finger prints to West Germany's *Ostpolitik*, Kohl left the foundations of Brandt's and Schmidt's *Ostpolitik*, which was based on a mixture of reconciliation and economic rewards, untouched. Moreover, his liberal coalition partner and his foreign minister Hans-Dietrich Genscher (who also served as foreign minister under Schmidt) ensured a continuation in Germany's *Ostpolitik*. Kohl had, however, to operate in an international environment which was characterized by confrontation rather than cooperation. The American government at that time treated the SU as a threat that should be contained and dealt with only from a position of strength. Under these circumstances, which some named a second cold war, Kohl and Genscher wanted to limit the damage as much as possible and to focus on the *détente* between the two Germanies. The FRG and the GDR concluded several agreements, and the East German leader Honecker visited the Federal Republic for the first time, which symbolized the recognition of the GDR by the FRG as its equal (Hanrieder, 1989: 214–16).

The coming to power of Gorbachev as leader of the SU in 1985 and the change of atmosphere that it caused in the relations between the US and the SU had its effects on German–Soviet relations as well. Although West Germany kept its economic help to the SU despite American pressure to refrain from the export of high technology, the signing of several far-reaching arms reduction agreements between the two superpowers gave the SU and West Germany a chance to boost their bilateral relationship much further. This would culminate in the so-called Bonn declaration of June 1989, just before the upheaval in eastern Europe. In this document the two countries committed themselves to contribute to overcoming the division of Europe. As the declaration says: 'They are determined to work together on concepts of achieving this goal through the building of a European peace and cooperation – of a European order of peace or a common European home' (Ash, 1993: 113). Both parties called it a new page in their relationship. It was in fact the informal end of the cold war and indeed the beginning of a new era in Germany's postwar history.

Thus, by the time that the historic transformation in almost every eastern European country took place, the FRG had already built a web of economic and political ties with many former Communist countries. But Kohl understood very well that a united Germany would be tolerable for its neighbours only if it were part of a united Europe where national borders lose their political significance. Even though Germany has moved towards eastern Europe ahead of its European partners, Kohl has been very careful to present the shift of German attention to the east not as a German attempt to pursue its own national interest but as an effort to seek a European interest (cf. *The Economist*, 13 July 1996: 25). As from 1989 Kohl emphasized that Germany's policy towards the transformation in eastern Europe should be an integral part of the common EU policy and that the Germans were prepared to help the EU to realize its ambition to play a prominent role in the transformation process in central and eastern Europe. Thus, Germany was not only ready to pursue its foreign policy towards central and eastern Europe through the common EC framework, but it was also willing to act as the major paymaster of the EC/EU resources allocated to the central and eastern European countries. As a result of this economic leverage and the clear sense of direction that the German leaders hold regarding the preferred course of common action, Germany was able to play an exceptional part in the formulation of the common response towards the political and economic transformation in eastern Europe.

The common policy

Until the beginning of the political and economic reforms in eastern Europe in the mid-1980s, relations between the countries in western and eastern Europe were conducted essentially on a bilateral basis. The EC as such did not even have a formal relationship with its eastern counterpart the Council for Mutual Economic Assistance (CMEA), also known as Comecon. As the SU refused to recognize the EC as a distinct political entity, official relations between the EC and the SU or any of its satellite states were out of the question. The EC itself also had, for its part, little interest in a close relationship with the eastern countries or Comecon. The quantity of trade between the two economic blocs was not significant and Comecon itself had no competence in the handling of the trade relations of the eastern countries. The Commission could easily settle the access of certain products from eastern Europe through sectoral agreements on an *ad hoc* basis through informal contacts with the individual eastern governments. The only exceptions were Yugoslavia and

Romania which followed a foreign policy course independently of the SU. 1
signed a trade and cooperation agreement with Yugoslavia in 1970, and cor
a trade agreement with Romania in 1980.

The first formal contacts between the EC and Comecon were established after the
coming to power of Mikhail Gorbachev as leader of the SU in 1985. The normalization of relations between the EC and Comecon led to a mutual recognition in
1988, whereupon the SU allowed the individual eastern European countries to
enter into an official relationship with the EC. In the same year the first trade and
cooperation agreement was concluded between the EC and Hungary, followed a
year later by a similar agreement with Poland and the SU. By 1990 the EC had
comparable agreements with all the eastern European countries, but missed a coherent common *Ostpolitik*. As a matter of fact the EC, like its member-states, was
caught by surprise by the events in central and eastern Europe. The EC member-
states were nevertheless prompt in their response to the political and economic
reforms in eastern Europe. During the meeting of the European Council in Hanover
in June 1988 the EC leaders responded very positively to the change of spirit in the
East–West relationship under the new Soviet leadership. The EC leaders welcomed
the establishment of a climate of increased confidence and cooperation between the
two superpowers and the more outward-looking attitude expressed by the eastern
European countries. At the next meeting in December 1988 in Rhodes, the heads of
states and government expressed their satisfaction over the readiness of the eastern
European states to broaden economic ties with the EC, and declared their determination to overcome the division of Europe and to promote Western values. During the
European Council meeting in Madrid in June 1989, the member-states again paid
tribute to the important changes in the SU and the countries of central and eastern
Europe, and restated the firmness of the EC and its member-states to play an active
role by the support and the promotion of reforms in these countries. At the meetings
in Rhodes and Madrid the EU leaders made a linkage between economic help and
the building of democratic institutions as well as the creation of market economies.
This integrated approach, promoted by Germany and supported by Britain, France
and the other member-states, became the guiding principle in the EC's response to
the transitions in eastern Europe. It was established as the EC's official policy at the
meeting of the European Council in Strasbourg in December 1989, where the EC
leaders declared that they would use all available means to encourage the necessary
economic reforms and to continue the search for suitable ways of association with
countries that have started economic and political reforms (cf. Pinder, 1991: 30;
Wertz, 1992: 209–10; *Bulletin of the European Communities*, 1988 and 1989).

The policy instruments: the offer of membership

The EC itself has taken the lead in helping the central and eastern European countries in the transformation from planned economies to market economies. The EC
has accepted the major responsibility for organizing the collective effort of the
Western countries to provide economic aid to the former Communist countries. The
first major step in that direction was the PHARE programme (Poland and Hungary:

Assistance for Restructuring Economies), which was launched by the EC in 1989 to support the process of political and economic reforms in Poland and Hungary. The help programme was actually initiated during a meeting of the group of seven leading industrial countries (the so-called G-7, of which four were EC member-states) in July 1989 in Paris. The G-7 entrusted the European Commission, which already managed the collective help of the EC members to eastern Europe, with the coordination of Western aid to these two countries. The Commission was also assigned the task of organizing the multilateral aid of all the 24 members of the OECD, also known as the G-24. The EC itself and the EC member-states became, however, the largest contributors to Operation PHARE, as the help programme was labelled in EC terminology.

The main proposal of Operation PHARE was to reward Poland and Hungary for the progress they had already made towards a multi-party system and a market economy and to support the further process of political and economic reforms in the two countries. Operation PHARE was extended in 1990 to Czechoslovakia, Bulgaria, Romania, Yugoslavia and East Germany (until its unification with West Germany). The Baltic states, Albania, Slovenia and Croatia, were included in a later stage. The PHARE programme offered the central and eastern European countries immediate food aid, tariff-free access to the EC market for a large number of products, technical and financial training necessary for the management of market-oriented economies, support for the development of the private sector, contribution in the financing of projects aimed at economic restructuring, assistance to major infrastructure projects and help in the process of democratic institution building. To complement the PHARE programme, the EC member-states decided during the Strasbourg European Council meeting of 1989 to set up a European Bank for Reconstruction and Development (EBRD). The EBRD, which was established in Paris in 1990, had to provide the central and eastern European states with the necessary funds to finance the transition towards a market-oriented economy, in addition to the loans from the World Bank. The EC itself, the member-states and the European Investment Bank have been the major sponsors of the EBRD, generating the lion's share of the ERBD's starting capital (cf. Pinder, 1991: 30–2; Van Ham, 1993: 167–73; *General Reports EC/EU*, 1989–95).

The PHARE programme and the EBRD have become major tools in the hands of the EC/EU member-states to create in eastern Europe conditions that encourage the development of a market economy, based on the principle of free enterprise, and strengthen the consolidation of a democratic order. Since economic and financial help was made conditional upon the requirement of progress towards democratic and economic reforms and discriminated in favour of the countries that were judged to have the most credible reform programmes, the PHARE grants and the ERBD loans gave the EC/EU member-states powerful instruments to support the prospects for success of the reforms towards democracy and market economy in the former Communist countries (Pinder, 1991: 33). So the largest share of the PHARE aid was allocated to Poland and Hungary, which have satisfied the condition of movement towards plural democracy and competitive market economy. The other eastern countries received only small amounts of the PHARE aid and could qualify for more help by the adoption of further political and economic reforms. The connection between financial help and economic and political reforms was also made explicit in the first article of the EBRD statute which says that 'The purpose of the Bank shall be to foster the transition towards open-market economies and to promote private and entrepreneurial initiative in the Central and Eastern European countries committed to and applying the principle of multiparty democracy, pluralism and market economics' (cited in Van Ham, 1993: 181).

But the most important instrument that the EC member-states have used to stir the adoption of Western values of political and economic freedom, has been the offer of EU membership to the central and eastern European countries that qualify for such a membership. It took some time before the EU members could agree on the opening of that perspective and compromise on the way the entry to the EU could be realized. With the benefit of hindsight, we may say that the member-states chose a stage-by-stage strategy whereby the movement from one stage to another was not automatic and depended on internal developments in the central and eastern European countries and the internal developments in the EC/EU itself.

The first stage was the granting of associated membership, which was considered by Germany and some other states to be a first step in an enlargement towards central and eastern Europe. Although the possibility of association between the EC and the central and eastern European states was already mentioned in the conclusions of the Strasbourg European Council of 1989, the member-states were divided over a proposal of the Commission for a special type of association agreement with these countries, the so-called Europe agreements. Besides the reluctance of some member-states to open their markets for imports from eastern Europe in sectors where the eastern countries have comparative advantages like agriculture, steel, coal and textiles, the main political obstacle has been the initial resistance of some member-states to the inclusion of the possibility of future membership. France and other southern member-states wanted to delay the entry of the central and eastern European states not only for protectionist reasons. They were also concerned about the consequences of full membership for the EC budget and especially their country's revenue from the CAP and the cohesion funds. Under pressure from Germany and Britain, which were in favour of an EU enlargement towards the east, France finally agreed to refer to the possibility of membership in the preamble of the Europe agreements, but only as an ultimate goal and not before it was made clear to the potential associated countries in central and eastern Europe that accession to the EC would not be automatic.

The Europe agreements, which were endorsed by the European Council in April 1990, have replaced the existing trade and cooperation agreements. They are, however, more than a simple upgrading of a trade and cooperation agreement. Besides new and closer forms of economic, scientific and technical cooperation, increased EC financial aid and technical support and common projects to improve infrastructure and greater cultural cooperation, the Europe agreement also encourages the free movement of goods and services, leading ultimately to the creation of a free trade area and a phased introduction of the free movement of capital and people. In addition, the Europe agreement institutionalizes a political dialogue between the EC and the associated state, with association councils to act as fora for decision and discussion, association committees composed of senior officials and parliamentary association committees composed of members of Parliament of the associated country and members of the European Parliament (Nello, 1991: 206–7).

The Europe agreements have become the keystone of the EU's policy to ensure a rapid transition to a market economy and democracy. Since the countries in central and eastern Europe considered the association agreements as a stepping stone to full-fledged EC membership, the Europe agreements also became an effective policy instrument to secure the establishment of pluralist democracy and a competitive market economy in the former Communist countries. A crucial element in this policy is the fact that the upgrading of the existing trade and cooperation agreement to a Europe agreement is not automatic. If the central and eastern European states want such an association agreement, they have to meet certain conditions. They can qualify by giving practical evidence of their commitment to the rule of law, respect for human rights including respect for religious and ethnic minorities, political pluralism, free elections and economic liberalization. As the preamble of the Europe agreements explicitly states, the full realization of the association agreement is linked to the actual accomplishment of political, economic and legal reforms in the associated country (Pinder, 1991: 59; Kramer, 1993: 228). The central European countries, the so-called Visegrad countries, Poland, Hungary and Czechoslovakia, were the first to negotiate such a Europe agreement with the Commission. The Europe agreement with Poland and Hungary took effect in 1994. The Europe agreements with the Czech Republic and Slovakia (as a result of the splitting of Czechoslovakia in 1993 into the Czech and Slovak republics) entered into force the next year. In 1993 the EU concluded another two Europe agreements with Romania and Bulgaria, which also started reform programmes, and these were followed by a similar agreement with the three Baltic states, Estonia, Latvia and Lithuania, in 1995, and Slovenia the next year. Thus by 1996 the Europe agreements have established an association between the EU and ten former Communist states in eastern Europe.

During the negotiations over the Europe agreement the central and eastern European countries demanded from the EU member-states a clear commitment to full EU membership. The EU member governments, for their part, were divided over the question of whether they should commit themselves to such a linkage between association and accession. The discussion among the EU member-states over a future enlargement eastward brought to the surface a diversity among the member-states regarding their commitment to such an enlargement. While Germany, Britain and Denmark clearly advocated an enlargement eastward, the other member-states were much more ambivalent about such an enlargement. Germany, which benefits more than any other EU member-state from its trade with the ten central and eastern European countries, was the most forceful supporter of the accession of these countries. Germany accounts for half of all EU exports to the ten central and eastern European countries and 20 per cent of the total foreign investments in these countries. But Germany had to accept the French conditions for such an enlargement: a deepening of the institutional structure of the EU before enlargement and the intensification of the EU policies towards the Mediterranean non-member-states. Britain supported an enlargement for the simple reason that an enlarged Union would potentially be also a looser Union. Denmark (like the other Scandinavian countries which would join the EU in 1995) strongly supported the integration of the Baltic countries into the EU because of their proximity and the mutual commercial ties. France, Italy and the Benelux countries were much more concerned about the negative effects that such an enlargement would have on further integration, as well as the budgetary consequences of enlargement. Spain, Portugal and Greece, despite their rhetoric about enlargement, were even more reluctant about a swift accession of the central and eastern European countries because of the likelihood of a financial reallocation of EU funds from the southern member-states to the new eastern ones as a result of such an extension eastward. While these southern member-states also had to worry about competition from the eastern European countries in several sectors, they had nothing to gain from enlargement due to the low degree of their economic involvement in eastern Europe (cf. Grabbe and Hughes, 1998; Wallace and Wallace, 1996: 366–72).

It would take a year of intensive deliberations before the member-states could agree on a common declaration which would recognize the central and eastern European countries' demand for EU membership. During the Copenhagen meeting of the European Council in June 1993, the EU leaders bridged their differences and acknowledged that the future cooperation with the associated states of central and eastern Europe (with which the EU has concluded Europe agreements) was geared to the objective of membership, and explicitly declared that the associated countries in central and eastern Europe that so desire can become members of the EU as soon as they are able to fulfil the necessary economic and political conditions for full membership. The requirements that the associated countries had to satisfy before the EU could consider the next step of full integration into the EU involved stable institutions guaranteeing democracy, the rule of law, human rights and respect for and protection of minorities; a functioning market economy as well as the capacity to cope with competitive pressure and market forces within the EU; and the ability to adopt the obligations of membership including the ability to adhere to the aims of political, economic and monetary union. In addition to the fulfilling of these conditions which depends on the progress in each associated state, entry of the central and eastern European states to the EU was also made conditional upon the EU's capacity to absorb new members, while maintaining the momentum of European integration and respecting its internal cohesion (*Bulletin of the European Communities*, June 1993). In other words, while the EU leaders agreed on the principle of enlargement to the east, they decided at the same time that such an enlargement must not be pursued at the expense of the deepening of European integration. Moreover, accession negotiations could begin only after the institutional conditions for ensuring the proper functioning of a much larger EU had been created at the 1996 intergovernmental conference.

Delaying the enlargement eastward

Germany used its EU presidency the next year to reinforce the credibility of the commitment made at the Copenhagen summit. At its meeting in Essen in December 1994, the European Council approved under the German presidency a detailed plan for the preparation of the associated states in central and eastern European for accession to the EU. The formal aim of the so-called pre-accession strategy was to institutionalize a structured relationship between the EU and the associated states, and to help the associated states to integrate into the internal market. The pre-accession strategy has established a structured process of political consultation between the Council of the EU on the one hand and all the associated states in central and eastern Europe on the other. The meetings are held in the form of annual joint sessions of the EU leaders with the associated states' leaders on the margin of the European Council and similar gatherings at ministerial level between the ministers of foreign affairs and other sectoral ministers of the EU and the counterparts from the central and eastern European countries. In addition, regular meetings and exchange of information take place at ambassadors and working groups levels. The structured dialogue covers not only matters that are related to the progressive integration of the associated states into the internal market of the EC, but also topics that fall within the scope of the common foreign and security policy and justice and home affairs. The pre-accession strategy also specifies a number of measures which will assist the associated states to take on the obligations of EU membership such as the incorporation of hundreds of EC regulations in their legislation, and to develop their capacity to cope with competitive pressure and market forces within the EU (*Bulletin of the European Union*, December 1994).

The EU member-states considered the pre-accession stage a new phase in the integration process of the central and eastern European countries into the EU. It was presented as a necessary middle stage in a process of integration. But actually the preparation of the associated states for accession delayed their entry to the EU. The member-states were, for example, unable to agree on a timetable for accession due to the differences among the three larger EU members in particular, about the priority that such an enlargement to the east should have, and the possibility of pursuing at the same time a deepening as well as a widening of the EU. While France had a preference for deepening before widening and Britain gave priority to widening over deepening, Germany wanted to follow a strategy of deepening as well as widening. As a matter of fact, France agreed to accept the pre-accession only after Germany was willing to support the French intention to launch a new Mediterranean policy during its presidency. After the adoption of the pre-accession strategy at the Essen summit, France championed a cautious approach towards the upgrading of the associated membership of individual countries in central and eastern Europe to full membership, while Germany, with the support of Britain, continued to push for further steps towards full membership. At the request of Germany the Commission conducted in 1997 a survey on the extent to which the ten central and eastern European countries met the conditions of membership defined by the European Council in Copenhagen. In the opinion of the Commission, five central and eastern European countries had made sufficient progress in satisfying the political and economic conditions for accession and were able to take on the obligations of membership. The commission recommended that negotiations for accession could start in 1998 with the Czech Republic, Hungary, Poland, Estonia and Slovenia. The five that did not earn the crucial conclusion were Latvia, Lithuania, Slovakia, Romania and Bulgaria. But even in the countries that passed the Commission test, the EU continued to dictate the full implementation of pluralist democracy and a competitive market economy. In an effort to encourage further efforts, the Commission stated in its report that these countries could be in a position to satisfy all the conditions of membership in the medium term but only if they maintain and strongly sustain their preparation efforts (*European Voice*, 17–23 July 1997). In March 1998 the Commission started accession talks on behalf of the member-states with the five central and eastern European applicants, but it was made clear from the beginning that this would be an evolutionary and inclusive process, whereby the Commission would submit regular reports on each candidate's progress towards accession. At the same time the Commission continued its efforts to prepare the other five central and eastern European countries for membership.

The opening of the accession negotiations forced the EU member-states to make progress in the institutional revisions and policy reforms that were necessary before the entry of the central and eastern European states to the EU. This was the fourth condition for accession defined by the European Council in Copenhagen which made accession also conditional upon the EU's capacity to absorb new members, while maintaining the momentum of European integration and respecting its internal cohesion. With the prospect of a future membership of 20 or even 27 members (if we also include the proposed enlargement southward), the existing EU member-states had to inprove the functioning of the EU institutions before the first enlargement round. This implied a recalculation of the weight of national votes in the Council of Ministers and the introduction of more qualified majority voting in several policy areas, as well as a reorganization of the Commission and a fundamental change in the distribution of the number of commissioners among the existing member-states. During the intergovernmental negotiations on the Treaty of Amsterdam, the member-states failed to realize these institutional changes which would have reduced the voting power of some states in the Council of Ministers and would have reduced the number of commissioners that the larger member-states have on the Commission. However, the biggest obstacle has been the need to reform the CAP and the structural and cohesion funds. These reforms touch upon vested interests of some existing member-states, which have the ability to hold the enlargement talks hostage in exchange for concessions and compensations in both policy areas. After all, each existing member-state can veto the negotiation result in the Council of Ministers. Moreover, enlargement depends as well on the national governments' willingness to convince their national Parliament to ratify the accession agreements. France, Belgium and Italy have already declared that they will support enlargement only after the necessary institutional reforms have been achieved. Other countries, notably Spain, Portugal and Greece, have indicated that they may block enlargement if this will lead to major cuts in transfers from the structural and cohesion funds to the three countries (cf. Grabbe and Hughes, 1998).

Thus, the difficulty of the EU member-states to reorder their own house has not only become the main obstacle along the road to enlargement, but it has also revealed the weaknesses in the EU ambition to play the leading regional power. Notwithstanding these problems, the EU and its member-states were able to take a leading role in helping the central and eastern European countries to transform their former economic and political systems, and to dictate as well further political and economic reforms in exchange for full EU membership.

Chapter 8

The impotence in former Yugoslavia: setting up the missing military capability

When fighting broke out in Yugoslavia in the summer of 1991 the leaders of the EU made no secret of their ambition to intervene as mediators in the Yugoslav crisis. Frustrated by the EU's inability to play a major mediating role in the Middle East peace process, but encouraged by its ability to play a leading role in the transformation process in central and eastern Europe, the EU leaders were sure that this was the hour of Europe, a chance to show the world that the EU is able to cope with the crisis in its own backyard. The foreign minister of Luxembourg, acting as the president of the EU Council of Ministers, was confident that the EU could handle the crisis: 'If one problem can be solved by the Europeans, it is the Yugoslav problem. This is a European country and it is not up to the Americans and not up to anybody else' (cited in Gow, 1997: 50). His views were echoed by Jacques Delors, at that time president of the European Commission, who remarked: 'We do not interfere in American affairs. We hope they will have enough respect not to interfere in ours' (cited in Danchev and Halverson, 1996: 183). Four years later, after a number of abortive attempts by the EU to end the war, the EU leaders had to realize that the EU as such was not taken seriously by the concerned parties. It was actually the US that managed to break the stalemate in former Yugoslavia, to push the various parties to the negotiations table and to conclude at the end of 1995 the Dayton accords, which ended the fighting and created the conditions for a settlement of the war. Moreover, the West European Union (WEU), which is projected as the future military arm of the EU, has proved irrelevant in the crisis in former Yugoslavia.

The inability of the EU and the WEU to cope successfully with the crisis in former Yugoslavia has revealed a fundamental weakness of the CFSP, namely the lack of a military capability to support its foreign policy. At the same time it has raised some serious questions as to whether such a military capability is of any significance without the active participation of American military power. It has also faced the EU member-states with the dilemma of whether they should develop such a military capability within or outside the EU framework, given the experience in former Yugoslavia where some EU member-states managed very well to organize their military contribution through the existing integrated military structures of the North Atlantic Treaty Organization (NATO). Hence, this chapter places the EU experience in former Yugoslavia against the ongoing debate between the EU member-states as to whether the WEU or NATO should be the definite organizational framework for the common defence. The EU member-states have confirmed in the recent Amsterdam Treaty their intention to formulate a common defence policy. But there was still disagreement among the member governments about whether and, if so, how far and how fast it was wise to incorporate WEU within the EU. While the merger of the WEU into the EU was not precluded, the commitment to NATO was also reaffirmed (Duff, 1997b: 126). Actually little progress has been made so far in making the WEU a concrete alternative to NATO. As a consequence NATO still represents the most integrated defence organization in Europe, and it is the only military organization in Europe that has the decision-making structure and the military resources to conduct complex peacekeeping and peace enforcement operations.

However, the debate about the role of NATO in the EU's common defence cannot be isolated from the different views the member-states hold regarding the role of the US in European defence, which touches immediately upon the distinct conceptions that the European member-states have with respect to the nature of the transatlantic relationship. NATO and the transatlantic relationship are, so to say, two sides of the same coin. In the debate among the member-states over the emerging common defence policy, which is actually a discussion over the role of the WEU versus the role of NATO (and implicitly that of the US) in the future common defence structure, the views of the three larger states, Britain, France and Germany, are most relevant. They not only embody the voices that really count in the internal debate over the future EU defence structures, but they also represent the different views with respect to the desired involvement of the US in European security. In addition, France and Britain are the EU member-states that are expected to make the largest military contribution to the setting up of an EU military capability, as the peacekeeping and peace enforcement operations in former Yugoslavia have already illustrated. Since the present attitudes of Britain, France and Germany towards a common defence policy are deeply rooted in their postwar history, we will start with a brief review of this history and relate it to the position that the three countries take in the current debate over the setting up of an integrated defence structure. We will move then to discuss the lessons that the EU member-states, and France in particular, have drawn from the experience in the war in former Yugoslavia for the setting up of the still missing European defence capability.

Britain: maintaining the special transatlantic relationship

The British position towards the role of the US in European defence originates in what successive British governments considered a cornerstone of Britain's postwar foreign policy: a special relationship with the US. Building on the wartime Anglo-American diplomatic and military cooperation, British policy makers pursued through a central orientation on the Atlantic alliance two major British foreign policy goals: first, to maintain a global role, and second, to give Britain and western Europe the security and stability that Britain was unable to provide on its own. To escape the condition of becoming less in importance, successive British governments tried to derive a powerful international position from the cultivation of a special relationship with the US, and used NATO as a main forum to exercise this special relationship. Almost all the British nuclear and conventional forces have been devoted to NATO and many military bases on British soil were used by the Americans. The two countries also worked closely in the areas of military intelligence, nuclear research and the development of weapon programmes, building a whole network of regular meetings, consultations and back-channel contacts at all levels of government (Newsom, 1987: 226–9). As Kissinger has noted, although Britain's physical power had declined, British governments have succeeded very effectively in using the relationship between the two countries to maintain political influence. British leaders made it psychologically impossible for American presidents to ignore British views and have created a situation in which 'American leaders saw it in their self-interest to obtain British advice before taking major decisions' (Kissinger, 1979: 90).

But the Atlantic alliance also served the British government's aim throughout the cold war of binding the US, militarily as well as politically, to Europe. The British main concern at the end of the Second World War was to avoid an American return to isolationism, just like the American detachment from European politics at the end of the former world war. The British policy makers realized, especially after the SU had demonstrated in 1949 its possession of a nuclear weapon, that neither Britain nor an Anglo-French coalition was capable of balancing the Soviet military power independently of the US. In their view a joint conventional military effort of the West European states could serve as an effective deterrence *vis-à-vis* the military power of the SU only by means of binding the American military conventional and nuclear power to Europe. The security guarantees given to western and southern Europe through NATO institutionalized in British eyes the American commitment to European security, and marked the American willingness to take the leading role in the protection of western and southern Europe against the spread of communism.

The British were not as troubled as the French by the American nuclear hegemony within the Alliance. Such an American dominance, which was softened in British perception by the Anglo-American special relationship, offered the best guarantee for a decisive American military presence in Europe. Moreover, British leaders, in contrast to French leaders, have always considered the development of a nuclear strategy independently of the US as incredible. They believed that the ability of a British nuclear force to deter a Soviet nuclear attack against Britain or any other country in western Europe depended on a link between such a force and the American atomic umbrella (Hanrieder and Auton, 1980: 190). As Freedman has argued, although the development of a British independent nuclear force was justified by stressing the political and strategic importance of such an independent contribution, it has always been regarded by British governments as a contribution to NATO's nuclear forces and the Alliance's deterrence power. The creation of a second centre of nuclear decision has increased, in the view of British policy makers, the potential for Britain to exercise influence within NATO and at the same time has reinforced the reliability of NATO's deterrence by making it less dependent on American willingness to use nuclear weapons (Freedman, 1983: 310–12).

But the creation and maintenance of an expensive British independent nuclear force (likewise the French independent nuclear force which we will discuss in the next section) has, besides a deterrent value of course, also a symbolic value: the preservation of Britain's international standing as a world power (Tugendhat and Wallace, 1988: 68–9).

Keeping the predominance of NATO

Throughout the 1960s and 1970s, a period in which a shift in priorities from the Commonwealth to Europe has taken place, British governments had more and more difficulty in maintaining Britain's demand for a great power status and keeping their privileged position alongside the Americans. The need to retreat from empire and the necessity to give up most of its overseas bases stripped Britain of a vital power base and deprived the British of their ability to live up to their claim of a shared responsibility with the Americans for global security. Moreover, the special relationship has increasingly turned into a one-sided relationship, as the Americans were actually more concerned with their strategic relationship with the SU than with their traditional partnership with Britain. Notwithstanding Kissinger's observation mentioned above, during major international crises, such as the Cuba crisis in 1962 or the Middle East war in 1973 where the two superpowers were on the edge of nuclear confrontation, American decisions were taken almost without consultation with the British leaders. British policy makers also had no part in the American–Soviet strategic arms limitation negotiations and had a limited knowledge about their progress. All in all, in spite of the Anglo-American military partnership in the Gulf War in 1991, the British leaders had to witness a weakening of the close relationship with the US, which was further subverted by the increased importance of Germany which is seen by the Americans as the key European actor in the Alliance and the crucial player in the EU.

Despite the cooling in the special Anglo-American relationship, British policy makers have ascribed great value to its preservation. Acting as a bridge between the US and its European allies, they made every effort to keep the American commitment to Europe's defence and to maintain NATO as the essential institutional framework for the organization of a western European defence (Tugendhat and Wallace, 1988: 27–8). In the intergovernmental negotiations among the EC member-states in 1991 about the institutionalization of the CFSP, the British government resisted a fundamental choice between European integration in the defence field within the EU and the continuation of the existing defence cooperation in NATO. However, the British clear preference for NATO does not imply a British opposition to closer European defence cooperation or a European grouping within NATO, as long as it is based on intergovernmental decision-making structures and does not jeopardize the American commitment to European security. The British established with the West Germans in 1969 the so-called Eurogroup within NATO, which provided the European members of NATO with a European pillar within the Alliance. It offered some counterweight to the American dominance within NATO and met the American demand for more cooperation among the European members of NATO. The

British were also in favour of revitalizing the WEU as a framework for the development of a European defence identity which would reflect a stronger and more integrated European pillar within NATO. But to secure an American military presence in Europe even after the ending of the cold war and the removal of the Russian threat, the British persisted in linking the WEU to NATO and opposed any attempt by France to establish the WEU as an alternative to NATO. The British insisted on a firm commitment to NATO and followed a negotiating tactic which was aimed at postponing a decision on the merger of the WEU into the EU for as long as possible (Laursen and Vanhoonacker, 1992: 198–9; Howorth and Menon, 1997: 115–18).

France: aspiring independence from the United States

Although France, like Britain, belonged to the victorious powers of the Second World War, as a result of the French military collapse in 1940 followed by five years of German occupation, it had to accept an inferior position in the decision making about the postwar global and European order. De Gaulle, the leader of the Free French who presided over the French war effort on the side of the Allies, was hardly treated by the Allied leaders as their equal and was denied a full share in the joint decision making about the future peace settlement. The decline in the international status of France was underscored by the absence of France from the wartime summits of the Big Three at Yalta and Potsdam in 1945, where the American, Russian and British leaders discussed the proposed boundary changes in eastern Europe and the partition of Germany. The diminishing international influence of France was only partially smoothed over by the final recognition of France as one of the four powers in occupied Germany and the acceptance of France as a permanent member alongside the Big Three and China in the Security Council of the newly established United Nations.

De Gaulle, who experienced the demotion in France's international ranking as humiliation, and the French leaders that succeeded him were not willing to embrace a simple supporting role for their country. To advance their concept of European defence, France signed the Brussels pact in 1948 with Britain and the Benelux countries, which was succeeded in 1955 by the WEU. But as the wartime grand alliance began to crumble and the division in ideology as well as the conflict of interests between the Western powers and the SU came to the surface, the French policy makers realized that France had to adapt to the altered international circumstances and to accept American supremacy. They understood that, to satisfy the French wish to participate in the control of Germany, France had to rely on American and British help. The French leadership also recognized that, given the country's limited military power, the defence of France had to be organized jointly with Britain and the US. As a matter of fact, after the Communist coup in Prague in February 1948 and the Russian blockade of the access routes to the western sectors of Berlin in June 1948, the French government, in common with the British government, pressed the Americans for such an alliance to ensure American commitment to their security. Thus, the fear of Russian domination in Europe outweighed the French political reservations about joining an Anglo-American alliance and paved the way for the French accession in April 1949 to NATO (Wiggershaus and Foerster, 1993: 125–31).

The growing feeling of insecurity after the outbreak of the Korean war in 1950 reinforced French readiness to accept dependence on the US and to embrace the dominant position of the Americans within the organization. The French were even in favour of the complete integration of western European defence within NATO under American leadership. As a senior French foreign policy maker wrote at that time to his foreign minister Robert Schuman:

> While it is true that France has an interest, in political and diplomatic terms, to keep the maximum possible freedom of action and to avoid the Atlantic Alliance turning into a kind of Comniform under the direction of the United States, it is nonetheless essential to involve the Americans in ever-closer cooperation and to freely accept the limitations on our sovereignty which will place us in a better position to safeguard our national independence. (Wiggershaus and Foerster, 1993: 137)

However, right from the beginning the French leaders regarded NATO as the second best option for the organization of West Europe's defence. Contrary to the British, who gave absolute priority to NATO, the French leaders saw NATO simply as an insurance against a Russian military attack. They were convinced that while the Atlantic Alliance was of temporary nature, the Brussels pact was one of the seeds of a permanent European federation (Wiggershaus and Foerster, 1993: 133). The first French attempt to set up an integrated European army was triggered by an American demand during the Korean war in 1950 for a West German contribution to NATO. Since the proposed German participation in NATO provoked the French obsession with the German danger as it stirred up the dormant problem of German rearmament, the French came with an alternative proposal in the form of a unified European army, which placed the German military contribution within the institutional framework of a European Defence Community (EDC).

The French policy makers used, for the integration of the West German army into a larger West European framework, the same concept that they used at the same time for the integration of the West German coal and steel industry into a European Coal and Steel Community (ECSC), which was discussed in Chapter 2. The far-reaching proposal encompassed the creation of a unified European army composed of French, Benelux, West German and Italian units, directed by a European minister of defence who would operate under the direction of a council of ministers of the participating countries and would be responsible to a European assembly. Such a unified structure had to build satisfactory safeguards into the EDC against a German military revival. No less important was, of course, the absence of the US and Britain from the EDC, which offered France a chance to take the lead in the proposed common European defence structure. However, the EDC agreement, which was signed in Paris in 1952 by the same six countries who signed the ECSC treaty a year earlier, failed to achieve in 1954 the final approvement of the French Parliament (Fursdon, 1980). After the abortive French plan for an EDC, the French had to compromise with the Americans and the British about the future participation of West Germany in the defence of Europe through both NATO and the Brussels pact which was transformed at that occasion into the WEU.

With the return of de Gaulle to political power in 1958, the French concern for its standing in the world and its independence from the two superpowers would dominate the French foreign and security policy agenda. Although de Gaulle deeply believed in France's *grandeur*, he recognized that France lacked a sufficient power base to match the military and economic power of the US and the SU to claim a great-power status. His basic foreign policy premise was therefore that France could acquire a forceful international position only by seeking French diplomatic and military independence from the two superpowers. As he has expressed in his much-quoted statement: 'France defends herself, by herself, for herself and in her own way' (Hayward, 1983: 273). To achieve such a military self-reliance, de Gaulle created an independent French nuclear force (*force de frappe*), which would become the symbol of French independence. It was de Gaulle's conviction that nuclear independence could establish France again as a major world power, since nuclear weapons were the major source of military power and the principal basis of international influence (Freedman, 1981: 313; Hayward, 1983: 273).

De Gaulle also opposed the reliance of former French governments on the Atlantic alliance and believed that in order to achieve self-reliance it was necessary to withdraw the French forces from NATO's military command. The French leader believed that the alliance was in fact dominated by a British–American directorate, as a result of which French national interests were subordinated to Anglo-American interests. In his view the disadvantages of NATO membership outweighed the benefits of membership. This belief was reinforced by the American and British rejection in 1958 of his proposal to form a tripartite directorate within NATO that would include the US, Britain and France. It would have enabled France to deal on an equal footing with the US and Britain and would lead to a greater French involvement in all matters of international security. In a number of consecutive decisions the French leader demonstrated France's independence of the US. It began in 1959 with the French refusal to allow the Americans to stockpile tactical nuclear weapons on French soil and to place in France American intermediate-range ballistic missiles armed with nuclear warheads under American control. In addition, de Gaulle rejected in 1962 the American proposal to establish within NATO a Multilateral Nuclear Force. The friction between France and the US culminated in the decision of the French leader in 1966 to withdraw French military forces from NATO's command and to place them under an independent French authority, even though France remained formally a member of the Atlantic alliance.

A major incentive for the French military withdrawal from NATO was the American advocacy in 1962 of a new NATO strategy of 'flexible response', replacing an early use of nuclear weapons in reaction to a Soviet attack by an early response with conventional forces. The proposed strategy affirmed in French eyes the unreliability of the American nuclear guarantee and reinforced the general French doubt about American readiness to take the necessary risks for a defence of Europe with nuclear weapons if its own homeland were at stake (Freedman, 1981: 313–24). However, as Henry Kissinger has rightly stated, de Gaulle's decisions were not shaped by a principled anti-American position. De Gaulle's uncompromising style of diplomacy was rather guided by a single-minded devotion to the French national interest. He refused therefore to subordinate France's security to the interests of the

US, but was ready to collaborate with the Americans whenever the interests of the two countries converged (Kissinger, 1994: 606–7). De Gaulle, for instance, criticized the American military intervention in Vietnam but supported the US during the Cuban missile crisis in 1962. He disapproved of the bilateral arms control negotiations between the US and the SU which he considered as a *tête-à-tête* between the two superpowers, but sought a rapprochement with the Americans after the Russian invasion of Czechoslovakia in 1968.

The Europeanization of NATO

The basic Gaullist conception of France's diplomatic independence and nuclear self-reliance has been endorsed by de Gaulle's successors after his resignation in 1969. Pompidou, Giscard d'Estaing, Chirac and even the socialist President Mitterrand accepted the Gaullist legacy. In spite of the heavy costs of maintaining an independent nuclear force, all of them kept the *force de frappe* as a symbol of France's independence. However, his successor adopted a more pragmatic approach to NATO. After the invasion of Czechoslovakia the French leaders came to realize that the defence of France and the defence of western Europe were indivisible and adjusted the French military strategy to that of NATO. The new French military strategy of a gradual response and active defence supplemented NATO's strategy of flexible response and forward defence. French military units were also allowed to participate in NATO exercises, although the French troops remained under French national command outside NATO's control (Hanrieder and Auton, 1980: 111–14). The fact that the French leaders remained preoccupied with the French obsession with its independence from NATO came again to the foreground during the intergovernmental negotiations on the TEU that coincided with the end of the cold war, when Mitterrand challenged the predominance of NATO in European security.

The French policy makers strongly believed at that time that the revised European security environment, as a consequence of the disintegration of the SU and the breakdown of the Warsaw pact, would lead in the long term to the collapse of NATO. This offered France a unique opportunity to seek a broad institutional context for the organization of a common European defence with an autonomous European security identity. To that purpose the French policy makers followed a twofold strategy. In the context of the intergovernmental negotiations over the proposed European Union, the French initiated the revival of the WEU as the future common defence framework of the proposed EU. At the same time the French pushed from within NATO for a restructuring of the Atlantic alliance which would legitimize the evolving role of the EU and the WEU in the new European defence structures and would lead to a diminishing military role for the US in European security and defence.

Mitterrand clearly used the intergovernmental negotiations among the EC member-states on economic, monetary and political union in 1991 to launch several proposals that would allow the European Council and the Council of Ministers to deal with common defence issues and would make the WEU an integral part of the European unification process. In the final negotiations on the TEU the French had to water down their ambition to make the WEU the sole military arm of the EU, but with German backing they were successful in opening up the prospects for a future integration of the WEU into the EU (cf. Laursen and Vanhoonacker, 1992: 122–5). The French managed to incorporate in the TEU an indication that the newly established CFSP would also deal with all questions related to the security of the Union, including the eventual framing of a common defence policy which might in time lead to a common defence. The WEU, which was referred to as an integral part of the development of the Union, was requested to elaborate and implement decisions and actions of the Union that have defence implications. NATO as such was given no specific role although the TEU assured the EU members that were also NATO members that the CFSP would respect their obligations under the North Atlantic Treaty and that the CFSP would be compatible with the common security and defence policy established within the NATO framework (TEU, Article J.4). In that way the French policy makers laid down a fundament for the creation of an autonomous European defence structure outside the NATO framework which goes beyond the British wish to limit the establishment of a common European defence to the strengthening of the European pillar within NATO.

Within NATO, where the French were actively involved in the discussions over the restructuring of NATO, the French pressed for a recognition by NATO of the development of the EU's own joint defence, the so-called European Security and Defence Identity (ESDI). The French also suggested a division of labour between NATO and the WEU, according to which NATO would continue to take care of the Soviet threat, while the WEU would be responsible for the limited new threats (like the one in former Yugoslavia). The French, with the support of the Germans who were always quick to emphasize that such an ESDI would not weaken but rather strengthen the transatlantic solidarity, received indeed on several occasions the blessings of the alliance for the development of such an ESDI, which the US in particular considered to be the European pillar within NATO. But the US and the other NATO partners were much more critical over the proposed relationship between NATO and the WEU. Such a relationship should indeed be complementary but it should not lead to a separate European military structure which would be an expensive duplication of NATO (de Wijk, 1997: 25). The US actually introduced the Combined Joint Task Force (CJTF) concept that allowed the WEU to use collective assets of NATO for WEU operations undertaken by the European allies in pursuit of their CFSP. The American initiative had to encourage a development of 'separable but not separate' capabilities which could respond to European desire to develop its own defence capability (de Wijk, 1997: 80). Moreover, the French had to witness that NATO under American leadership, instead of becoming irrelevant because of a diminishing Soviet threat, was able to adapt to the changed security situation by taking responsibility for new defence tasks like crisis management, peacekeeping, peace enforcement and humanitarian operations in Europe and outside the original NATO area.

Notwithstanding French rhetoric about the separate ESDI and the French sponsorship of the WEU as a rival to NATO and its potential successor, in recent years the French have started a process of gradual reintegration into NATO. The French policy makers had to realize that NATO will not fade away simply because the cold war came to an end – on the contrary. After the successful adaptation of NATO to the new security environment, the French had to recognize that, given the unwillingness of the crucial military partners, Britain and Germany, to support the replacement of NATO by the WEU, NATO, not the WEU, will continue to be the prominent defence organization in Europe. Thus, almost three decades after the French military withdrawal from the Atlantic alliance, the Gaullist President Chirac had to conclude that 'the necessary rebalancing of relations within the Atlantic Alliance, relying on existing European institutions as the WEU, can only take place from the inside, not against the United States, but in agreement with it' (cited in Howorth and Menon, 1997: 34). Since the French reorientation towards NATO is closely related to the French experience in former Yugoslavia, we will discuss this process of reintegration in more detail later in this chapter.

Germany: from dependency to partnership in leadership

The relationship between Germany and the US was dominated over the five post-war decades by the security needs of Germany. Since the US was, in the view of successive German governments, the only superpower that could counterbalance the military power of the SU, in the cold war period the German leaders had in fact little other choice than the cultivation of a close relationship with the American ally. Only an American military commitment to the defence of Germany and western Europe and a linkage to the American nuclear deterrence could offer West Germany a security guarantee against a military threat from the SU. A German independent nuclear deterrence power was out of the question as West Germany took upon itself the obligation to refrain from the production of nuclear weapons. The option of a policy of declared neutralism was rejected by the West German government in the first postwar years.

The process that would lead to West Germany's accession to NATO was triggered by the outbreak of the war in Korea in 1950, when both the Americans and the British wanted the Federal Republic to participate as soon as possible in the defence of its eastern borderline – a contribution that the Federal Republic's first postwar Chancellor Konrad Adenauer was willing to make. Adenauer also understood that the whole issue of rearmament could not be considered in terms of an independent West German army, as West Germany's rearmament was only possible on the condition that the newly established West German army would be placed under international supervision. The first scheme in the form of a European Defence Community (EDC), which was basically a French design aimed at restraining Germany from making independent use of its military troops, failed to acquire the approval of the French national assembly. To make the West German participation in the defence of western Europe acceptable to the French, the Germans joined the WEU which was linked to NATO, hence facilitating the admission of West Germany to NATO (Hanrieder and Auton, 1980: 4–7).

Although the German army was the backbone of NATO's conventional forces on the front line between East and West, during the whole cold war period West Germany failed to gain equality with the Americans on security matters. The West

German government had to accept the presence in Germany of a large number of tactical nuclear weapons systems over which they had no control at all, since the nuclear warheads remained under American control. The Germans had also very little say in the American change in military strategy in the 1960s from massive retaliation to that of flexible response which was adopted by NATO in 1967. The new emphasis upon conventional forces instead of nuclear weapons enabled NATO to respond to a conventional attack from the East without the need for an immediate use of nuclear weapons, but it also raised some questions about the credibility of the American nuclear guarantee. As in France, also in Germany the question of American willingness to use its own nuclear weapons against the SU in the event of an attack against western Europe has been a recurring concern. After the two superpowers had reached a nuclear parity, thus increasing the American vulnerability to Soviet nuclear weapons, the distrust of American readiness to risk a nuclear retaliation from the SU for the sake of Germany has even intensified. German politicians followed with great suspicion the debate among American policy makers and academics about the first use of nuclear weapons in Europe. In fact they told the West Europeans that they could no longer count on an American nuclear commitment to the defence of Europe. Some even argued that the nuclear commitment had made the alliance more of a liability to the US than an asset (cf. Hanrieder, 1989: 63–82).

But the West German leaders took a more assertive attitude towards the question of the credibility of the American nuclear guarantee in the mid-1970s, when the Germans and the rest of western Europe were faced with a Soviet expansion of its modernized intermediate-range nuclear forces. The Germans were the first to demand in NATO an appropriate Western reaction to the Russian challenge. The outcome was the so-called NATO double-track decision of 1979, which stated an American commitment to deploy in Germany (and, on German insistence, also in a number of other western European countries) the new intermediate-range weapon system of ground-launched cruise missiles and to replace the existing intermediate missiles with a modernized version. The same decision contained also, at the insistence of Germany and other western European governments, an offer to the SU to negotiate an arms control agreement on intermediate nuclear weapons. The arms control proposal was made even more attractive later by the proposal to destroy the entire category of American and Soviet intermediate missiles. This so-called zero option was indeed the ultimate outcome of the negotiations. As Risse-Kappen has suggested, NATO's double-track decision can be seen as the first decision in NATO where the West Europeans, and West Germany in particular, were directly involved in an American nuclear decision affecting Europe. This participation in the US decision making far exceeded the usual consultation and gave the West German government, for the first time, the right of veto (Risse-Kappen, 1988: 179–80).

The unforeseen ending of the cold war and the unexpected realization of German unification offered Germany the opportunity to restructure its relationship with the US. As the military threat from the SU faded away, the military dependency of Germany on the American military resources and nuclear deterrence, which predominated this relationship over the first five postwar decades, could be replaced by a much more balanced relationship. In 1989 President Bush himself offered the

German leaders 'partnership in leadership' (Smith, Paterson, Merkel and Padgett, 1992: 144). With this new watchword in the transatlantic rhetoric, the US clearly upgraded its relationship with Germany, giving Germany at least the privileged position that Britain used to enjoy.

Balancing between the WEU and NATO

Besides the change in the German–American relationship, the ending of the cold war has also modified the German attitude towards NATO. The removal of the Soviet threat placed the importance of NATO for the security of Germany in a completely different context. In the cold war days only the integrated defence of NATO and only the American nuclear commitment provided through NATO could give Germany the security it needed. The new security environment has placed the whole issue of conventional and nuclear warfare in Europe in a different perspective and, as a consequence, has made the continued existence of NATO questionable. In the debate among its two large partners, Britain and France, about the question of whether NATO should remain the most important European military organization or that the WEU should develop into an autonomous defence organization, linked to the EU but independent of NATO, Germany has chosen a middle-of-the-road position. Germany is still fully integrated in NATO. Almost all the German forces have been assigned to an integrated NATO command and national military planning is subjected to NATO. As a matter of fact, Germany is the only country in the world without a general staff that exercises full command over its military forces. German leaders have therefore always considered their relationship to NATO not in terms of autonomy in the conduct of its defence policy, but in terms of the security the alliance provided through the American commitment to NATO (Howorth and Menon, 1997: 56–8). This has not changed after German unification. Germany continues to consider NATO the main military organization in Europe and it still wants to keep the vital role of the US within NATO, which would preserve the American nuclear commitment to its European NATO partners. The German leaders could of course exchange the American nuclear deterrent for a French nuclear deterrent or encourage the development of a French–British nuclear force as a nucleus of a future European nuclear deterrent. But this is, in German eyes, no more appealing, since this would mean the trading of one nuclear dependence for another. Although the German leaders can never be sure that the US will use its nuclear weapons to defend Germany, the chances that France or Britain will risk a nuclear war for the defence of Germany are even less. In addition, a security dependence on France would cause a radical change in the nature of the Franco-German alliance, which has always been based on equality between the two partners.

But at the same time the German leaders have been, with France, the motor behind the CFSP which implies the development of a military dimension. However, in German eyes, the development of a European defence identity does not exclude the continuation of full military integration within NATO. The German leaders truly believe that the different views of the British and the US on the one hand and that of France on the other over the restructuring of European defence could be reconciled. They actually took it upon themselves to serve as an intermediary between the French and the British and Americans, but with a clear intention to bring France closer to NATO. So for example the Eurocorps, which was created by Germany and France to embody the aspiration of a European defence identity, was placed in 1993 under NATO command (Howorth and Menon, 1997: 51–2). Also in the controversy among the EU partners over the future role of the WEU in the proposed common defence policy Germany clearly fulfils the role of a bridge builder between the opposing French and British views. Balancing between the NATO option and WEU option, Germany pursues a middle course, supporting the development of the WEU as both the defence arm of the EU and the European pillar within NATO. In the German view the WEU is not a substitute for NATO but a link between NATO and the EU. In this respect the concept of Combined Joint Task Forces which makes NATO resources available to the WEU fits exactly the German conviction that the WEU and NATO do not preclude each other.

The experience in former Yugoslavia

With hindsight we may say that the aspiration of the EU to solve on its own the crisis in former Yugoslavia, as indicated at the beginning of this chapter, was too high, and that the expectation of the EU leaders that they would be able to deal with the escalating conflict simply by diplomatic mediation and conference diplomacy, backed by economic measures, was mistaken. The EU and its member-states indeed missed the chance to make the management of the crisis in former Yugoslavia the hour of Europe. Again with the benefit of hindsight, we may conclude that the failure of the EU to fulfil a decisive role in resolving the conflict on its own doorstep had very much to do with the lack of both a political will and a military capability to reinforce its political authority. The EU as such was reluctant to use intimidation in the form of a limited use of military force in order to get the parties involved in the conflict to comply with the EU wishes. This is what Alexander George calls 'coercive diplomacy'. The general intent of coercive diplomacy is, according to George, to back a demand on an adversary with a threat of punishment for non-compliance that will be credible enough to persuade him that it is in his interest to comply with the demand. In other words, to help persuade the opponent to back down, instead of the blunt use of force, just enough force is used to demonstrate resolution and to give credibility to the threat that greater force will be used if necessary (George and Simons, 1994: 2, 10).

At the start of the crisis in former Yugoslavia, provoked by the decision of both Slovenia and Croatia in June 1991 to break away from the Yugoslav federation and the attempt of the Serbs to prevent the disintegration of the country, the EU member-states were quite confident that they would be able to get the crisis under control simply through diplomatic mediation, using as leverage the trade agreements and the economic aid and financial help programmes, as well as their ability to deny the self-declared independent states international recognition. The initial success of the EU troika (comprising, at that time, the foreign ministers of the member-states that serve as the present, former and coming EU Presidency) to receive in July 1991 the agreement of all the parties concerned to a ceasefire which would be monitored by the EU, and to start negotiations over a political settlement of the new situation in Yugoslavia, reinforced this belief. On the basis of this agreement the EU tried to encourage a political dialogue between Slovenia, Croatia, Bosnia-Hercegovina, Macedonia, Montenegro and Serbia by means of a conference on Yugoslavia which was organized by the Dutch Presidency in The Hague in September 1991 under the chairmanship of Lord Carrington (a former British foreign minister and a former secretary-general of NATO).

The talks in The Hague could not prevent the reopening of the fighting, but it removed the resistance of the Serbian leadership to recognize the right of other republics in the Yugoslav federation to self-determination, on the condition of adequate arrangements for minorities including the possibility of special status for certain areas. The Serbian leadership, however, rejected an EU plan for a political settlement based on the existing borders of the republics, despite an EU threat that such a dismissal may lead to an EU recognition of the other republics and economic sanctions against Serbia. The EU plan offered in Serbian eyes insufficient autonomy to the Serb communities outside Serbia. They proposed an alternative plan for a 'mini-Yugoslavia' to include Serbia, Montenegro and any others who wanted to remain part of a Yugoslav federation. In addition, the large Serb enclaves in Croatia and Bosnia had to become 'autonomous federal units' (Gow, 1997: 53–60). The Serbian uncompromising attitude stalemated further negotiations and paved the way for the final recognition of Slovenia, Croatia, Bosnia and Macedonia by the EU.

At that early stage in the conflict in former Yugoslavia the first debate among the EU member-states began over a possible military intervention to enforce a peace settlement. The EU had already established in the summer of 1991 teams of unarmed ceasefire monitors, the so-called European Community Monitoring Mission (ECMM), to control the implementation of an agreed ceasefire and to mediate in the event of local violations of such a ceasefire. At that time France was planning for military intervention with the aim of ending the hostilities. In line with the French ambition to upgrade the WEU as the military arm of the EU, France proposed to its WEU partners in August 1992 and again in September that year to send to Yugoslavia a European peacekeeping force to supervise the ceasefire. France was, however, unable to win substantial support for this idea among the other WEU members. Especially Britain, whose participation in such a force would have been crucial, was very cautious towards any form of military intervention, arguing that such an intervention would probably need a large military force. On French insistence a WEU working group examined several options for a WEU intervention in Yugoslavia. A first option referred to logistic support for EC monitors which required 2,000 to 3,000 personnel. A second option, related to the escort and protection of monitors by armed military forces, involved 5,000 to 6,000 personal. A third option concerned a lightly armed peacekeeping force of between 4,500 and 5,000 military personnel and 3,000 to 5,000 additional monitors to police the ceasefire. A fourth option referred to a fully fledged peacekeeping force of 20,000 to 30,000 personnel. However, none of these options, which were considered by the WEU council at the end of September, was adopted (Gow, 1997: 160–2; Edwards, 1997: 186–7; Holland, 1997: 150–1, 169).

As the EU member-states were unable to agree on an armed peacekeeping force, they turned to the United Nations (UN), and the Security Council in particular, to take over the responsibility for the effort to impose a durable ceasefire backed by a UN peacekeeping force. This marked, in fact, the end of an independent EU intervention in former Yugoslavia. From then on any involvement of the EU member-states would be part of the international effort to seek a peaceful solution to the war in former Yugoslavia, through successive international conferences which were co-chaired by the EU and the UN, or by means of mediation carried out by a joint team composed of an EU and a UN representative. However, it is not our intention to review the diplomatic effort undertaken by the international community to cope with the war in former Yugoslavia, nor is it our purpose to examine the peacekeeping and the peace enforcement activities of the UN in former Yugoslavia. In what follows we will simply focus on some salient features of these activities, which may considered to be relevant for any attempt to set up a common European defence.

The first noticeable point is the crucial role that France and Britain have fulfilled in the creation of the UN Protection Force (UNPROFOR), which was originally created by the Security Council in February 1992 to support the implementation of the ceasefire agreement between Serbian and Croatian forces in Croatia, negotiated by the UN's secretary-general special envoy (the former American foreign minister Cyrus Vance). The two countries also made the largest contributions to UNPROFOR, in terms of military personnel as well as commanding officers, when the activities of UNPROFOR extended step-by-step to Bosnia and Macedonia. In Bosnia, which proved to be the most problematic of the three former Yugoslav republics, the UNPROFOR commanding officers were essentially French and British. From the experience in former Yugoslavia we may conclude that whatever the future organizational structure of a European common defence would be, the two countries would clearly form the backbone of any future European military force. Germany's active military commitment remained doubtful despite the removal of the formal objection to participation in peacekeeping operations. Germany's experience in the Second World War would probably continue to set limits to its military contribution to such an operation beyond that of general logistical and technical support.

A second remarkable characteristic of the experience in peacekeeping and peace enforcement military operations in former Yugoslavia is the central role that NATO has played in the actual conduct of these operations, which were formally carried out under the authority of the UN. NATO's Northern Army Group Forward Headquarters in Germany was in fact moved to Bosnia to form the UNPROFOR Command. It provided UNPROFOR with the necessary command infrastructure, experienced military staff and established working procedures to set up the military operations in former Yugoslavia. The enforcement of the naval sanctions against Serbia and Montenegro by a combined NATO–WEU task force in the Adriatic Sea and the Danube River was also based around NATO's Standing Naval Force Mediterranean. Moreover, the implementation of the no-flight zone over Bosnia, the close air support for UNPROFOR and the so-called UN 'safe areas' were all directed from a headquarters at a NATO air base in Italy (cf. Gow, 1997: 113, 130, 133).

The key role played by NATO in former Yugoslavia had an unintended consequence for the reintegration of France into NATO. Since German officers were not allowed to participate at that stage in UNPROFOR, due to the self-imposed restrictions of the German government on the deployment of German military personnel outside NATO's area, their vacant places in the Northern Army Group Headquarters were taken by French officers designated to UNPROFOR. Although the military operations of UNPROFOR were carried out in the name of the UN, the French, who also participated in the NATO-led maritime and air force operations, actually took part again in the military structure of NATO from which they withdrew in the mid-1960s. This development would have far-reaching consequences, as we will see in the next section, for the probable organization of a common European defence.

A third striking feature of the peacekeeping operations in former Yugoslavia is the unavoidable conclusion that a diplomatic resolution of a conflict requires the use of force to make a political demand more credible and to support a peacekeeping or peace enforcement operation. The peacekeeping operations in Croatia and Macedonia were more in line with the traditional peacekeeping tasks of maintaining a peace settlement by the presence along the ceasefire lines which separate the former belligerent parties or the active mediation in local conflicts. But the peacekeeping operations in Bosnia were much more complex. As Gow has argued, the tasks of armed protection of humanitarian convoys and the protection of UN-designated 'safe areas' required the explicit threat to use force and the capability to use force. UNPROFOR was allowed to use force in self-defence and had the authority to use force to enable the humanitarian convoys to reach their destination when attacked. However, the actual use of air force in support of the UNPROFOR ground troops and in defence of the 'safe areas' was limited due to the reluctance of the UN secretary-general and his representative in former Yugoslavia to rely on military means which may have jeopardized the UN position in Bosnia, as well as the fear of the governments that participated in UNPROFOR to endanger their troops on the ground (cf. Gow, 1997: 127–40). In retrospect we may say that the failure of the Europeans to stop the fighting in former Yugoslavia had little to do with a division among the EU member-states about their political objectives regarding the war in former Yugoslavia. They were quite united in their support of the peace plans and the diplomatic efforts on behalf of the EC/EU to push the parties concerned to agree to the peace proposals. Their failure had very much to do with the differences of approach towards the use of force to underscore their political demands for a peaceful solution. All in all, the basic disagreement between the French and the British (as well as the other EU members that delivered military troops to UNPROFOR) over the use of their ground forces to enforce the peace plans made their political credibility, and thus their chances of success, almost nil.

In the events where an unequivocal threat of the use of force was made, or a limited force had been employed in a decisive manner, it produced the desired outcome, as the response to the Sarajevo market square massacre on 5 February 1994 in the form of an ultimatum issued by NATO illustrates. In the ultimatum, which was a joint French–American proposal, NATO demanded that the Bosnian Serbs withdraw their heavy weapons at least 20 kilometres from the Bosnian capital

Sarajevo within ten days. Any heavy weapons still in place after the ten days' deadline would be destroyed by air strikes. The diplomatic negotiations that followed resulted, just before the end of the deadline, in the agreement of the Bosnian Serbs to withdraw their heavy weapons (Silber and Little, 1995: 343–53). The guns around Sarajevo were silenced for almost 18 months, until another mortar attack on the market place in Sarajevo on 28 August 1995. The immediate response was a sustained bombing campaign against the Bosnian Serbs.

The air strikes carried out by NATO airplanes were followed by an American diplomatic offensive, which actually started in May 1995 and was also supported by a bombing of ammunition dumps at the Bosnian Serb headquarters in Pale. After several years of abortive attempts by high-ranking representatives of the EC/EU and the UN to reach a settlement on an agreed division of Bosnia among the Bosnian Muslims, the Bosnian Serbs and the Bosnian Croats, the Americans – who actually stood on the sideline – decided to step into the Bosnian diplomatic quagmire to bring the fighting in Bosnia to an end. The American intensive shuttle diplomacy between the belligerent parties, accompanied by the use of NATO air power against Bosnian Serb strongholds and the deployment of a powerful rapid reaction force (composed of British, French and Dutch combat troops), made the talks at the American air base in Dayton possible. However, it should be said that the successful conclusion of the negotiations at the end of 1995 was also helped by the circumstances at that stage of the crisis in former Yugoslavia, namely, the readiness of the Serbian leadership to impose a settlement on the Bosnian Serbs to remove the sanctions against Serbia and Montenegro, and the Bosnian Serbs' loss of territory as a consequence of the shift in the military balance between the Croatian–Bosnian coalition and the Bosnian Serbs in favour of the former (Gow, 1997: 276–87).

The American success in ending the fighting in Bosnia, and the success of the NATO Implementation Force (IFOR) – to which the Americans made a substantive contribution – in enforcing the line of separation between the federation of Bosnia–Hercegovina and the Serb area, as agreed in the Dayton accords, stand in sharp contrast to the EU (and the UN) failure to have an important influence of its own on the developments in former Yugoslavia and the inability of UNPROFOR to prevent the fighting. It highlights the fourth noticeable point, namely the indispensability of the US and NATO for any security in Europe, in spite of the significant change in the nature of the security threat. As NATO's IFOR has proven so far in former Yugoslavia, while the WEU is almost non-existent, NATO is still the only military organization that has the capability of managing the new tasks of crisis management, peacekeeping and peace enforcement.

Separable but not separate

As the war in former Yugoslavia illustrates, the ending of the cold war has not jeopardized the position of NATO, which has remained the major forum for consultation on security issues between the US and the individual member-states. In the security field the EU member-states started to formulate a collective security policy only after the signing of the TEU. While the substance of the common defence policy is still vague and sometimes ambiguous, the general outline is less obscure. So is it clear that the member-states, for different reasons, want a continuing military presence of the US in Europe. Of the larger states Britain feels that, irrespective of the threat to European security, Europe needs the American military resources as long as the EU governments are unable to replace the American capabilities with European-based defence capabilities. Germany wants to prevent the renationalization of defence in western Europe and sees the continuation of a strong American presence in Europe as a guarantee for the conservation of the multinational defence framework that was established during the cold war period. Even France, which wants the Europeans to handle their defence on their own and considers the US more as a reserve force, nevertheless seeks a preservation of the American contribution to European security (Gebhard, 1994: 20–5). Also the other EU member-states want to preserve NATO as a forum for the transatlantic decision making in security matters and consider NATO as the essential organizational framework wherein the military cooperation with the US should be carried out. However, the US has lost its hegemonical position in NATO. Not only France but also Germany want to deal with the US on the basis of equality. Gone are the days when the US controlled NATO and NATO's strategic doctrines and military policies were in fact formulated in the US.

There is a consensus among the European members of NATO that the alliance should become more European in the sense that it should deal with European security problems from a European regional perspective rather than an American global view. Although the WEU is seen as the framework for the elaboration and implementation of decisions and actions of the EU that have defence implications, there is still no consensus over the integration of the WEU into the EU. Agreement has nevertheless developed over the making of the WEU the European pillar within NATO and the creation of a linkage between the WEU and NATO, but how decision making in the two organizations would be linked is still blurry. In practice NATO, which is at present the most integrated military organization in Europe, remains the main defence organization in Europe. Moreover, there is a broad consensus that as long as the WEU lacks a useful command and control system and is deprived of an adequate military infrastructure, the organizational structures of NATO are indispensable. The WEU members have agreed in principle on the building of a military command structure within the WEU which would provide the member-states with an autonomous decision-making centre to deal with international crises. But even France realizes that such an effort would need huge financial resources which at the moment no EU government is ready to generate. France also understands that none of the WEU members would be ready to contribute the necessary funds to give the WEU the operational capacity to conduct large-scale military operations, since such an investment in fact implies a duplication of the already existing infrastructure of NATO. This reality, combined with the French participation in NATO's command structure in former Yugoslavia, has led to a more flexible attitude from France towards NATO.

But the turning point in the French stance towards NATO has, however, been a result of the American willingness to endorse a significant change in the way the alliance manages its military operations. The US agreed in June 1996 to a restructuring of NATO that would allow the Europeans to take the lead of future NATO peacekeeping operations, in the event that American troops do not participate in such an operation. The creation of special headquarters, the so-called Combined Joint Task Forces (CJTF), for the management of specific military missions such as peacekeeping operations, opened the possibility of running a NATO operation under the political and strategic leadership of the WEU. Moreover, to carry out the military mission the WEU will be allowed to use military equipment borrowed from NATO, including American-owned intelligence and communication systems. Whenever American troops are part of such a combined joint task force, NATO (and in fact the US) keeps its control over NATO operations. As de Wijk has argued, the CJTF concept provided for the use of 'separable but not separate' NATO resources for WEU operations and in so doing gave further interpretation to the formation of a European Security and Defence Identity (de Wijk, 1997: 127). The CJTF concept was in fact already put into practice in the peacekeeping military operations in former Yugoslavia, where the French commanding officers of UNPROFOR have used the NATO command structure to conduct military operations.

The CJTF concept could have great significance for the set-up of a common European defence, as it offers a way out of the controversy between France and Britain over the prominence of either the WEU or NATO as the major defence organization in Europe. It satisfies the British (and German) call for closer military cooperation between NATO and the WEU and at the same time it reflects the French desire for a European identity within NATO. Although the French have not yet given up their position that the WEU should become in the long term the prominent defence organization of the EU, it seems that they have nevertheless come to the inescapable conclusion that only NATO has the capability to run a complex military operation and should therefore, at least in the short term, be kept as the major defence organization in Europe. Thus, the decision to create the CJTF could be the beginning of the setting up of a real European defence capability.

Chapter 9

The reality of European foreign policy making

In this concluding chapter I will reflect on the central question raised in the Introduction. As the reader may recall, it concerns the question as to whether the individual member-states dominate the common foreign policy making of the EU or whether the institutions and structures of foreign policy making in the EU dictate the foreign policy behaviour of the individual member-states. In answering this question we should keep in mind that international organizations do not simply happen. As David Chuter has argued, 'their structures, organization and working methods are generally imitated from national models, depending on who the founding nations are and what the power relationships are between them' (Howorth and Menon, 1997: 113).

The institutional setting

The analysis of the way that foreign policy is made in western Europe in the first part of this book leads to the conclusion that, in spite of the creation of an institutionalized framework for the making of a common foreign policy at the EU level, foreign policy making in western Europe is still the foreign policy of 15 nation-states rather than the foreign policy of one supranational state. The founding member-states, as well as those that joined the EC/EU in the successive enlargement rounds, were and actually still are very cautious in the transfer of sovereignty to the EU institutions. They have not only defined and limited very carefully the shift of sovereignty, but they have also structured the integrationist framework so as to preserve a balance of power within that structure in favour of the member-states (cf. Milward and Sorensen, 1993: 19). From the very beginning the member-states have ensured that it is not the European Commission, which was supposed to represent the supranational interest, but the Council of Ministers, which represents the interests of the national governments, that would be given ultimate control over the foreign and external policies of the EC. This has not changed over the years – on the contrary. In the area of the common trade policy, where the member-states had already moved much of their powers to the Commission when the EEC was created even though the final decisions on the common trade policies remained the competence of the Council, the member-states have become more restrictive in the extension of these powers of the Commission to new trade areas such as services and intellectual property.

The concern about the loss of sovereignty has very much determined the resistance of most member-states to the merger of the EPC and the later CFSP into the EC structure, as this would have made it much more difficult to prevent the extension of the system of qualified majority voting to the CFSP. While all member-states recognize the need to improve the performance of the EU in the CFSP area, the member-states hold very diverse opinions on the introduction of qualified majority voting in the CFSP field. Many share the view that a government must be free to act in defence of its national interests whenever such an interest is at stake. A system of qualified majority voting is, in this view, an infringement of the ability of a government to advance and protect national interests, especially in the highly sensitive field of national security. Not only large states like Britain and France, but also smaller states like Denmark and Greece, consider qualified majority voting in CFSP matters a real threat to national sovereignty as it would end the government freedom of action or would force it to accept an obligation that the government does not support. Many member-states argue, for instance, that decisions on military missions, involving the sending of armed forces to war zones, could be taken only by national governments, not by a majority in the European Council of Ministers. In particular the member-states that practice a policy of neutrality consider the preservation of the present system of unanimous voting to be the best safeguard to make sure that decisions in the CFSP area take proper account of vital national interests. However, we witness some change in the unwillingness of most member-states to subject decision making in the CFSP field to the rule of qualified majority voting. A key member-state like France, which used to hold strongly to the idea that it is the national interest rather than the European interest (whatever this may be) that should be the guiding principle of French foreign policy, has modified its traditional objection to any revision in the existing voting rule of unanimity in CFSP matters. In the run-up to the intergovernmental negotiations over the Treaty of Amsterdam, Germany, which is an outspoken supporter of a movement towards majority voting in CFSP matters, managed to receive the support of France for a German idea – the so-called 'constructive abstention' concept – which offers a way out of the paralysing vetoes in the CFSP. As we discussed in Chapter 5 the member-states have agreed to employ more flexibility in the application of the veto right, which means a real breakthrough in the stalemated positions of the member-states regarding the introduction of qualified majority voting to the CFSP area. Even Britain, which still sticks to the principle that unanimity should remain the norm in all CFSP issues, did not oppose the new decision rule which allows those member-states that are unwilling to take part in a particular joint action (and find themselves in a minority) to abstain rather than block further decision making, although the use of a veto is still permissible.

Although the member-states are unlike one another in form of government, the national styles of foreign policy making have clearly affected the way the member-states have organized their common foreign policy making at the European level. From the description of the mode of foreign policy making at both the national level and the European level in Chapters 4 and 5, we may conclude that the style of foreign policy making in the larger EU member-states in particular has led to a development whereby the European Council and the Council of Ministers rather than the European Commission have emerged as the key actors in the making of the Union's foreign policy. In France, Britain and Germany the head of state or government plays a central role in the formulation of the country's foreign policy. Although the smaller member-states reveal more diversity in the role of the prime minister in the making of foreign policy, in many of these countries the head of government also fulfils a prominent function in the management of his country's foreign policies. The predominance of the national leaders in the larger states in the making of national foreign policies and the increasing prominence in this respect of government leaders in the smaller states is reflected in the dominant position that the European Council of heads of state and government has acquired in shaping the common foreign policy at the EU level. It is noticeable that those smaller countries where the prime minister traditionally plays a more modest part in the making of foreign policy have not prevented the development of the European Council into the pivotal policy-making body of the EU.

All the institutional innovations that were meant to improve the international performance of the EU as a single actor have not weakened the control of the chiefs of state and government over the common foreign policy of the EU. Although the TEU has given the Commission an associated role in the CFSP area, the former EPC secretariat which, under the provisions of the TEU, had to be included in the institutional framework of the EU, has been interwoven in the administrative machinery of the Council of Ministers instead of the bureaucratic apparatus of the Commission. To frustrate a development of the CFSP unit into an autonomous policy-making body that would form the nucleus of a future European foreign ministry, the permanent officials of the CFSP unit from the Council secretariat (who are supposed to act independently of the government of their country of origin) were matched by an equal number of national civil servants, sent on secondment to the CFSP unit from the diverse national ministries of foreign affairs. Most member-states wanted the CFSP unit in the Council secretariat to be just an administrative unit that would provide assistance to the Political Committee, composed of the political directors of the national foreign ministries. The same procedure is applied in the implementation of the more recent decision to create a CFSP analysis and planning unit, that will contribute to a better planning and analysis of the common foreign policies and in that way will give more substance to the CFSP. This unit is also located within the Council secretariat, even though officials from the Commission are not excluded from participation in the work of this CFSP analysis and planning unit. But even the creation of the CFSP unit and the CFSP analysis and planning unit has not eroded the prominent role of the Political Committee in the definition of foreign policy options and the implementation of agreed policies. In practice the political directors of the foreign ministries in the member-states still bear the main responsibility for managing the CFSP.

The decision to appoint a High Representative for the CFSP – the so-called Mr or Mrs CFSP – designed to improve and strengthen the coherence and continuity in the representation of the EU to the outside world, also secures the continuing predominance of the member-states in the making of the CFSP. The High Representative (a civil servant or a heavyweight politician) is nominated by the European Council from which he also receives his instructions. He is answerable to the Council of Ministers and is not allowed to make any decisions in CFSP matters on his own. The creation of the position of High Representative reflects not only the continuing tendency to keep power in the CFSP well away from the Commission, but it also illustrates how little most member-states are concerned about the position of the Commission in the foreign policy area and how little support the Commission enjoys for its ambition to obtain a greater role in the making of the Union's foreign policy.

The common policies

National considerations have also determined the commitment of the member-states to reach agreement on common positions and to implement joint actions. The importance of safeguarding the individual interests of the member-states and their tendency to define issues in terms of national interests have constrained the member-states in their ability to formulate a common foreign policy. However, in issue areas where the member-states, and especially the 'big three', were able to reach agreement on a set of consensually based rules for action, based on a common set of shared goals and agreed criteria for joint actions, namely the common policy towards the Middle East conflict and peace process as well as the common policy towards the transformation in eastern Europe, the common policies moved over the years from vagueness to clarity.

Genuine national interests have driven the member-states to agree on a common policy towards the Arab–Israeli conflict and the Middle East peace process. As demonstrated in Chapter 6, France, the major architect behind the building of a European consensus on a common policy towards the Arab–Israeli conflict, was led from the very beginning by a mixture of political and economic interests. The French support for the Arab demand for a full withdrawal of Israel from Arab territories occupied during the June war of 1967 and the Palestinian right to self-determination was part of a French strategy to break with the support of former French governments to Israel and to distance itself from the American Middle East policy. In that way France wanted to strengthen its leverage in the acquisition of oil agreements in the oil-producing Arab countries and the export of French arms and other goods to the Middle East.

Britain, like France, had a vested interest in protecting and promoting its commercial and financial interests in the fast-growing markets of the oil-exporting Arab countries. Although the British did not want to undermine the American policy in the Middle East, they had little interest in helping France, its main European competitor in the Arab world, to become the champion of the Arab cause in Europe. To maintain their goodwill in the Arab countries the British felt compelled to take a more pro-Arab attitude towards a settlement of the Arab–Israeli dispute. While the Americans tried to balance the Arab demand for Israeli withdrawal from the occupied territories against the Israeli requirement of peace and security, a policy that the Arabs perceived as pro-Israel since it neglected the Arab demand for Palestinian state-hood, the British were ready to acknowledge the right of the Palestinians to have some sort of a Palestinian homeland as part of an overall Arab–Israeli settlement.

The other European countries, Germany and the Netherlands in particular, joined France and Britain in this so-called even-handed policy towards the Arab–Israeli conflict only after the Arabs decided in 1973 to use the oil weapon against those countries that they perceived as pro-Israel. The German interest in securing the free flow of oil from the Middle East and the Dutch interest in lifting the Arab oil embargo against the Netherlands caused Germany and the Netherlands, which in the initial days of EPC refused to accommodate themselves to the French views on the desired settlement, to move towards a more pro-Arab position. In their ambition to create the right political conditions for the activities of German and Dutch business in the Arab world, these two traditional supporters of Israel and loyal partners of the US went, step by step, as far as supporting the Palestinian aspiration to have an independent state and recognizing the PLO as the representative of the Palestinian people. Thus, it is obvious that naked national interests were the driving force behind the willingness of the member-states to establish a common policy towards the Arab–Israeli conflict, even if it has limited their own range of permiss-ible options to deal with that conflict.

As we illustrated in Chapter 7, Germany is committed to an enlargement of the EU to the east as a result of historical responsibility and a mixture of geopolitical and economic interests. The legacy of the Second World War, the chance to re-cover its position as the central power on the European continent and the economic opportunities for German business and industry in the east, have made Germany the motor behind the developing consensus among EU members over the need to integrate the countries of central Europe in the EU. But at the same time the Germans realize that an institutional adjustment and the alteration of certain cur-rent common policies are necessary preconditions for such an enlargement. Being already the largest net contributor to the EU budget, the Germans are reluctant to bear the main financial responsibility of such an enlargement. Britain and the other northern member-states are also driven by a special responsibility for the economic and democratic stability in central and eastern Europe. Like Germany they consider the prospect of EU membership the best incentive for the continuation of the democratization process and the strengthening of the free market in the central and eastern European countries. But Britain's support of the integration of these coun-tries into the EU is motivated by an additional purely selfish British interest as well. The British believe that an enlargement to the east will complicate the func-tioning of the EU and will set limits to the ability of the EU to decide on common policies. Thus, in the British view a larger Union will not only water down the move towards deeper integration but it will also open the perspective for a looser union, whereby EU membership does not require participation and cooperation in all areas. As a matter of fact the British, who have always wanted the EC/EU to be simply a single market, see any enlargement of the EU as the best safeguard against an ever closer Union.

The reasoning behind the French reluctant attitude to a fast enlargement to the east, which is shared by the other southern member-states, lies also in sheer national interest. The French and the other Mediterranean members fear that such an enlargement, which will bring into the EU a number of relatively poor countries with a huge agricultural sector, will lead to an immense reduction in the money transferred from the EU budget to the farmers in the southern member-states and will result in severe cuts in the funds that the less developed southern regions of the Union receive from the collective resources of the EU. However, Germany has managed to build a consensus among all member-states on a common policy towards the central and eastern European countries that bridges the gap that separates those member-states that are in favour of a fast accession of the central and eastern European states and those that want to delay the expansion to the east. It consists of an agreement in principle on an enlargement to the east, but at the same time it acknowledges that the entry of any new members, including countries from the east, could take place only when the present 15 members have accomplished a reform of the existing decision-making structure of the EU that would make an enlarged Union manageable, and not before an applicant meets the qualifications for membership. In practice this means a waiting time of several years followed by a lengthy accession period.

Their common policy towards the Arab–Israeli conflict and the Middle East peace process helped the member-states to build a distinguished international identity, while their common policy towards the transformation in central and eastern Europe has made them a powerful regional actor. The member-states had, however, great difficulty in the setting up of a common defence policy, the lack of which accounts to a large extent for the impotence of the EU during the war in former Yugoslavia. As we saw in Chapter 8, France and Britain, the major players in this respect, have conflicting views over the desired structure of a common European defence and the role of the US and NATO in this connection, rooted in opposing beliefs over the desired nature of the Atlantic partnership. While Britain wants to keep NATO as the foundation of any future European defence structure and regards a strong US commitment to European security as the bedrock of European security, France has always pressed for a separate European defence organization which can act independently of the US.

However, as we argued in Chapter 8, the inability and unwillingness of the other European partners to duplicate the existing NATO military structure, the restructuring of NATO and the introduction of the CJTF concepts which allows the use of NATO resources for peacekeeping military operations under a European commanding officer, as well as the French participation in the NATO peacekeeping and peace enforcement military operations in former Yugoslavia, have marked a reintegration of France into the military structure of NATO and has opened the prospect of a linkage between the WEU and NATO which will help to set up the missing European military capability.

It is noteworthy, in this connection, that the larger and powerful member-states rather than the smaller member-states have clearly left their finger prints on the formation of the European common foreign policies. Whenever France, Germany and Britain were able to reach agreement on a common stand, the EU came forward with a unified position. This has been the case with respect to the common policies towards the Arab–Israeli conflict and the transformation in eastern Europe. If these three countries were unable to compromise then the EU lacked a collective stance, as the absence of a common policy towards the setting up of a common defence illustrates. In other words, the willingness of the three larger states in particular to converge their different national interests in the various issue areas has in fact dictated the extent to which the member-states were able to project a single European view on the global stage. Thus, notwithstanding the consensus rule in CFSP matters, in practice the foreign policy preferences of the larger states sets the limits to the common foreign policy options, to which the smaller member-states have to adjust. In a similar way the three larger states also play a principal role in shaping the institutional structure of the European foreign policy decision regime. Whenever the powerful French–German coalition has received the approval of Britain for additional procedural rules or supplementary organizational arrangements to improve the machinery of common foreign policy making, progress is made in the institutionalization of the foreign policy decision regime. Of course the agreement between the three larger states could be blocked by a veto of a smaller state, but the smaller member-states have actually little other choice than to go along with the consensus reached among the three larger states. Does this mean that the EU is in fact moving towards an informal triangular directorate responsible for the framing of a European foreign policy? It seems that this is indeed the case, although France and Britain have not completely given up their perceived right to act in defence of their own national interests when it suits them. But France, Germany and even Britain came to realize that acting in concert as leaders of a unified European bloc, with the economic weight of the EU as an important power resource, will allow them to exercise more influence on the global stage than individually.

Does the European foreign policy decision regime matter?

This brings us to the fundamental question of whether the European foreign policy decision regime created and shaped by the EU member-states matters. Before I deal with this question it is important to bring forward an observation made by Friedrich Kratochwil concerning the casual influence of rules in shaping behaviour. Discussing the impact of international regimes, Kratochwil reminds us that although international regimes obviously influence interaction patterns, they do not influence behaviour in the manner of antecedent causes. The relationship is not one in which a factor X causes Y. Kratochwil rejects the notion that regimes exist and influence decisions only if they satisfy the regulatory requirement of being a constraint. Although rules do have a regulative role, and as such have a casual influence in shaping behaviour, rules have in his view a constitutive function as well which has to be taken into consideration in judging the influence of regimes (Ruggie, 1993: 459–60). Keeping these remarks in mind, the question of whether the European foreign policy decision regime matters may then be answered in the affirmative. Although the European foreign policy decision regime is not always the direct cause of foreign policy outcomes in western Europe, it does make a difference in an indirect way by influencing the interaction patterns among the member-states in two ways.

First, the decision regime mediates the foreign policy outcomes that the member-states produce at the EU level. It helps to settle differences between member-states over the desired common position in specific foreign policy issues, by trying to find things to which they can agree. This does not always have to result in a consensus along the lowest common denominator; it might also lead to a consensus by persuasion, whereby one or more countries are convinced to accept a common position which they were at first unwilling to do. Second, once established, the structure of common foreign policy making at the EU level is conceived as a constraint on foreign policy making at the national level. The member-states not only adapt their own national views to that of the others, but they also comply with the common positions and joint actions agreed upon in a specific issue area, once the member-states manage to reach a consensus on such a common position or a joint course of action. Although one may argue that the Arab use of the oil weapon would have changed the foreign policies of Germany and the Netherlands towards the Arab–Israeli conflict irrespective of the existence of the EPC, it is clear that the EPC framework was not used simply as an alibi to legitimize that change. The EPC framework actually became the decisive institutional framework wherein the western European powers were able to resolve their divergent views *vis-à-vis* the Middle East conflict. As we have seen, the agreed common positions over the desired settlement of the Arab–Israeli conflict became also the parameters of the national foreign policies in this respect.

The close examination of the interaction at the national and EU levels in the three case studies allows us to draw the conclusion that the member-states also follow strictly the formal procedural rules and observe the informal procedural rules for common foreign policy making. The major principles of the common Middle East policy and the basic components of the collective policy towards eastern Europe were indeed formulated and expressed by the European Council. It is during the meetings of the heads of state and government in the European Council that the major knots were cut and the guidelines for the common foreign policy were defined. The role of the Council of Ministers in the two related areas has been essentially to search for common ground in advance of the meetings of the European Council and to take the major decisions that would put the agreed principles into effect afterwards. In the intervals between the regular Council meetings the member-states made a real effort to harmonize their national views with respect to the two issue areas. Consultations between the member-states on all levels, aimed at the formation and presentation of a common stand in the two specific issues, have become a habit. Unilateral actions in these issue areas have become rather an exception. Even though the distinction between the political and economic aspects of foreign policy issues had become blurred, the Council of Ministers and the Commission have observed nevertheless a rigid division of labour in the preparation as well as the implementation of the agreed common policies. The Council of Ministers and the Presidency (assisted by the machinery of the Council's secretariat) have dealt almost exclusively with all the issues where political and security considerations predominated, whereas the Commission and its officials have played a prominent part only when economic questions prevailed. So the Commission was heavily involved in the groundwork regarding the common strategy towards the transformation in eastern Europe and the management of the common economic help programmes, but had much less interference with the framing of the common positions towards the Arab–Israeli conflict and the Middle East peace process or the common positions regarding the war in former Yugoslavia.

To round up, this book has illustrated that the European Union's foreign policy is more than the sum of the foreign policy of its member-states. The interaction among the member-states has created a structure at the European level, which does not shape the behaviour of the individual states but has clearly imposed some constraints on the substance and the process of foreign policy making in the individual member-states. This means that the conclusion we drew earlier in this chapter, that foreign policy outcomes and foreign policy making in western Europe are still dominated by the national states, has to be modified. It is obvious that the European foreign policy decision regime, which has been generated by the interacting member-states of the European Union, has affected to some extent the substance of national foreign policies as well as the way that foreign policy is made at the national level.

Bibliography

Agostini, M.V. (1990a) The role of Italian regions in formulating Community policy, *The International Spectator*, vol. 25, no. 2: 87–97.

Agostini, M.V. (1990b) Italy and its Community policy, *The International Spectator*, vol. 25, no. 4: 347–55.

Allen, D. and Pijpers, A. (eds) (1984) *European Foreign Policy-making and the Arab–Israeli Conflict* (The Hague: Martinus Nijhoff).

Almond, M. (1994) *Europe's Backyard War: The War in the Balkans* (London: Mandarin).

Archer, C. (1994) *Organizing Europe* (London: Edward Arnold).

Aronson, S. (1978) *Conflict and Bargaining in the Middle East: An Israeli Perspective* (Baltimore: Johns Hopkins University Press).

Aronson, S. (1992) *The Politics and Strategy of Nuclear Weapons in the Middle East: Opacity, Theory, and Reality, 1960–1991: An Israeli Perspective* (Albany: State University of New York Press).

Ash, T.G. (1993) *In Europe's Name: Germany and the Divided Continent* (London: Jonathan Cape).

Baldwin, D.A. (ed.) (1993) *Neorealism and Neoliberalism: The Contemporary Debate* (New York: Columbia University Press).

Beling, W. (ed.) (1986) *Middle East Peace Plans* (London: Croom Helm).

Blondel, J. and Müller-Rommel, F. (1988) *Cabinets in Western Europe* (London: Macmillan).

Booth, K. and Smith, S. (eds) (1995) *International Relations Theory Today* (Cambridge: Polity Press).

Brzezinski, Z. (1983) *Power and Principle* (New York: Farrar, Straus, Giroux).

Buchan, D. (1993) *Europe: The Strange Superpower* (Aldershot: Dartmouth).

Bull, H. (1977) *The Anarchical Society* (London: Macmillan).

Bulletin of the European Communities (Luxembourg: Office for Official Publications of the European Communities).

Bulmer, S. (1983) Domestic politics and European Community policy-making, *Journal of Common Market Studies*, vol. XXI, no. 4: 349–63.

Bulmer, S. (1991) Analysing EPC: the case for two-tier analysis, in M. Holland (ed.) *The Future of the European Political Cooperation* (London: Macmillan).

Bulmer, S. and Paterson, W. (1987) *The Federal Republic of Germany and the European Community* (London: Allen & Unwin).

Bulmer, S. and Paterson, W. (1988) European policy-making in the Federal Republic – internal and external limits to leadership, in *Federal Republic of Germany and the European Community: The Presidency and Beyond* (Bonn: Europa Union Verlag).

Bulmer, S. and Paterson, W. (1989) West Germany's role in Europe: man-mountain or semi-Gulliver?, *Journal of Common Market Studies*, vol. 28, no. 2: 95–117.

Büren, R. (1978) West German policy towards the Arab states, in I. Rabinovich and H. Shaked (eds) *From June to October: The Middle East between 1967 and 1973* (New Brunswick: Transaction Books).

Buzan, B. (1995) The level of analysis problem in international relations reconsidered, in K. Booth and S. Smith (eds) *International Relations Theory Today* (Cambridge: Polity Press).

Buzan, B., Jones, C. and Little, R. (1993) *The Logic of Anarchy: Neorealism to Structural Realism* (New York: Columbia University Press).

Carlsnaes, W. and Smith, S. (eds) (1994) *European Foreign Policy: The EC and Changing Perspectives in Europe* (London: Sage).

Christakis, M.G. (1993) *Greece and the European Community* (Canterbury: University of Kent).

Church, C.H. and Phinnemore, D. (1994) *European Union and European Community: A Handbook and Commentary on the Post-Maastricht Treaties* (Hemel Hempstead: Harvester Wheatsheaf).

Churchill, W.S. (1950) *The Second World War*, vol. 4 (Boston: Houghton Mifflin).

Cini, M. (1996) *The European Commission: Leadership, Organization and Culture in the EU Administration* (Manchester: Manchester University Press).

Clarke, M. (1992) *British External Policy-making in the 1990's* (London: Macmillan).

Cohen, R. (1981) *International Politics: The Rules of the Game* (London: Longman).

Danchev, A. and Halverson, T. (eds) (1996) *International Perspectives on the Yugoslav Conflict* (London: Macmillan).

Destler, I.M. (1972) *Presidents, Bureaucrats and Foreign Policy* (Princeton: Princeton University Press).

de Wijk, R. (1997) *Nato on the Brink of the New Millennium* (London: Brassey's).

Dinan, D. (1994) *Ever Closer Union? An Introduction to the European Community* (London: Macmillan).

Duff, A. (1997a) *Reforming the European Union* (London: Federal Trust).

Duff, A. (ed.) (1997b) *The Treaty of Amsterdam: Text and Commentary* (London: Federal Trust).

Duff, A., Pinder, J. and Pryce, R. (eds) (1994) *Maastricht and Beyond: Building the European Union* (London: Routledge).

Edwards, G. (1997) The potential and the limits of the CFSP: the Yugoslav example, in E. Regelsberger, P. Schoutheete de Tervarent and W. Wessels (eds) (1997) *Foreign Policy of the European Union: From EPC to CFSP and Beyond* (Boulder, CO: Lynne Rienner).

Edwards, G. and Pijpers, A. (eds) (1997) *The Politics of European Treaty Reform: The 1996 Intergovernmental Conference and Beyond* (London: Pinter).

Edwards, G. and Spence, D. (eds) (1994) *The European Commission* (London: Longman).

Europe Documents (Brussels: Agence Europe).

European Voice (Brussels: The Economist Group).

Evans, G. and Newnham, J. (1990) *The Dictionary of World Politics* (New York: Harvester Wheatsheaf).

Evans, P.B., Jacobson, H.K. and Putnam, R.D. (eds) (1993) *Double-Edged Diplomacy: International Bargaining and Domestic Diplomacy* (Berkeley: University of California Press).

Freedman, L. (1981) *The Evolution of Nuclear Strategy* (New York: St Martin's Press).

Fursdon, E. (1980) *The European Defence Community: A History* (London: Macmillan).

Gebhard, P.R.S. (1994) *The United States and European Security*, Adelphi Paper, No. 286 (London: The International Institute for Strategic Studies).

General Report on the Activities of the European Communities 1989 (1990) (Brussels: European Commission).

General Report on the Activities of the European Communities 1990 (1991) (Brussels: European Commission).

General Report on the Activities of the European Communities 1991 (1992) (Brussels: European Commission).

General Report on the Activities of the European Communities 1992 (1993) (Brussels: European Commission).

General Report on the Activities of the European Communities 1993 (1994) (Brussels: European Commission).

General Report on the Activities of the European Union 1994 (1995) (Brussels: European Commission).

General Report on the Activities of the European Union 1995 (1996) (Brussels: European Commission).

George, A.L. and McKeown, T. (1985) Case studies and theories of organizational decision making, in *Advances in Information Processing in Organizations*, vol. 2: 21–58.

George, A.L. and Simons, W.E. (eds) (1994) *The Limits of Coercive Diplomacy*, 2nd edn (Boulder, CO: Westview Press).

George, S. (1990) *An Awkward Partner: Britain in the European Community* (Oxford: Oxford University Press).

George, S. (ed.) (1992) *Britain and the European Community: The Politics of Semi-Detachment* (Oxford: Clarendon Press).

Ginsberg, R.H. (1989) *Foreign Policy Actions of the European Community: The Politics of Scale* (Boulder, CO: Lynne Rienner).

Gow, J. (1997) *Triumph of the Lack of Will: International Diplomacy and the Yugoslav War* (London: Hurst & Co.).

Grabbe, H. and Hughes, K. (1998) *Enlarging the EU Eastward* (London: Pinter).

Greilsammer, I. and Weiler, J. (1984) European political cooperation and the Palestinian–Israeli conflict: an Israeli perspective, in D. Allen and A. Pijpers (eds) (1984) *European Foreign Policy-making and the Arab–Israeli Conflict* (The Hague: Martinus Nijhoff).

Griffiths, R.T. (ed.) (1980) *The Economy and Politics of the Netherlands since 1945* (The Hague: Martinus Nijhoff).

Haas, E.B. (1958) *The Uniting of Europe: Political, Social and Economic Forces* (Stanford, CA: Stanford University Press).

Haas, E.B. (1964) *Byond the Nation-state: Functionalism and International Organizations* (Stanford, CA: Stanford University Press).

Haas, E.B. (1970) The study of regional integration: reflections on the joy and anguish of pre-theorizing, *International Organization*, vol. 24: 607–46.

Haas, E.B. (1990) *When Knowledge Is Power* (Berkeley: University of California Press).

Hanf, K. and Soetendorp, B. (eds) (1998) *Adapting to European Integration: Small States and the European Union* (London: Longman).

Hanrieder, W.F. (1989) *Germany, America, Europe: Forty Years of German Foreign Policy* (New Haven: Yale University Press).

Hanrieder, W.F. and Auton, G.P. (1980) *The Foreign Policies of West Germany, France and Britain* (Englewood Cliffs, NJ: Prentice Hall).

Hayes-Renshaw, H.F., Lequesne, C. and Lopez, P. (1989) The Permanent Representation of the member states to the European Communities, *Journal of Common Market Studies*, vol. 28, no. 2: 119–37.

Hayes-Renshaw, F. and Wallace, H. (1997) *The Council of Ministers* (London: Macmillan).

Hayward, J.E.S. (1983) *Governing France: The One and Indivisible Republic* (New York: Norton).

Hermann, C.F., Kegley, C.W. and Rosenau, J.N. (eds) (1987) *New Directions in the Study of Foreign Policy* (Boston: Allen & Unwin).

Hermann, C.F. and Peacock, G. (1987) The evolution and future of theoretical research in the comparative study of foreign policy, in C.F. Hermann, C.W. Kegley and J.N. Rosenau (eds) *New Directions in the Study of Foreign Policy* (Boston: Allen & Unwin).

Hermann, M.G. and Hermann, C.F. (1989) 'Who makes foreign policy decisions and how: an empirical enquiry', *International Studies Quarterly*, vol. 33, no. 4: 361–87.

Hill, C. (ed.) (1983) *National Foreign Policies and European Political Cooperation* (London: Allen & Unwin).

Hill, C. (ed.) (1996) *The Actors in Europe's Foreign Policy* (London: Routledge).

Hine, D. (1993) *Governing Italy* (Oxford: Oxford University Press).

Hoffmann, S. (1987) *Janus and Minerva: Essays in the Theory and Practice of International Politics* (Boulder, CO: Westview Press).

Holland, M. (ed.) (1997) *Common Foreign and Security Policy: The Record and Reforms* (London: Pinter).

Hollis, M. and Smith, S. (1991) *Explaining and Understanding International Relations* (Oxford: Clarendon Press).

Holsti, K.J. (1989) Mirror, mirror on the wall, which are the fairest theories of all?, *International Studies Quarterly*, vol. 33, no. 3: 255–61.

Hopmann, T.P. (1994) French perspectives on international relations after the cold war, *Mershon International Studies Review*, vol. 38, no. 1: 69–93.

Howorth, J. and Menon, A. (eds) (1997) *The European Union and the National Defence Policy* (London: Routledge).

Ifestos, P. (1987) *European Political Cooperation: Towards a Framework of Supranational Diplomacy* (Aldershot: Avebury).

Jopp, M. (1994) *The Strategic Implications of European Integration*, Adelphi Paper, No. 290 (London: The International Institute for Strategic Studies).

Jordan, R.S. (ed.) (1991) *Europe and the Superpowers* (London: Pinter).

Karvonen, L. and Sundelius, B. (1987) *Internationalization and Foreign Policy Management* (Aldershot: Gower).

Katzenstein, P.J. (ed.) (1997) *Tamed Power: Germany in Europe* (Ithaca: Cornell University Press).

Keatinge, P. (ed.) (1991) *Ireland and EC Membership Evaluated* (London: Pinter).

Kegley, C.W. (1987) Decision regimes and the comparative study of foreign policy, in C.F. Hermann, C.W. Kegley and J.N. Rosenau (eds) *New Directions in the Study of Foreign Policy* (Boston: Allen & Unwin).

Kegley, C.W. (1995) *Controversies in International Relations Theory: Realism and the Neoliberal Challenge* (New York: St Martin's Press).

Kegley, C.W. and Wittkopf, E.R. (1987) *American Foreign Policy: Pattern and Process* (New York: St Martin's Press).

Kelstrup, M. (ed.) (1992) *European Integration and Denmark's Participation* (Copenhagen: Copenhagen Political Studies Press).

Keohane, R.O. (1984) *After Hegemony* (Princeton: Princeton University Press).

Keohane, R.O. (1989) *International Institutions and State Power* (Boulder, CO: Westview Press).

Keohane, R.O. and Nye, J.S. (1989) *Power and Interdependence*, 2nd edn (New York: HarperCollins).

Keohane, R.O., Nye, J.S. and Hoffmann, S. (eds) (1993) *After the Cold War: International Institutions and State Strategies* (Cambridge, MA: Harvard University Press).

Khader, B. (1984) Europe and Arab–Israeli conflict: an Arab perspective, in *European Foreign Policy-making and the Arab–Israeli Conflict* (The Hague: Martinus Nijhoff).

Kissinger, H. (1979) *The White House Years* (Boston: Little, Brown).

Kissinger, H. (1982) *Years of Upheaval* (London: Weidenfeld & Nicolson).

Kissinger, H. (1994) *Diplomacy* (New York: Simon & Schuster).

Kramer, H. (1993) EC response to the new eastern Europe, *Journal of Common Market Studies*, vol. 31, no. 2: 213–44.

Krasner, S.D. (ed.) (1983) *International Regimes* (Ithaca: Cornell University Press).

Kratochwil, F. and Ruggie, J.G. (1986) International organization: a state of the art on an art of the state, *International Organization*, vol. 40, no. 4: 753–75.

Kupchan, C.A. (1987) *The Persian Gulf and the West: The Dilemmas of Security* (Boston: Allen & Unwin).

La Serre, F., Leruez, J. and Wallace, H. (eds) (1990) *French and British Foreign Policies in Transition: The Challenge of Adjustment* (New York: Berg).

Laffan, B. (1991) 'Sovereignty and national identity', in P. Keatinge (ed.) *Ireland and the EC Membership Evaluated* (London: Pinter).

Laurence, M. and Garnett, J. (1997) *British Foreign Policy: Challenges and Choices for the Twenty-first Century* (London: Pinter).

Laursen, F. and Vanhoonacker, S. (eds) (1992) *The Intergovernmental Conference on Political Union: Institutional Reforms, New Policies and International Identity of the European Community* (Maastricht: European Institute of Public Administration).

Lequesne, C. (1993) *Paris-Bruxelles: Comment se fait la politique européenne de la France* (Paris: Presses de la fondation nationale des sciences politique).

Levy, M.A., Young, O.R. and Zürn, M. (1995) The study of international regimes, *European Journal of International Relations*, vol. 1, no. 3: 267–330.

Licklider, R. (1988) *Political Power and the Arab Oil Weapon: The Experience of Five Industrial Nations* (Berkeley: University of California Press).

Lindberg, L.N. and Scheingold, S.A. (1970) *Europe's Would-be Polity: Patterns of Change in the European Community* (Englewood Cliffs, NJ: Prentice Hall).

Lodge, J. (ed.) (1993) *The European Community and the Challenge of the Future* (London: Pinter).

Luif, P. (1995) *On the Road to Brussels* (Vienna: Braumuller).

Lukacs, Y. (ed.) (1992) *The Israeli–Palestinian Conflict: A Documentary Record* (Cambridge: Cambridge University Press).

McLean, S. (ed.) (1986) *How Nuclear Weapons Decisions are Made* (London: Macmillan).

Macridis, R.C. (ed.) (1992) *Foreign policy in World Politics*, 8th edn (Englewood Cliffs, NJ: Prentice Hall).

Makovsky, D. (1996) *Making Peace with the PLO* (Boulder, CO: Westview Press).

Maull, H. (1980) 'Oil and influence: the oil weapon examined', in G. Treverton (ed.) *Energy and Security* (Westmead: Gower).

Mayes, D.G. (ed.) (1993) *The External Implications of European Integration* (New York: Harvester Wheatsheaf).

Mayhes, A. (1998) *Recasting Europe: The European Union's Policy towards Central and Eastern Europe* (Cambridge: Cambridge University Press).

Mény, Y., Muller, P. and Quermonne, J.L. (eds) (1996) *Adjusting to Europe: The Impact of the European Union on National Institutions and Policies* (London: Routledge).

Miles, L. (ed.) (1996) *The European Union and the Nordic Countries* (London: Routledge).

Miller, L.B. (1986) Through a glass darkly: western Europe and the Middle East, in M. Curtis (ed.) *The Middle East Reader* (New Brunswick: Transaction Books).

Milward, A.S. (1984) *The Reconstruction of Western Europe 1945–51* (London: Routledge).

Milward, A.S. (1992) *The European Rescue of the Nation-state* (London: Routledge).

Milward, A.S. and Sorensen, V. (1993) Interdependence or integration, in A.S. Milward, F.M.B. Lynch, R. Ranieri, F. Romero and V. Sorensen *The Frontier of National Sovereignty: History and Theory 1945–1992* (London: Routledge).

Moravcsik, A. (1991) Negotiating the Single European Act: national interests and conventional statecraft in the European Community, *International Organization*, vol. 45, no. 1: 19–56.

Moravcsik, A. (1993) Preference and power in the European Community: a liberal intergovernmentalist approach, *Journal of Common Market Studies*, vol. 31, no. 4: 473–524.

Morgenthau, H.J. (1951) *In Defense of the National Interest: A Critical Examination of American Foreign Policy* (New York: Alfred A. Knopf).

Morgenthau, H.J. (1952) Another great debate: the national interest of the United States, *American Political Science Review*, vol. 46: 961–88.

Morgenthau, H.J. (1973) *Politics Among Nations: The Struggle for Power and Peace*, 5th edn (New York: Alfred A. Knopf).

Most, B.A. and Starr, H. (1986) *Inquiry, Logic, and International Politics* (Columbia: University of South Carolina Press).

Nello, S.S. (1991) *The New Europe: Changing Economic Relations between East and West* (New York: Harvester Wheatsheaf).

Newsom, D.D. (1987) US–British consultation: an impossible dream?, *International Affairs*, vol. 63, no. 2: 225–38.

Nicoll, W. and Trevor, C.S. (1994) *Understanding the New European Community* (Hemel Hempstead: Harvester Wheatsheaf).

Norgaard, O., Pedersen, T. and Petersen, N. (eds) (1993) *The European Community in World Politics* (London: Pinter).

Northedge, F.S. (ed.) (1969) *The Foreign Policy of the Powers* (London: Faber & Faber).

Nugent, N. (1994) *The Government and Politics of the European Union* (London: Macmillan).

Nuttall, S.J. (1992) *European Political Co-operation* (Oxford: Clarendon Press).

Pappas, S.A. (ed.) (1995) *National Administrative Procedures for the Preparation and Implementation of Community Decisions* (Maastricht: European Institute of Public Administration).

Paterson, W. and Southern, D. (1991) *Governing Germany* (Oxford: Basil Blackwell).

Peterson, J. (1993) *Europe and America in the 1990s: The Prospects for Partnership* (Hants: Edward Elgar).

Peterson, J. and Sjursen, H. (eds) (1998) *A Common Foreign Policy for Europe? Competing Visions of the CFSP* (London: Routledge).

Piening, C. (1997) *Global Europe: The European Union in World Affairs* (Boulder, CO: Lynne Rienner).

Pinder, J. (1991) *The European Community and Eastern Europe* (London: Pinter).

Putnam, R.D. (1988) 'Diplomacy and domestic politics: the logic of two-level games', *International Organization*, vol. 42, no. 3: 427–60.

Quandt, W.B. (1977) *Decades of Decisions: American Policy toward the Arab–Israeli Conflict, 1967–1976* (Berkeley: University of California Press).

Quandt, W.B. (1986) *Camp David: Peacemaking and Politics* (Washington, DC: The Brookings Institution).

Regelsberger, E., Schoutheete de Tervarent, P. and Wessels, W. (eds) (1997) *Foreign Policy of the European Union: From EPC to CFSP and Beyond* (Boulder, CO: Lynne Rienner).

Richardson, J. (ed.) (1996) *European Union: Power and Policy-making* (London: Routledge).

Risse-Kappen, T. (1988) *The Zero Option: INF, West Germany, and Arms Control* (Boulder, CO: Westview Press).

Rittberger, V. (ed.) (1995) *Regime Theory and International Relations* (Oxford: Clarendon Press).

Rometsch, D. and Wessels, W. (eds) (1996) *The European Union and Member States: Towards Institutional Fusion?* (Manchester: Manchester University Press).

Ronzitti, N. (1987) European policy formulation in the Italian administrative system, *The International Spectator*, vol. 22, no. 4: 207–14.

Rosati, J.A. (1993) *The Politics of United States Foreign Policy* (Fort Worth: Harcourt, Brace, Jovanovich).

Rosenau, J.N. (1987) Introduction: new directions and recurrent questions in the comparative study of foreign policy, in C.F. Hermann, C.W. Kegley and J.N. Rosenau (eds) *New Directions in the Study of Foreign Policy* (Boston: Allen & Unwin).

Ruggie, J.G. (1993) *Multilateralism Matters: The Theory and Praxis of an Institutional Form* (New York: Columbia University Press).

Rummel, R. (ed.) (1990) *The Evolution of an International Actor: Western Europe's New Assertiveness* (Boulder, CO: Westview Press).

Rummel, R. (ed.) (1992) *Toward Political Union* (Boulder, CO: Westview Press).

Saba, K. (1986) The Spanish foreign policy decision-making process, *The International Spectator*, vol. 21, no. 4: 24–33.

Sandholtz, W. (1993) Choosing union: monetary politics and Maastricht, *International Organization*, vol. 47, no. 1: 1–39.

Schmitter, P.C. (1969) Three neo-functionalist Hypotheses about international integration, *International Organization*, vol. 23, no. 1: 161–6.

Shlaim, A. and Yannopoulos, G.N. (eds) (1976) *The EEC and the Mediterranean Countries* (Cambridge: Cambridge University Press).

Silber, L. and Little, A. (1995) *The Death of Yugoslavia* (London: Penguin).

Smith, G., Paterson, W.E., Merkel, P. and Padgett, S. (eds) (1992) *Developments in German Politics* (London: Macmillan).

Smith, M., Smith, S. and White, B. (eds) (1988) *British Foreign Policy: Tradition, Change and Transformation* (London: Unwin Hyman).

Smith, M. and Woolcock, S. (1993) *The United States and the European Community in a Transformed World* (London: Pinter).

Smith, S. (1986) Theories of foreign policy: an historical overview, *Review of International Studies*, vol. 12, no. 1: 13–29.

Smith, S.M. (1981) *Foreign Policy Adaptation* (Aldershot: Gower).

Sobel, L.A. (ed.) (1980) *Peace-making in the Middle East* (New York: Facts On File Inc.).

Soetendorp, R.B. (1982/83) *Pragmatisch of Principieel. Het Nederlandse Beleid ten aanzien van het Arabisch–Israelisch Conflict* (Groningen/Leiden: Krips Repro/Martinus Nijhoff).

Soetendorp, R.B. (1984) The Netherlands, in D. Allen and A. Pijpers (eds) *European Foreign Policy-making and the Arab–Israeli Conflict* (The Hague: Martinus Nijhoff).

Soetendorp, B. (1994) The evolution of the EC/EU as a single foreign policy actor, in W. Calsnaes and S. Smith, *European Foreign Policy* (London: Sage).

Spanier, J. (1988) *American Foreign Policy since World War II* (Washington, DC: Congressional Quarterly Press).

Spero, J.E. (1977) *The Politics of International Economic Relations* (New York: St Martin's Press).

Stein, A. (1990) *Why Nations Co-operate* (Ithaca: Cornell University Press).

Story, J. (ed.) (1993) *The New Europe: Politics, Government and Economy since 1945* (Oxford: Basil Blackwell).

Tanter, R. and Ullman, R.H. (1972) *Theory and Policy in International Relations* (Princeton, NJ: Princeton University Press).

Thatcher, M. (1993) *The Downing Street Years* (London: HarperCollins).

Tiilikainen, T. and Petersen, D.I. (eds) (1993) *The Nordic Countries and the EC* (Copenhagen: Copenhagen Political Studies Press).

Traxler, F. and Schmitter, P.C. (1995) The emerging Euro-polity and organized interests, *European Journal of International Relations*, vol. 1, no. 2: 191–218.

Treaty of Amsterdam (1997) (Luxembourg: Office for Official Publications of the European Communities).

Treaty on European Union (1992) (Luxembourg: Office for Official Publications of the European Communities).

Treverton, G. (ed.) (1980) *Energy and Security* (Hampshire: Gower).

Tugendhat, C. and Wallace, W. (1988) *Options for British Foreign Policy in the 1990s* (London: Routledge).

Urwin, D.W. (1972) *Western Europe since 1945* (London: Longman).

Urwin, D.W. (1991) *The Community of Europe: A History of European Integration since 1945* (London: Longman).

Van Ham, P. (1993) *The EC, Eastern Europe and European Unity: Discord, Collaboration and Integration since 1947* (London: Pinter).

Vasconcelos, A. de (1991) Portugal and European political cooperation, *The International Spectator*, vol. 26, no. 2: 127–40.

Wallace, H. and Wallace, W. (1995) *Flying Together in a Larger and More Diverse European Union* (The Hague: Scientific Council for Government Policy).

Wallace, H. and Wallace, W. (eds) (1996) *Policy-making in the European Union*, 3rd edn (Oxford: Oxford University Press).

Wallace, W. (1975) *The Foreign Policy Process in Britain* (London: The Royal Institute of International Affairs).

Wallace, W. (1990) *The Dynamics of European Integration* (London: Pinter).

Wertz, J.W. (1992) *The European Council* (Amsterdam: Elsevier).

Westlake, M. (1995) *The Council of the European Union* (London: Cartermill).

Westlake, M. (ed.) (1998) *The European Union beyond Amsterdam: New Concepts of European Integration* (London: Routledge).

Wiggershaus, N. and Foerster, R.G. (eds) (1993) *The Western Security Community, 1948–1950* (Oxford: Berg).

Young, J.W. (1993) *Britain and European Unity, 1945–1992* (London: Macmillan).

Young, O. (1989) *International Cooperation* (Ithaca: Cornell University Press).

Index